NEXT GEN

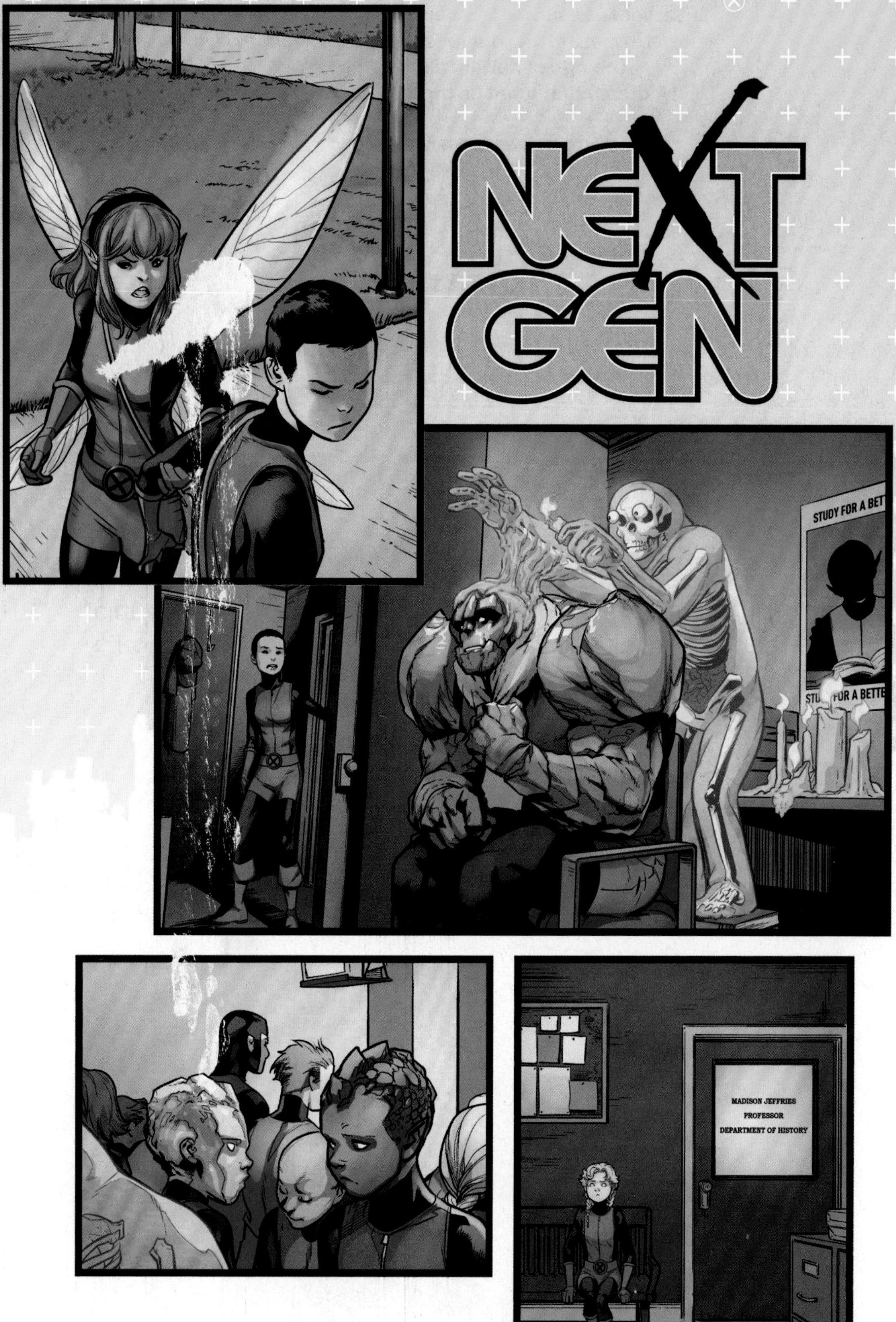
STUDY FOR A
MADISON JEFFRIES
PROFESSOR
DEPARTMENT OF HISTORY

Welcome to a perfect world.
Everyone is a mutant—special, powerful, individual.
No more strife, oppression or dependence.
The Age of X-Man: a dream made real.
A dream that must be protected...at any cost.

The Summers Institute for Higher Learning houses the
next generation of young minds, placing each student
on a ten-year track in one of four primary disciplines: law
enforcement, agriculture, medicine and history. Glob,
Armor, Anole, Pixie, Rockslide and Shark-Girl are a group of
friends who follow the rules...as all good students should.

WRITER **ED BRISSON**

ARTISTS **MARCOS TO** (#1-4)
& LUCAS WERNECK (#5)

COLOR ARTIST **JASON KEITH**

LETTERER **VC's CLAYTON COWLES**

COVER ART **CHRIS BACHALO** WITH
TIM TOWNSEND (#2, #4-5)
& AL VEY (#3)

ASSISTANT EDITORS **DANNY KHAZEM**
& LAUREN AMARO

EDITOR **DARREN SHAN**

X-MEN SENIOR EDITOR **JORDAN D. WHITE**

COLLECTION EDITOR **JENNIFER GRÜNWALD**   **CAITLIN O'CONNELL** ASSISTANT EDITOR
ASSOCIATE MANAGING EDITOR **KATERI WOODY**   **MARK D. BEAZLEY** EDITOR, SPECIAL PROJECTS
VP PRODUCTION & SPECIAL PROJECTS **JEFF YOUNGQUIST**   **JAY BOWEN** BOOK DESIGNER

SVP PRINT, SALES & MARKETING **DAVID GABRIEL**   **SVEN LARSEN** DIRECTOR, LICENSED PUBLISHING
EDITOR IN CHIEF **C.B. CEBULSKI**   **JOE QUESADA** CHIEF CREATIVE OFFICER
PRESIDENT **DAN BUCKLEY**   **ALAN FINE** EXECUTIVE PRODUCER

AGE OF X-MAN: NEXTGEN. Contains material originally published in magazine form as AGE OF X-MAN: NEXTGEN #1-5. First printing 2019. ISBN 978-1-302-91576-6. Published by MARVEL WORLDWIDE, INC., a subsidiary of MARVEL ENTERTAINMENT, LLC. OFFICE OF PUBLICATION: 135 West 50th Street, New York, NY 10020. © 2019 MARVEL No similarity between any of the names, characters, persons, and/or institutions in this magazine with those of any living or dead person or institution is intended, and any such similarity which may exist is purely coincidental. **Printed in Canada.** DAN BUCKLEY, President, Marvel Entertainment; JOHN NEE, Publisher; JOE QUESADA, Chief Creative Officer; TOM BREVOORT, SVP of Publishing; DAVID BOGART, Associate Publisher & SVP of Talent Affairs; DAVID GABRIEL, SVP of Sales & Marketing, Publishing; JEFF YOUNGQUIST, VP of Production & Special Projects; DAN CARR, Executive Director of Publishing Technology; ALEX MORALES, Director of Publishing Operations; DAN EDINGTON, Managing Editor; SUSAN CRESPI, Production Manager; STAN LEE, Chairman Emeritus. For information regarding advertising in Marvel Comics or on Marvel.com, please contact Vit DeBellis, Custom Solutions & Integrated Advertising Manager, at vdebellis@marvel.com. For Marvel subscription inquiries, please call 888-511-5480. **Manufactured between 6/28/2019 and 7/30/2019 by SOLISCO PRINTERS, SCOTT, QC, CANADA.**

10 9 8 7 6 5 4 3 2 1

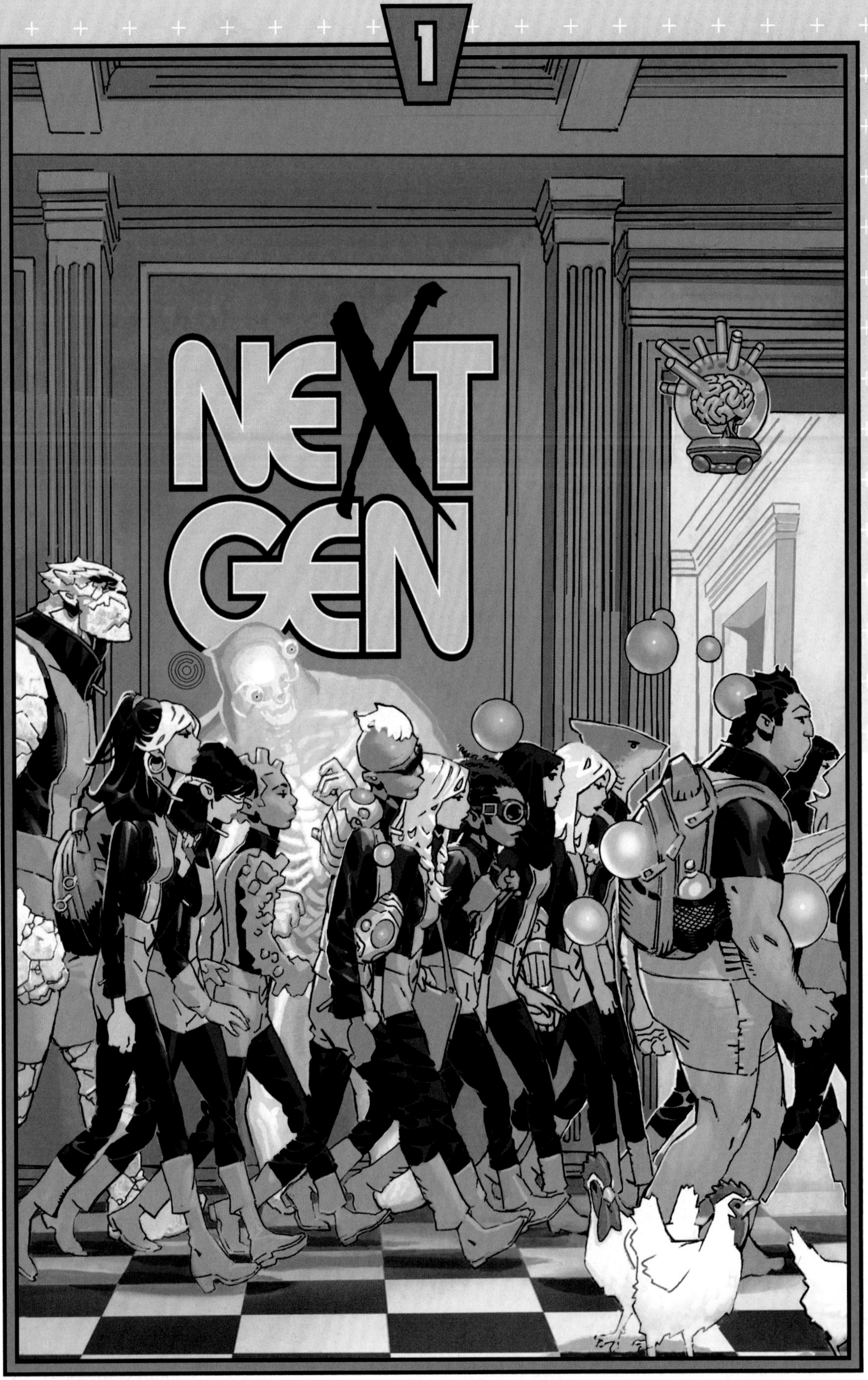
1
NEXT
GEN

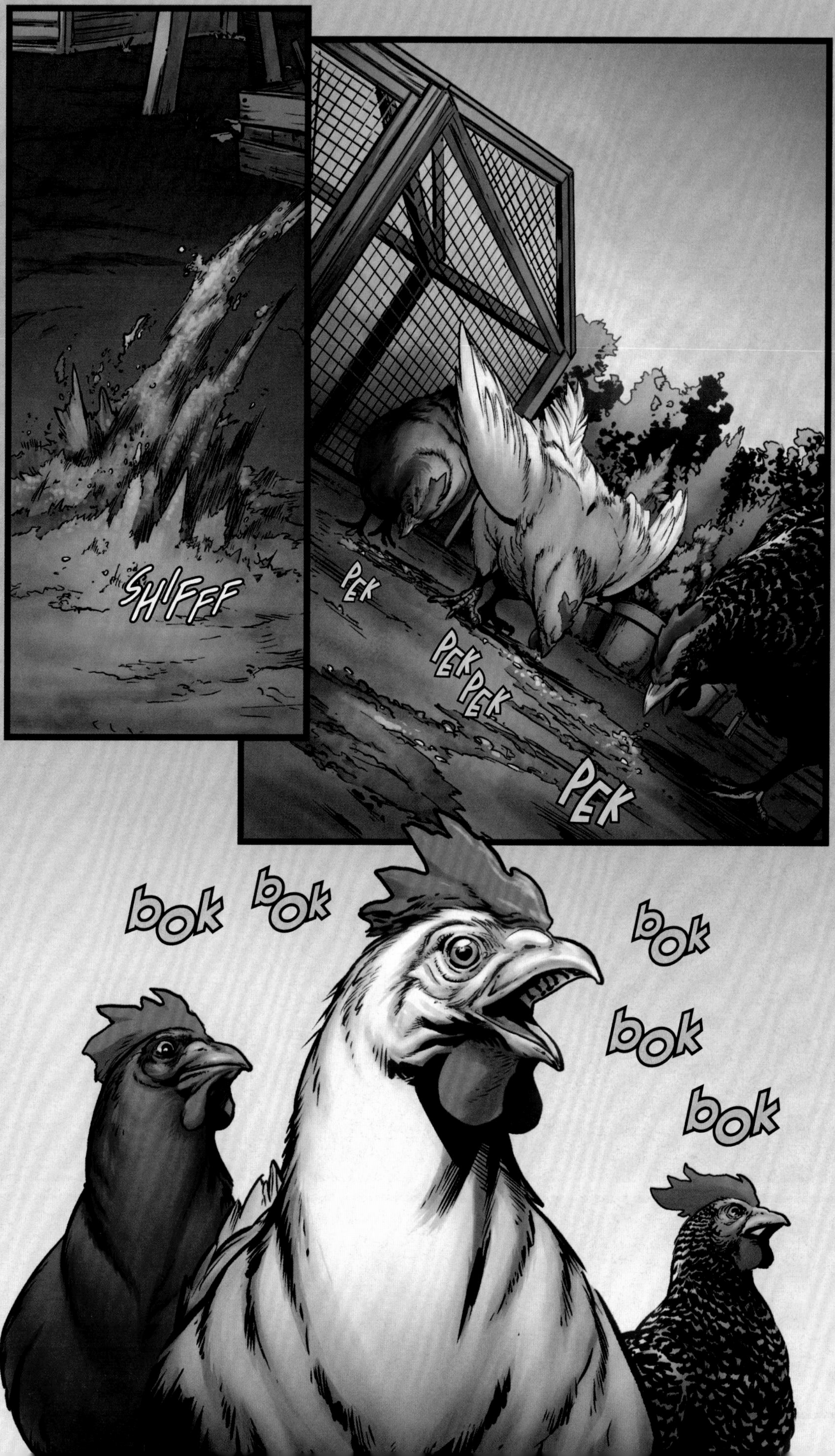
SHIFFF
PEK
PEKPEK
PEK
bok bok
bok
bok
bok

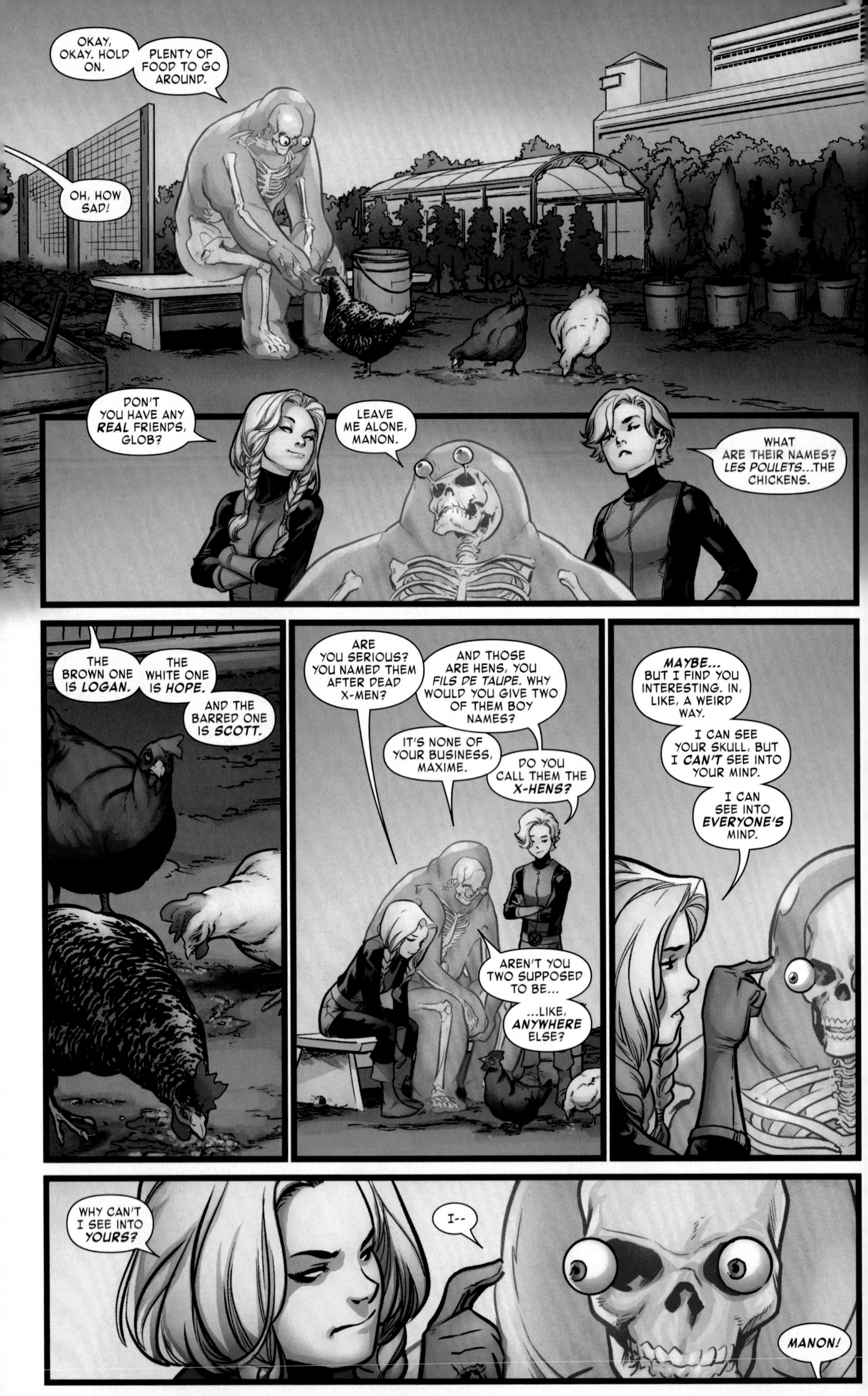
OKAY, OKAY. HOLD ON.
PLENTY OF FOOD TO GO AROUND.
OH, HOW SAD!
DON'T YOU HAVE ANY REAL FRIENDS, GLOB?
LEAVE ME ALONE, MANON.
WHAT ARE THEIR NAMES? LES POULETS...THE CHICKENS.
THE BROWN ONE IS LOGAN.
THE WHITE ONE IS HOPE.
AND THE BARRED ONE IS SCOTT.
ARE YOU SERIOUS? YOU NAMED THEM AFTER DEAD X-MEN?
AND THOSE ARE HENS, YOU FILS DE TAUPE. WHY WOULD YOU GIVE TWO OF THEM BOY NAMES?
IT'S NONE OF YOUR BUSINESS, MAXIME.
DO YOU CALL THEM THE X-HENS?
AREN'T YOU TWO SUPPOSED TO BE...
...LIKE, ANYWHERE ELSE?
MAYBE... BUT I FIND YOU INTERESTING. IN, LIKE, A WEIRD WAY.
I CAN SEE YOUR SKULL, BUT I CAN'T SEE INTO YOUR MIND.
I CAN SEE INTO EVERYONE'S MIND.
WHY CAN'T I SEE INTO YOURS?
I--
MANON!

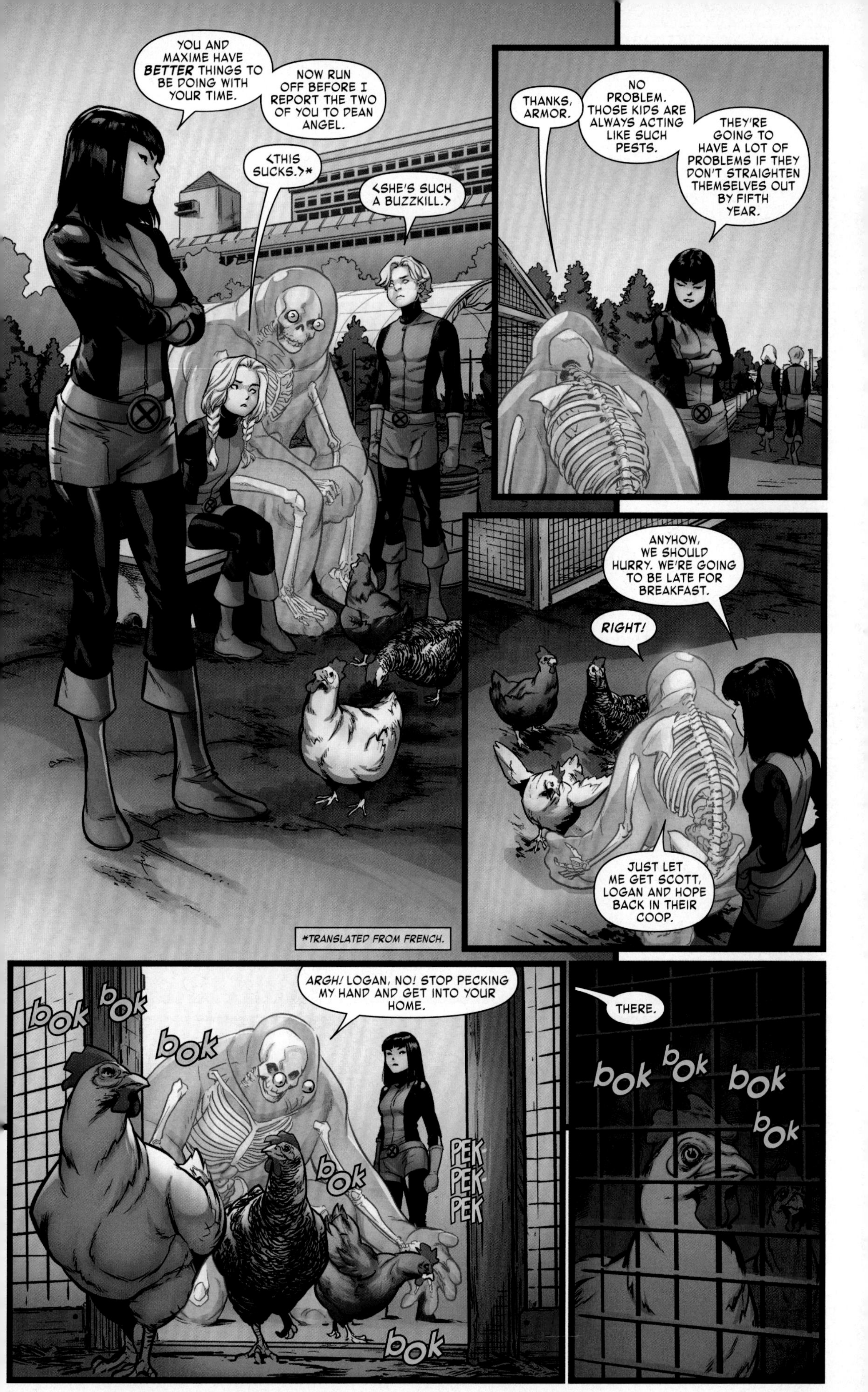

YOU AND MAXIME HAVE BETTER THINGS TO BE DOING WITH YOUR TIME.
NOW RUN OFF BEFORE I REPORT THE TWO OF YOU TO DEAN ANGEL.
<THIS SUCKS.>*
<SHE'S SUCH A BUZZKILL.>
*TRANSLATED FROM FRENCH.
THANKS, ARMOR.
NO PROBLEM. THOSE KIDS ARE ALWAYS ACTING LIKE SUCH PESTS.
THEY'RE GOING TO HAVE A LOT OF PROBLEMS IF THEY DON'T STRAIGHTEN THEMSELVES OUT BY FIFTH YEAR.
ANYHOW, WE SHOULD HURRY. WE'RE GOING TO BE LATE FOR BREAKFAST.
RIGHT!
JUST LET ME GET SCOTT, LOGAN AND HOPE BACK IN THEIR COOP.
bok bok
bok
ARGH! LOGAN, NO! STOP PECKING MY HAND AND GET INTO YOUR HOME.
bok
PEK-PEK-PEK
bok
THERE.
bok bok bok
bok

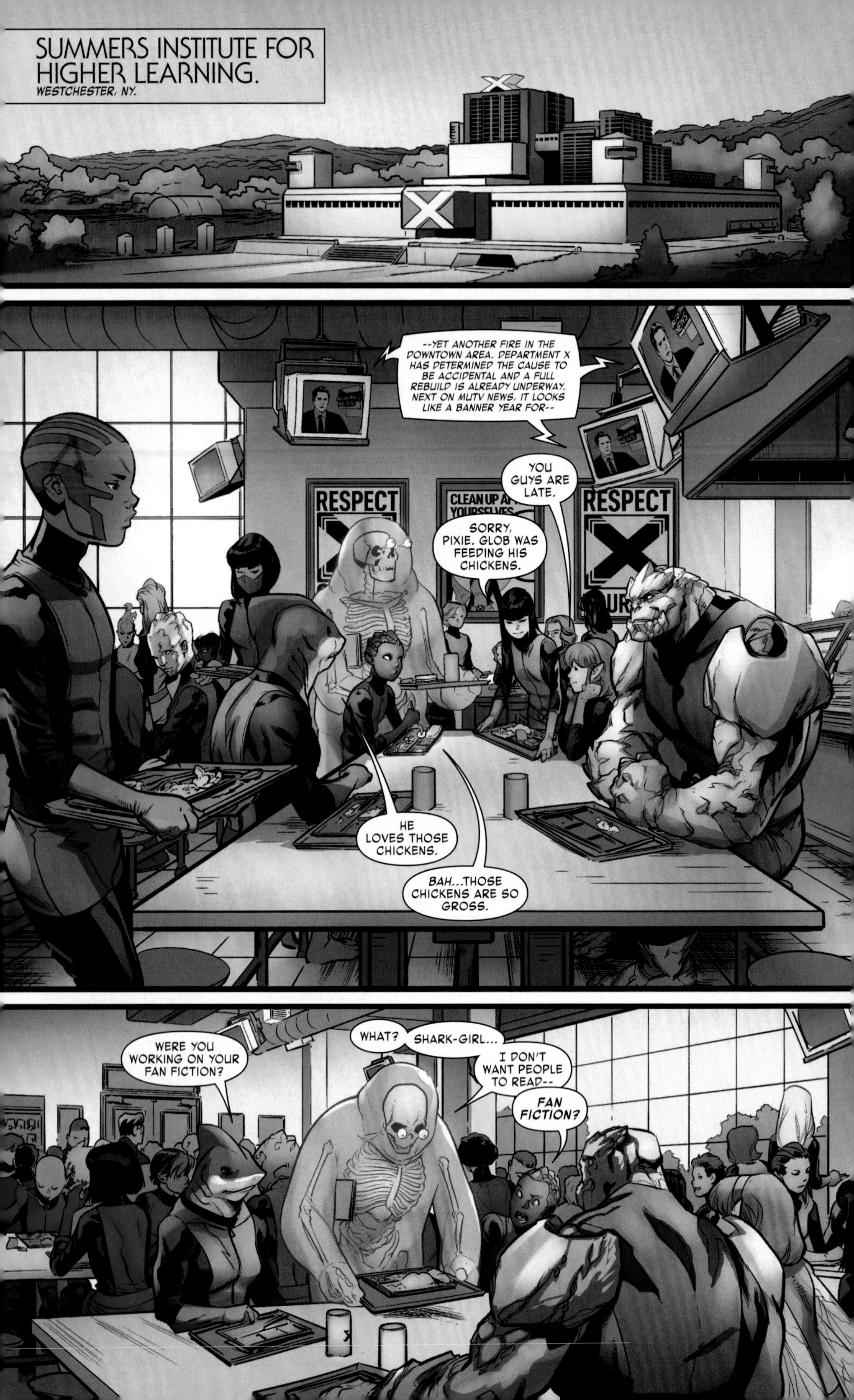
SUMMERS INSTITUTE FOR HIGHER LEARNING.
WESTCHESTER, NY.
--YET ANOTHER FIRE IN THE DOWNTOWN AREA. DEPARTMENT X HAS DETERMINED THE CAUSE TO BE ACCIDENTAL AND A FULL REBUILD IS ALREADY UNDERWAY. NEXT ON MUTV NEWS, IT LOOKS LIKE A BANNER YEAR FOR--
RESPECT
RESPECT
YOU GUYS ARE LATE.
SORRY, PIXIE. GLOB WAS FEEDING HIS CHICKENS.
HE LOVES THOSE CHICKENS.
BAH...THOSE CHICKENS ARE SO GROSS.
WERE YOU WORKING ON YOUR FAN FICTION?
WHAT?
SHARK-GIRL...
I DON'T WANT PEOPLE TO READ--
FAN FICTION?

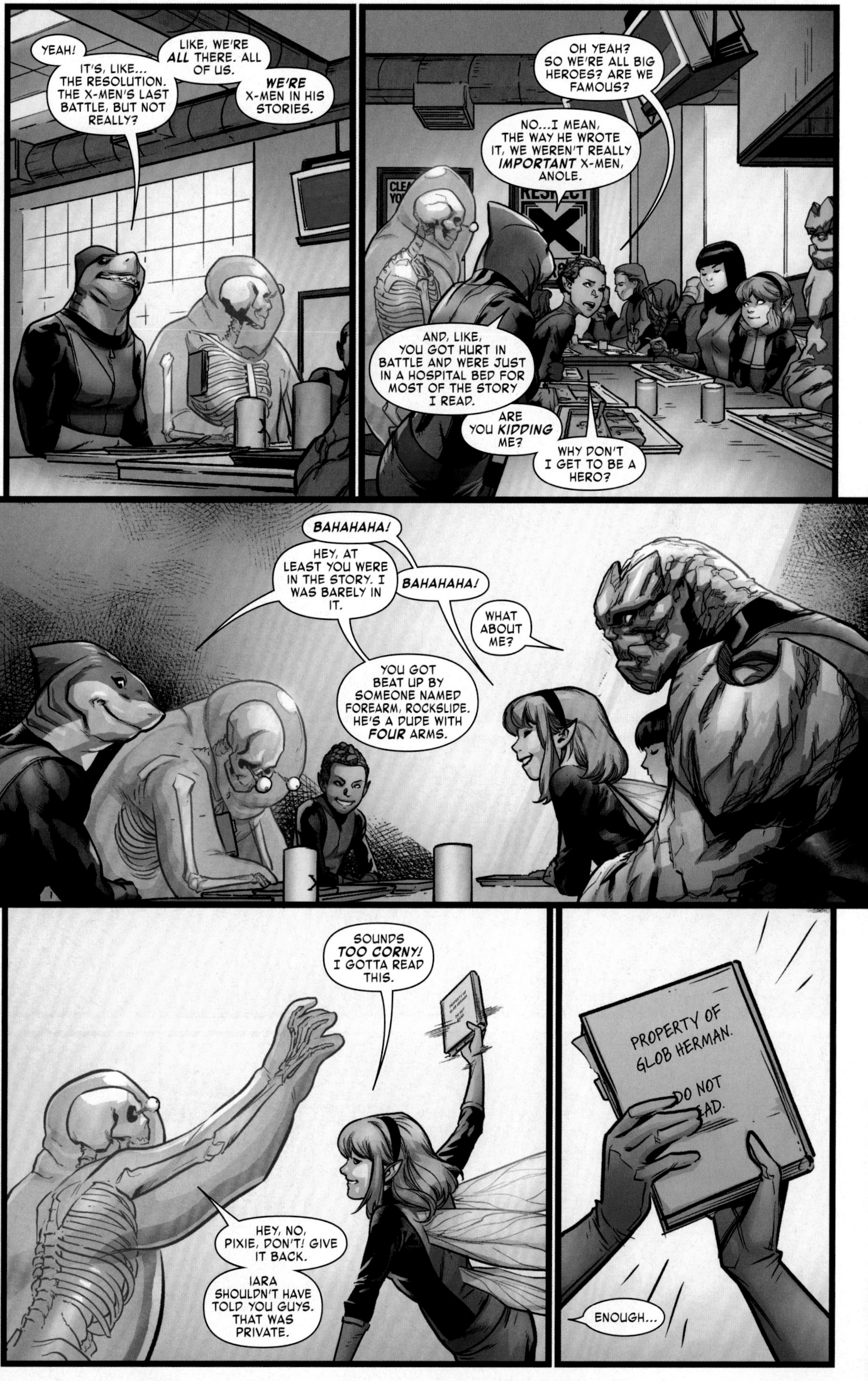

YEAH!
IT'S, LIKE... THE RESOLUTION. THE X-MEN'S LAST BATTLE, BUT NOT REALLY?
LIKE, WE'RE ALL THERE. ALL OF US.
WE'RE X-MEN IN HIS STORIES.
OH YEAH? SO WE'RE ALL BIG HEROES? ARE WE FAMOUS?
NO...I MEAN, THE WAY HE WROTE IT, WE WEREN'T REALLY IMPORTANT X-MEN, ANOLE.
AND, LIKE, YOU GOT HURT IN BATTLE AND WERE JUST IN A HOSPITAL BED FOR MOST OF THE STORY I READ.
ARE YOU KIDDING ME?
WHY DON'T I GET TO BE A HERO?
BAHAHAHA!
HEY, AT LEAST YOU WERE IN THE STORY. I WAS BARELY IN IT.
BAHAHAHA!
WHAT ABOUT ME?
YOU GOT BEAT UP BY SOMEONE NAMED FOREARM, ROCKSLIDE. HE'S A DUDE WITH FOUR ARMS.
SOUNDS TOO CORNY! I GOTTA READ THIS.
HEY, NO, PIXIE, DON'T! GIVE IT BACK.
IARA SHOULDN'T HAVE TOLD YOU GUYS. THAT WAS PRIVATE.
PROPERTY OF GLOB HERMAN.
ENOUGH...

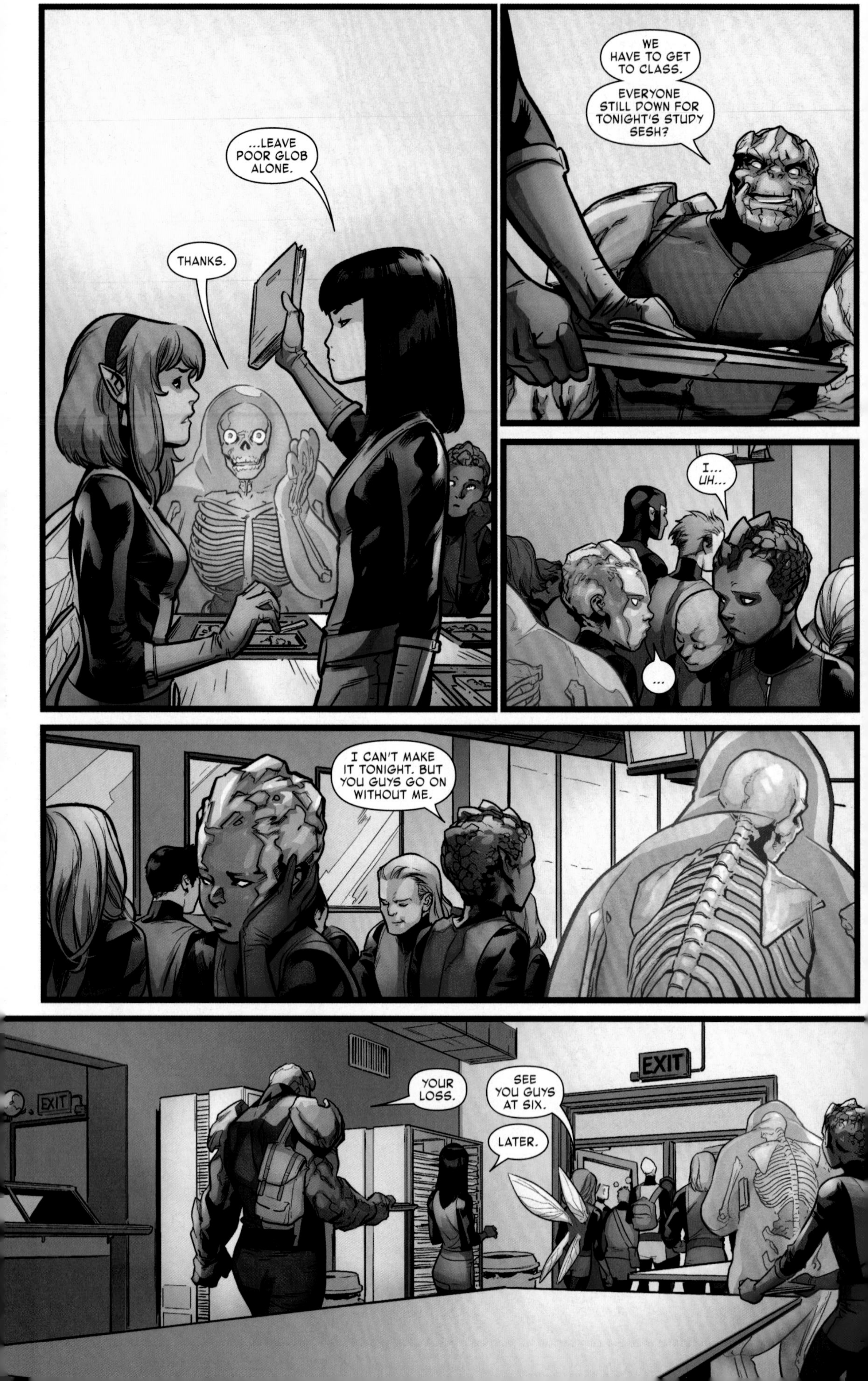
...LEAVE POOR GLOB ALONE.
THANKS.
WE HAVE TO GET TO CLASS.
EVERYONE STILL DOWN FOR TONIGHT'S STUDY SESH?
I... UH...
...
I CAN'T MAKE IT TONIGHT. BUT YOU GUYS GO ON WITHOUT ME.
EXIT
EXIT
YOUR LOSS.
SEE YOU GUYS AT SIX.
LATER.

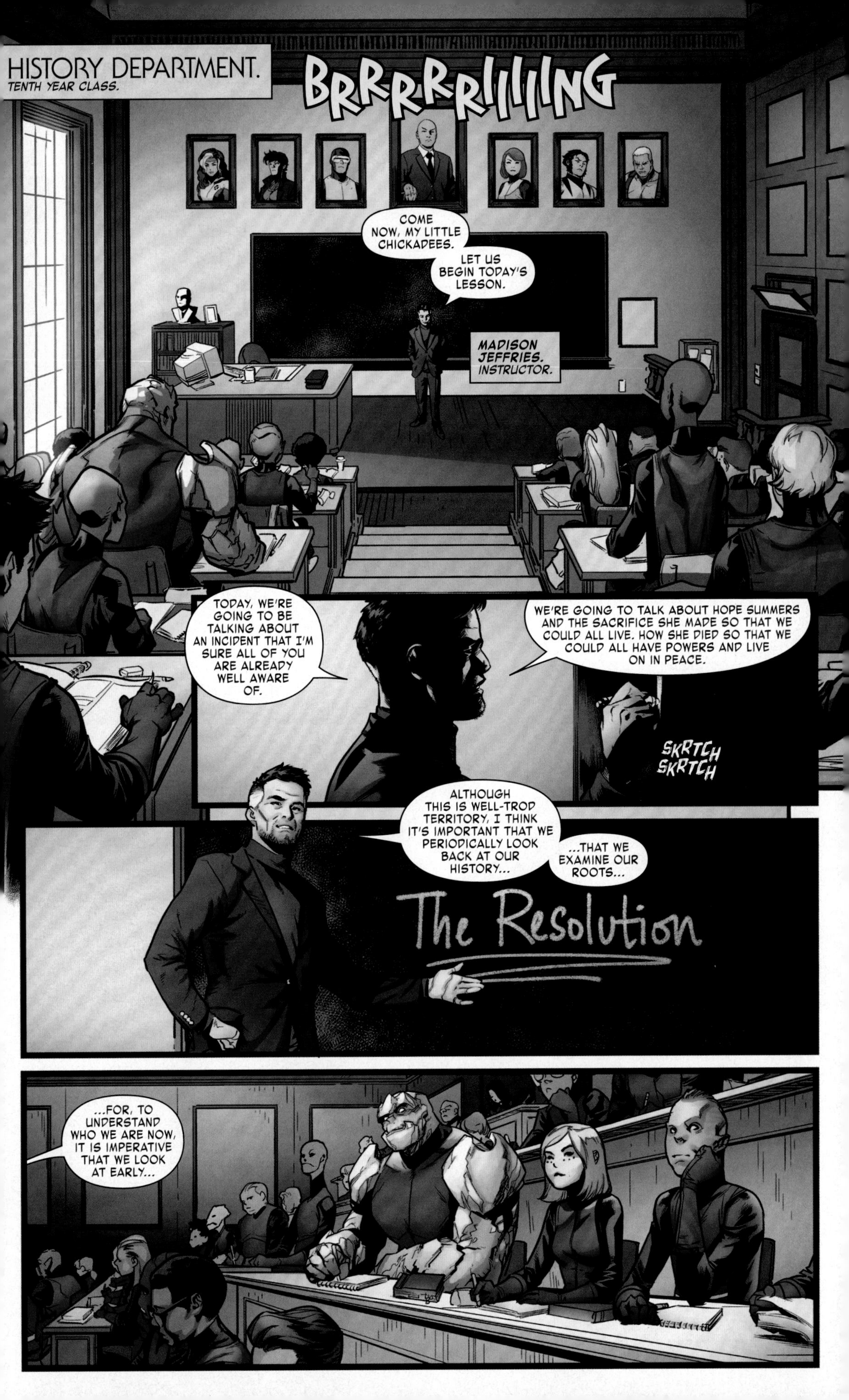
HISTORY DEPARTMENT.
TENTH YEAR CLASS.
BRRRRRIIIIING
COME NOW, MY LITTLE CHICKADEES.
LET US BEGIN TODAY'S LESSON.
MADISON JEFFRIES. INSTRUCTOR.
TODAY, WE'RE GOING TO BE TALKING ABOUT AN INCIDENT THAT I'M SURE ALL OF YOU ARE ALREADY WELL AWARE OF.
WE'RE GOING TO TALK ABOUT HOPE SUMMERS AND THE SACRIFICE SHE MADE SO THAT WE COULD ALL LIVE. HOW SHE DIED SO THAT WE COULD ALL HAVE POWERS AND LIVE ON IN PEACE.
SKRTCH SKRTCH
ALTHOUGH THIS IS WELL-TROD TERRITORY, I THINK IT'S IMPORTANT THAT WE PERIODICALLY LOOK BACK AT OUR HISTORY...
...THAT WE EXAMINE OUR ROOTS...
The Resolution
...FOR, TO UNDERSTAND WHO WE ARE NOW, IT IS IMPERATIVE THAT WE LOOK AT EARLY...

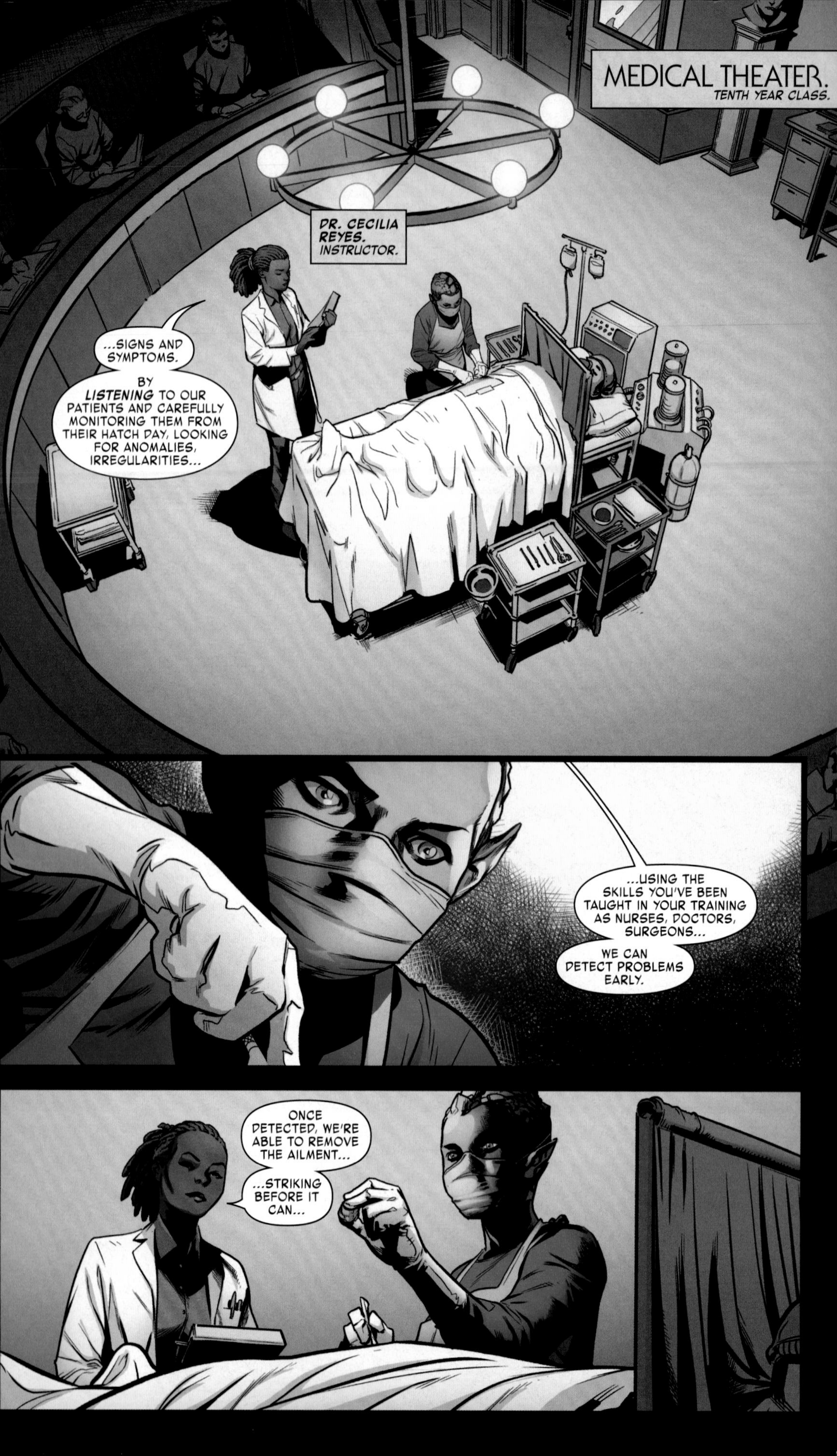
MEDICAL THEATER.
TENTH YEAR CLASS.
DR. CECILIA REYES. INSTRUCTOR.
...SIGNS AND SYMPTOMS.
BY LISTENING TO OUR PATIENTS AND CAREFULLY MONITORING THEM FROM THEIR HATCH DAY, LOOKING FOR ANOMALIES, IRREGULARITIES...
...USING THE SKILLS YOU'VE BEEN TAUGHT IN YOUR TRAINING AS NURSES, DOCTORS, SURGEONS...
WE CAN DETECT PROBLEMS EARLY.
ONCE DETECTED, WE'RE ABLE TO REMOVE THE AILMENT...
...STRIKING BEFORE IT CAN...

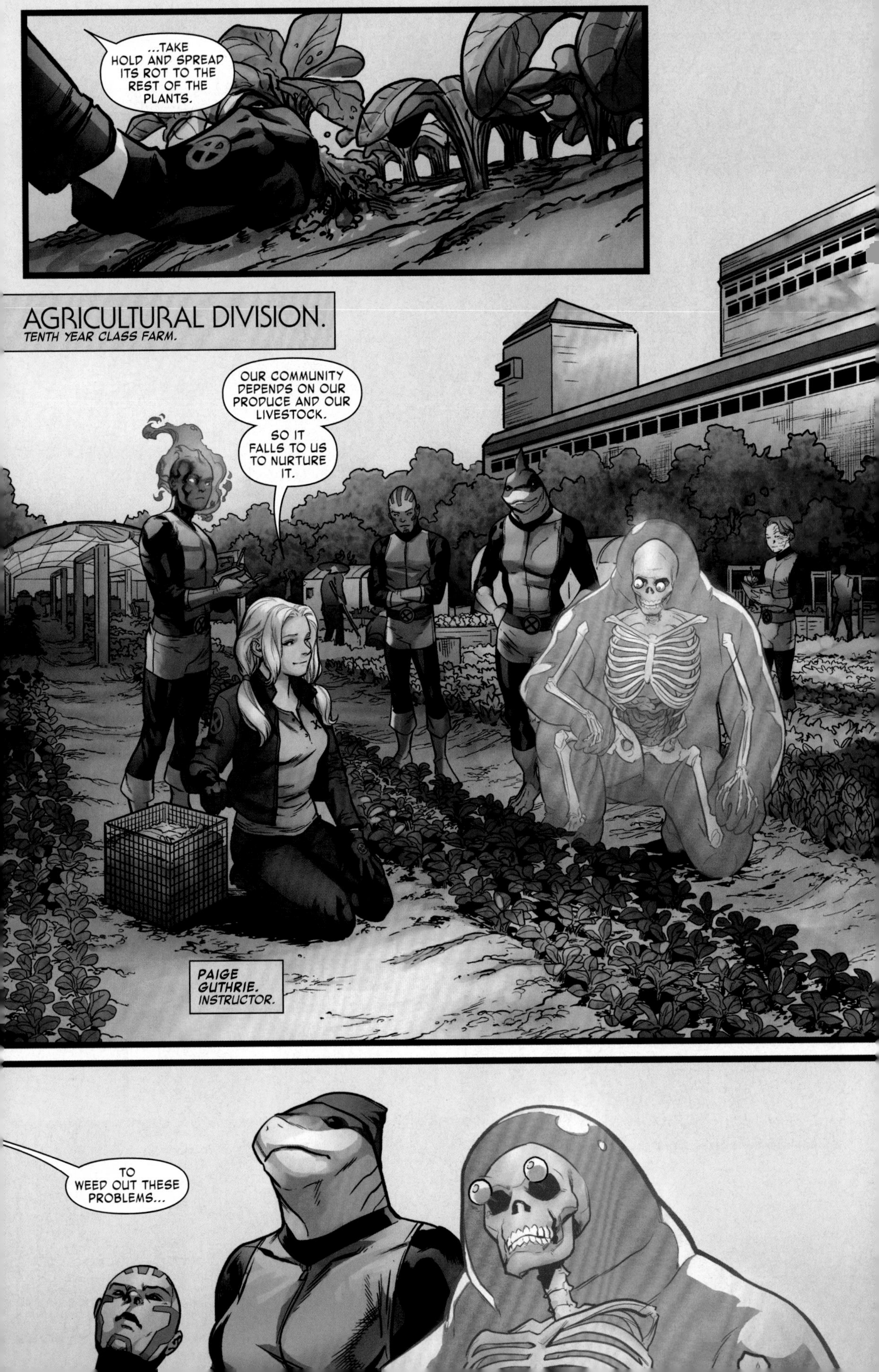
...TAKE HOLD AND SPREAD ITS ROT TO THE REST OF THE PLANTS.
AGRICULTURAL DIVISION.
TENTH YEAR CLASS FARM.
OUR COMMUNITY DEPENDS ON OUR PRODUCE AND OUR LIVESTOCK.
SO IT FALLS TO US TO NURTURE IT.
PAIGE GUTHRIE. INSTRUCTOR.
TO WEED OUT THESE PROBLEMS...

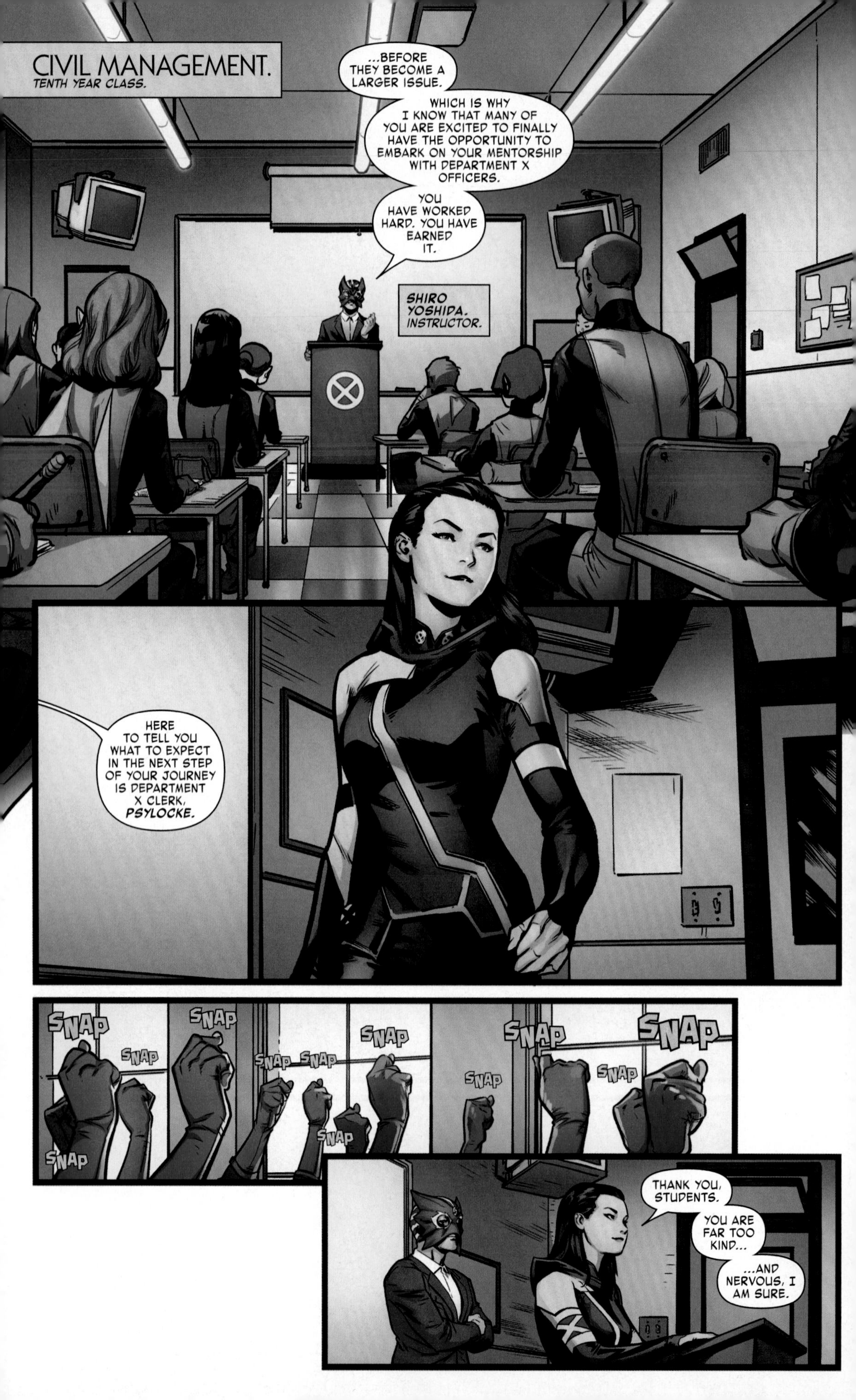
CIVIL MANAGEMENT.
TENTH YEAR CLASS.
...BEFORE THEY BECOME A LARGER ISSUE.
WHICH IS WHY I KNOW THAT MANY OF YOU ARE EXCITED TO FINALLY HAVE THE OPPORTUNITY TO EMBARK ON YOUR MENTORSHIP WITH DEPARTMENT X OFFICERS.
YOU HAVE WORKED HARD. YOU HAVE EARNED IT.
SHIRO YOSHIDA. INSTRUCTOR.
HERE TO TELL YOU WHAT TO EXPECT IN THE NEXT STEP OF YOUR JOURNEY IS DEPARTMENT X CLERK, PSYLOCKE.
SNAP SNAP SNAP SNAP SNAP SNAP SNAP SNAP SNAP SNAP SNAP SNAP
THANK YOU, STUDENTS.
YOU ARE FAR TOO KIND...
...AND NERVOUS, I AM SURE.

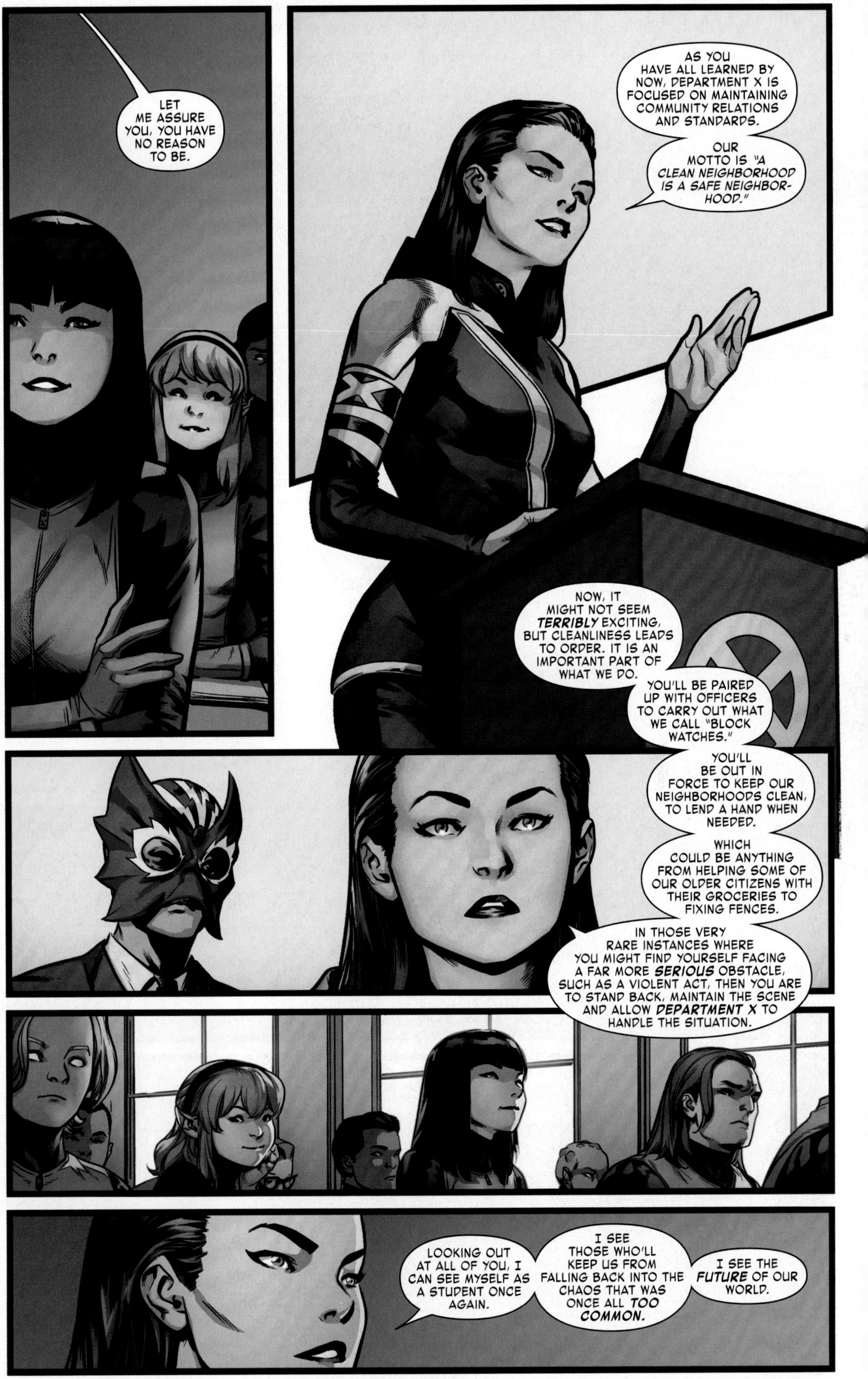
LET ME ASSURE YOU, YOU HAVE NO REASON TO BE.
AS YOU HAVE ALL LEARNED BY NOW, DEPARTMENT X IS FOCUSED ON MAINTAINING COMMUNITY RELATIONS AND STANDARDS.
OUR MOTTO IS "A CLEAN NEIGHBORHOOD IS A SAFE NEIGHBOR-HOOD."
NOW, IT MIGHT NOT SEEM TERRIBLY EXCITING, BUT CLEANLINESS LEADS TO ORDER. IT IS AN IMPORTANT PART OF WHAT WE DO.
YOU'LL BE PAIRED UP WITH OFFICERS TO CARRY OUT WHAT WE CALL "BLOCK WATCHES."
YOU'LL BE OUT IN FORCE TO KEEP OUR NEIGHBORHOODS CLEAN, TO LEND A HAND WHEN NEEDED.
WHICH COULD BE ANYTHING FROM HELPING SOME OF OUR OLDER CITIZENS WITH THEIR GROCERIES TO FIXING FENCES.
IN THOSE VERY RARE INSTANCES WHERE YOU MIGHT FIND YOURSELF FACING A FAR MORE SERIOUS OBSTACLE, SUCH AS A VIOLENT ACT, THEN YOU ARE TO STAND BACK, MAINTAIN THE SCENE AND ALLOW DEPARTMENT X TO HANDLE THE SITUATION.
LOOKING OUT AT ALL OF YOU, I CAN SEE MYSELF AS A STUDENT ONCE AGAIN.
I SEE THOSE WHO'LL KEEP US FROM FALLING BACK INTO THE CHAOS THAT WAS ONCE ALL TOO COMMON.
I SEE THE FUTURE OF OUR WORLD.

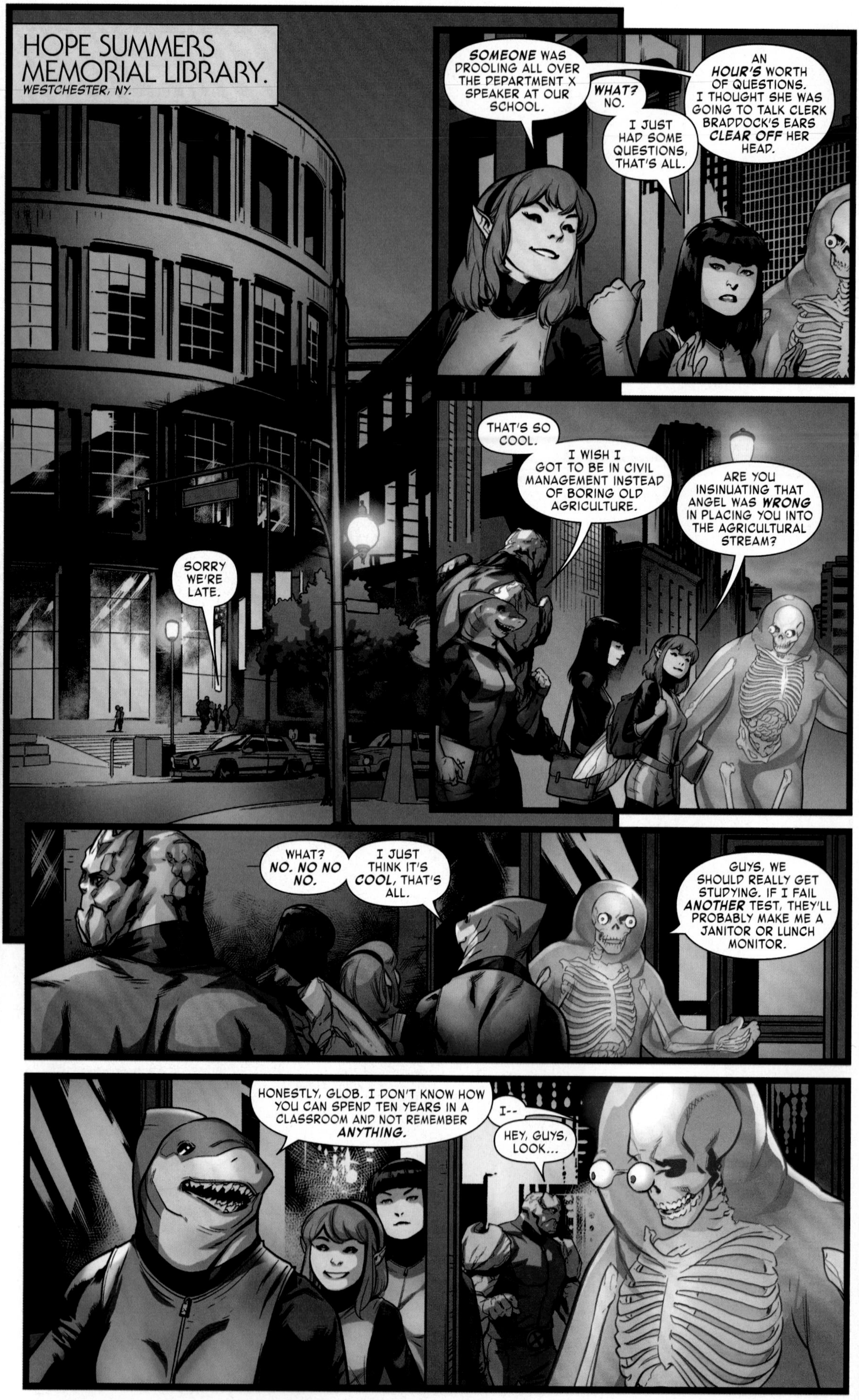
HOPE SUMMERS MEMORIAL LIBRARY.
WESTCHESTER, NY.
SORRY WE'RE LATE.
SOMEONE WAS DROOLING ALL OVER THE DEPARTMENT X SPEAKER AT OUR SCHOOL.
WHAT? NO.
I JUST HAD SOME QUESTIONS, THAT'S ALL.
AN HOUR'S WORTH OF QUESTIONS. I THOUGHT SHE WAS GOING TO TALK CLERK BRADDOCK'S EARS CLEAR OFF HER HEAD.
THAT'S SO COOL.
I WISH I GOT TO BE IN CIVIL MANAGEMENT INSTEAD OF BORING OLD AGRICULTURE.
ARE YOU INSINUATING THAT ANGEL WAS WRONG IN PLACING YOU INTO THE AGRICULTURAL STREAM?
WHAT? NO. NO NO NO.
I JUST THINK IT'S COOL, THAT'S ALL.
GUYS, WE SHOULD REALLY GET STUDYING. IF I FAIL ANOTHER TEST, THEY'LL PROBABLY MAKE ME A JANITOR OR LUNCH MONITOR.
HONESTLY, GLOB. I DON'T KNOW HOW YOU CAN SPEND TEN YEARS IN A CLASSROOM AND NOT REMEMBER ANYTHING.
I--
HEY, GUYS, LOOK...

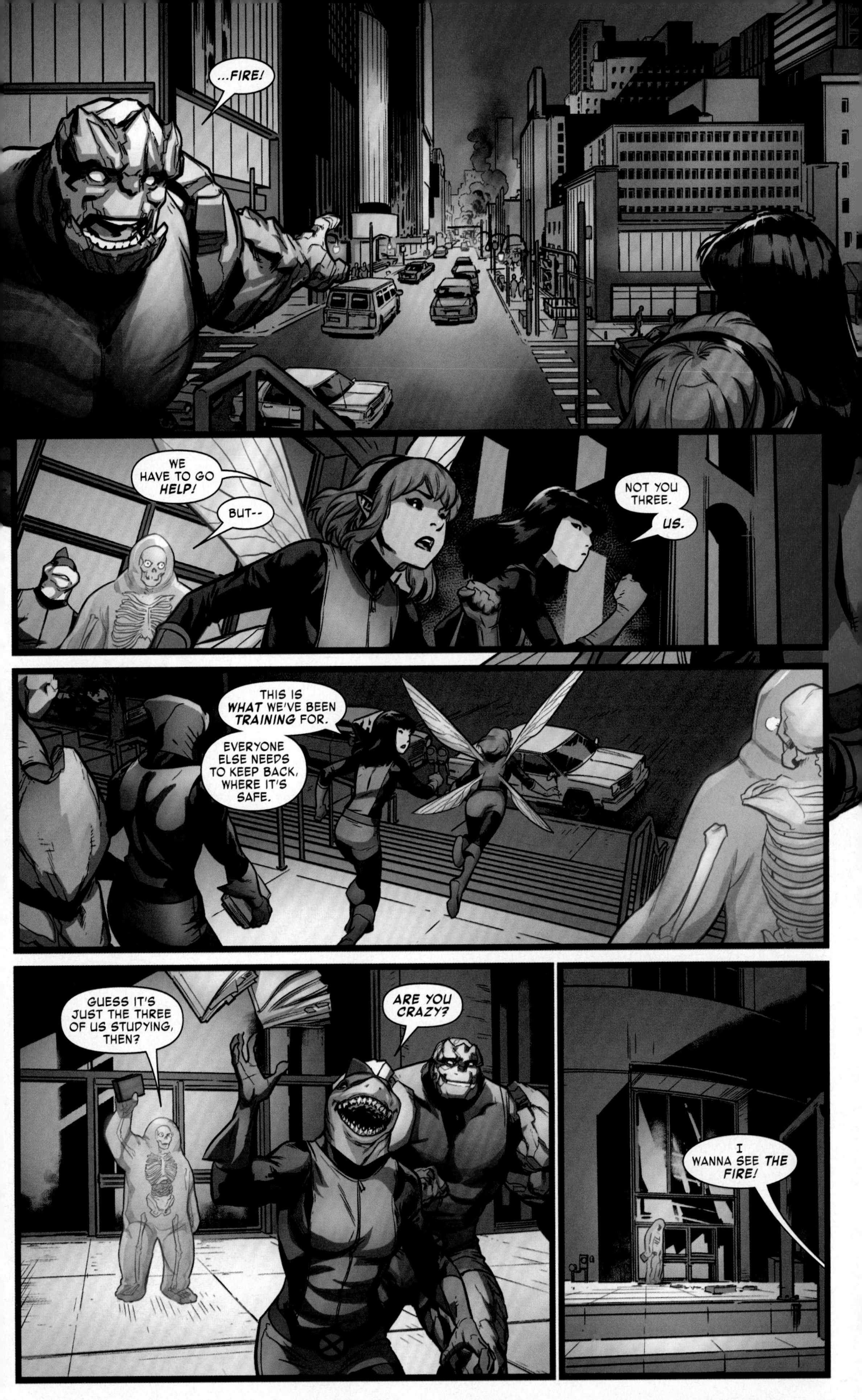
...FIRE!
WE HAVE TO GO HELP!
BUT--
NOT YOU THREE.
US.
THIS IS WHAT WE'VE BEEN TRAINING FOR.
EVERYONE ELSE NEEDS TO KEEP BACK, WHERE IT'S SAFE.
GUESS IT'S JUST THE THREE OF US STUDYING, THEN?
ARE YOU CRAZY?
I WANNA SEE THE FIRE!

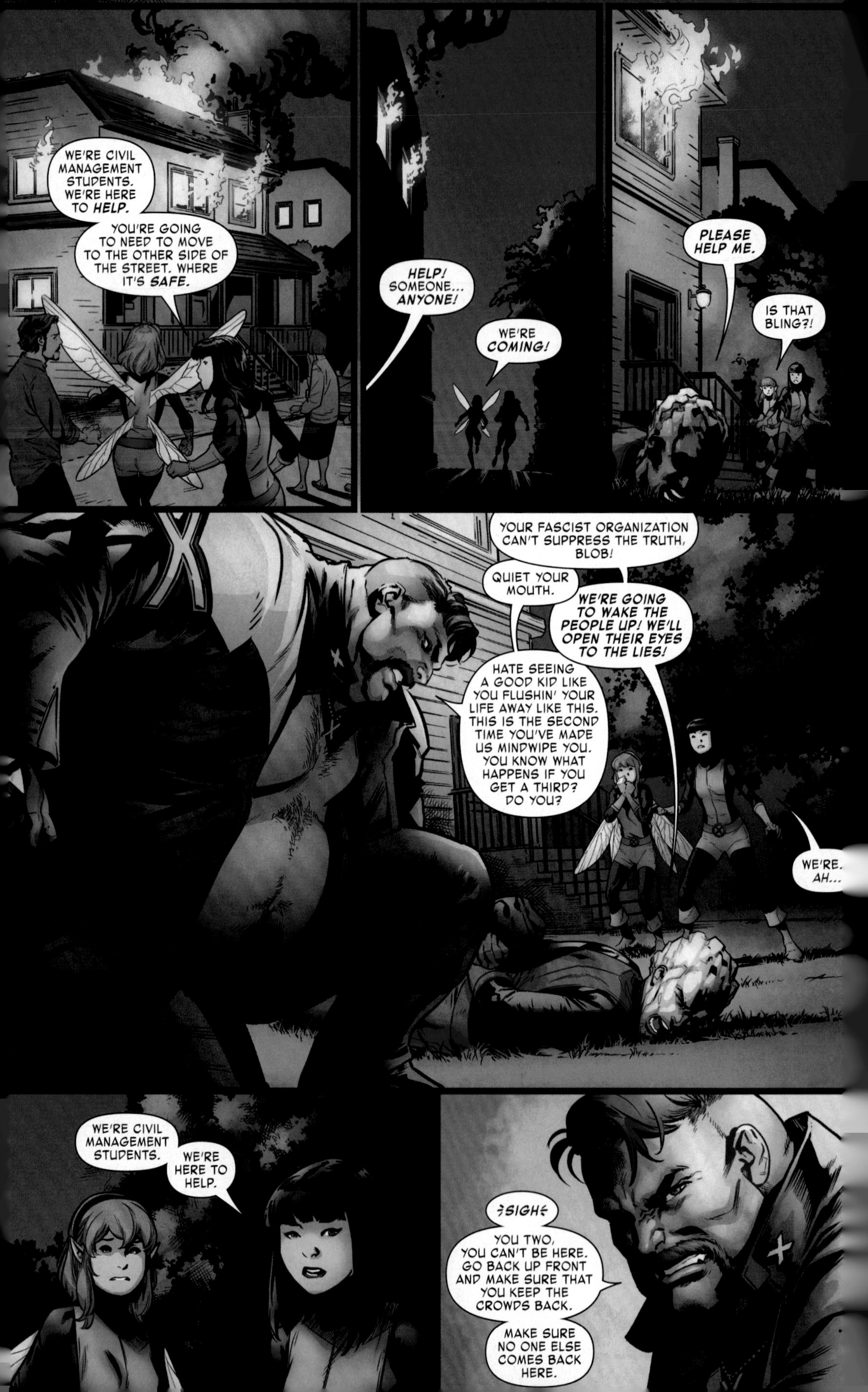
WE'RE CIVIL MANAGEMENT STUDENTS. WE'RE HERE TO *HELP.*
YOU'RE GOING TO NEED TO MOVE TO THE OTHER SIDE OF THE STREET. WHERE IT'S *SAFE.*
HELP! SOMEONE... *ANYONE!*
WE'RE *COMING!*
PLEASE HELP ME.
IS THAT BLING?!
YOUR FASCIST ORGANIZATION CAN'T SUPPRESS THE TRUTH, BLOB!
QUIET YOUR MOUTH.
WE'RE GOING TO WAKE THE PEOPLE UP! WE'LL OPEN THEIR EYES TO THE LIES!
HATE SEEING A GOOD KID LIKE YOU FLUSHIN' YOUR LIFE AWAY LIKE THIS. THIS IS THE SECOND TIME YOU'VE MADE US MINDWIPE YOU. YOU KNOW WHAT HAPPENS IF YOU GET A THIRD? DO YOU?
WE'RE. AH...
WE'RE CIVIL MANAGEMENT STUDENTS.
WE'RE HERE TO HELP.
SIGH
YOU TWO, YOU CAN'T BE HERE. GO BACK UP FRONT AND MAKE SURE THAT YOU KEEP THE CROWDS BACK.
MAKE SURE NO ONE ELSE COMES BACK HERE.

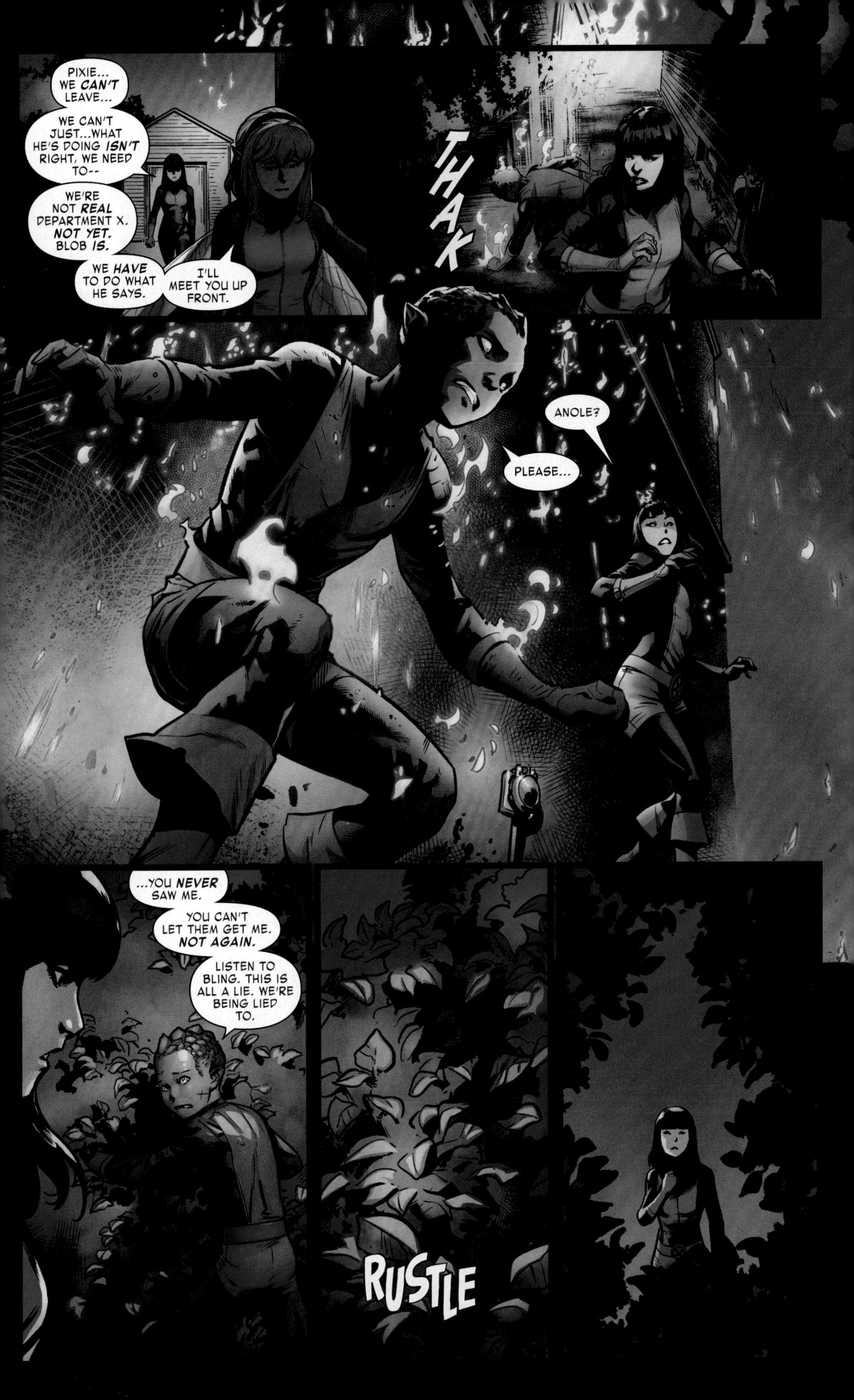
PIXIE... WE CAN'T LEAVE...
WE CAN'T JUST...WHAT HE'S DOING ISN'T RIGHT, WE NEED TO--
WE'RE NOT REAL DEPARTMENT X. NOT YET. BLOB IS.
WE HAVE TO DO WHAT HE SAYS.
I'LL MEET YOU UP FRONT.
THAK
ANOLE?
PLEASE...
...YOU NEVER SAW ME.
YOU CAN'T LET THEM GET ME. NOT AGAIN.
LISTEN TO BLING. THIS IS ALL A LIE. WE'RE BEING LIED TO.
RUSTLE

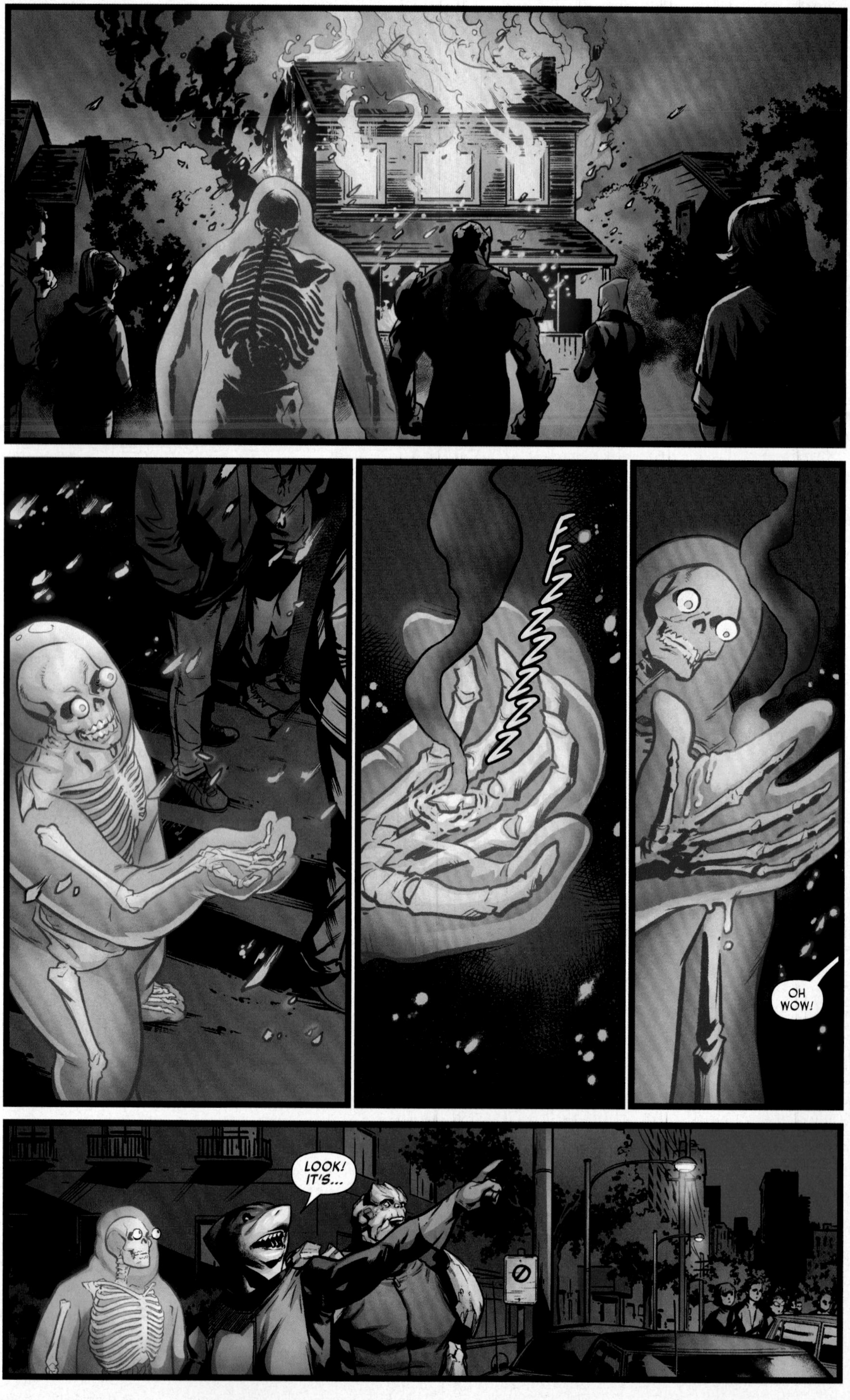

FFZZZZZZZZ
OH WOW!
LOOK! IT'S...

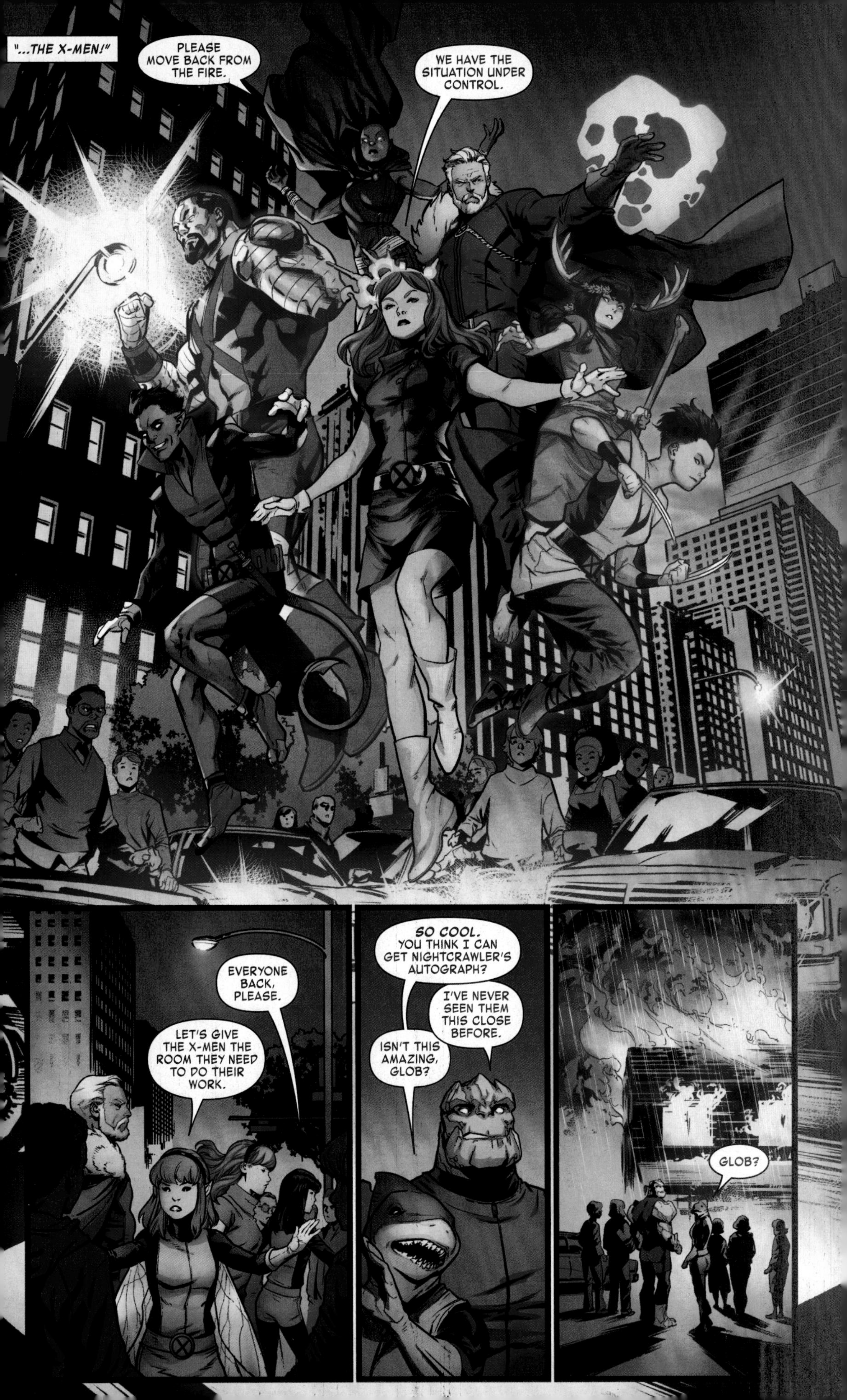
"...THE X-MEN!"
PLEASE MOVE BACK FROM THE FIRE.
WE HAVE THE SITUATION UNDER CONTROL.
EVERYONE BACK, PLEASE.
LET'S GIVE THE X-MEN THE ROOM THEY NEED TO DO THEIR WORK.
SO COOL. YOU THINK I CAN GET NIGHTCRAWLER'S AUTOGRAPH?
I'VE NEVER SEEN THEM THIS CLOSE BEFORE.
ISN'T THIS AMAZING, GLOB?
GLOB?

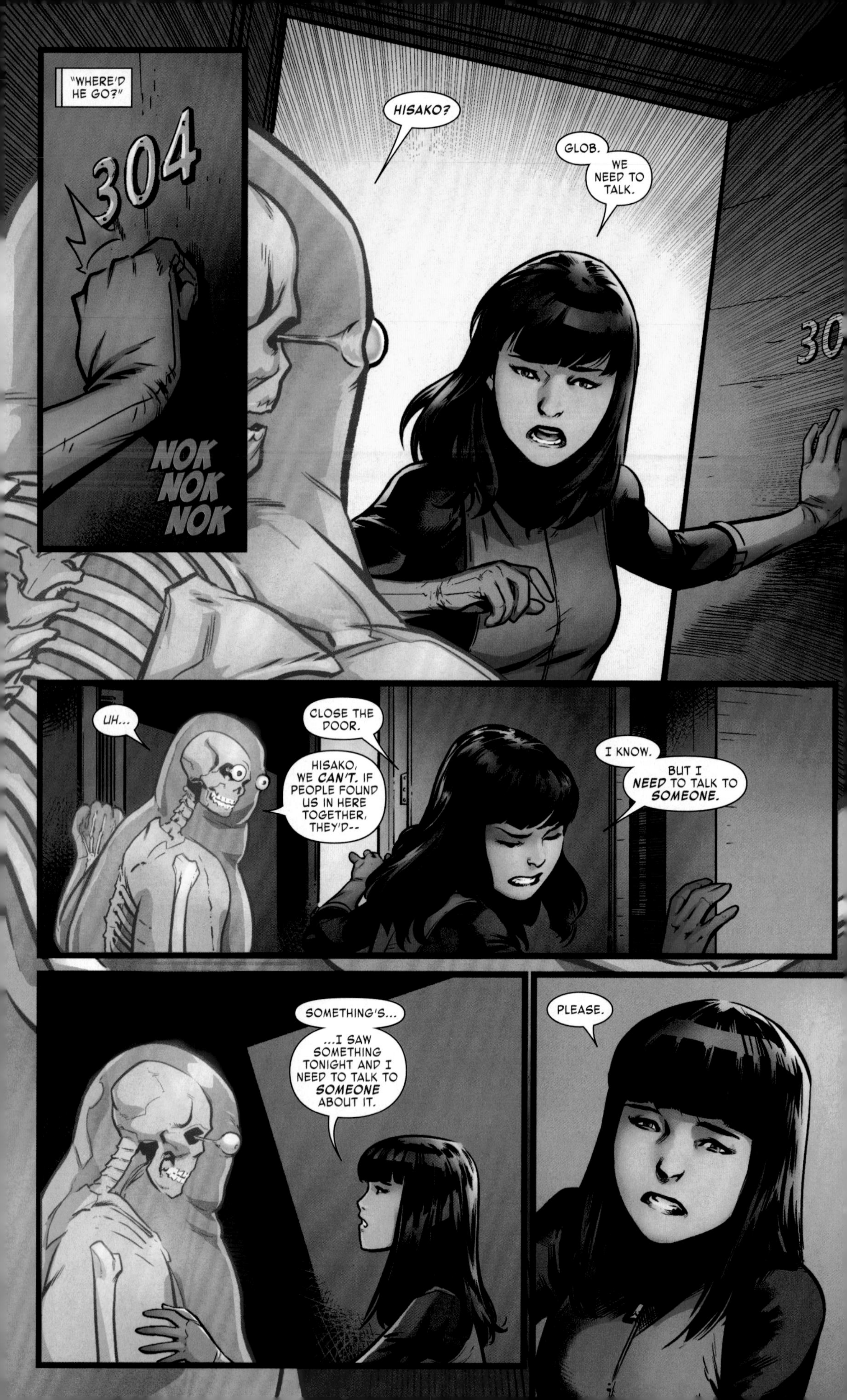
"WHERE'D HE GO?"
304
NOK NOK NOK
HISAKO?
GLOB.
WE NEED TO TALK.
30
UH...
CLOSE THE DOOR.
HISAKO, WE CAN'T. IF PEOPLE FOUND US IN HERE TOGETHER, THEY'D--
I KNOW.
BUT I NEED TO TALK TO SOMEONE.
SOMETHING'S...
...I SAW SOMETHING TONIGHT AND I NEED TO TALK TO SOMEONE ABOUT IT.
PLEASE.

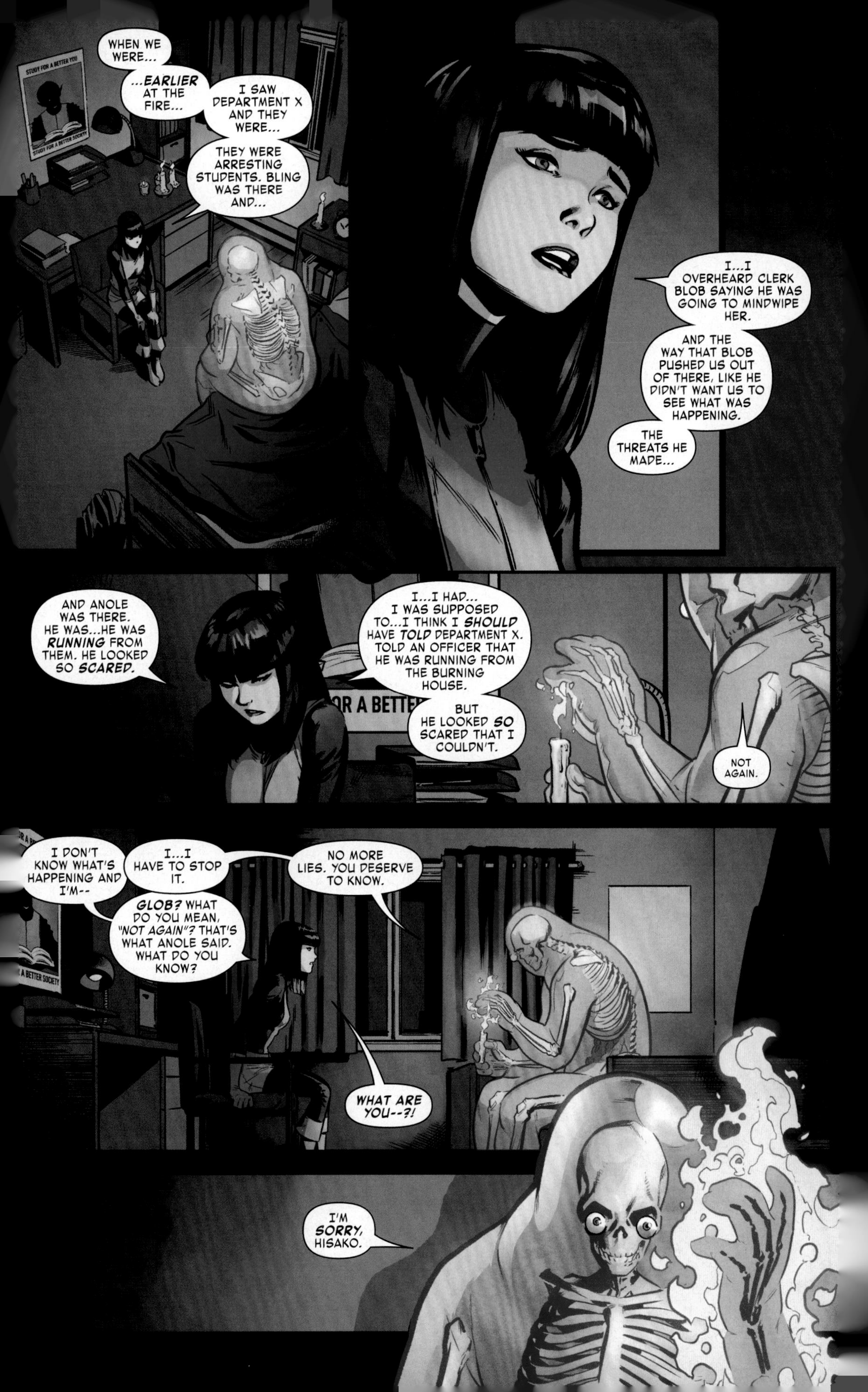
STUDY FOR A BETTER YOU
STUDY FOR A BETTER SOCIETY
WHEN WE WERE...
...EARLIER AT THE FIRE...
I SAW DEPARTMENT X AND THEY WERE...
THEY WERE ARRESTING STUDENTS. BLING WAS THERE AND...
I...I OVERHEARD CLERK BLOB SAYING HE WAS GOING TO MINDWIPE HER.
AND THE WAY THAT BLOB PUSHED US OUT OF THERE, LIKE HE DIDN'T WANT US TO SEE WHAT WAS HAPPENING.
THE THREATS HE MADE...
AND ANOLE WAS THERE. HE WAS...HE WAS RUNNING FROM THEM. HE LOOKED SO SCARED.
I...I HAD... I WAS SUPPOSED TO...I THINK I SHOULD HAVE TOLD DEPARTMENT X. TOLD AN OFFICER THAT HE WAS RUNNING FROM THE BURNING HOUSE.
BUT HE LOOKED SO SCARED THAT I COULDN'T.
NOT AGAIN.
I DON'T KNOW WHAT'S HAPPENING AND I'M--
I...I HAVE TO STOP IT.
GLOB? WHAT DO YOU MEAN, "NOT AGAIN"? THAT'S WHAT ANOLE SAID. WHAT DO YOU KNOW?
NO MORE LIES. YOU DESERVE TO KNOW.
WHAT ARE YOU--?!
I'M SORRY, HISAKO.

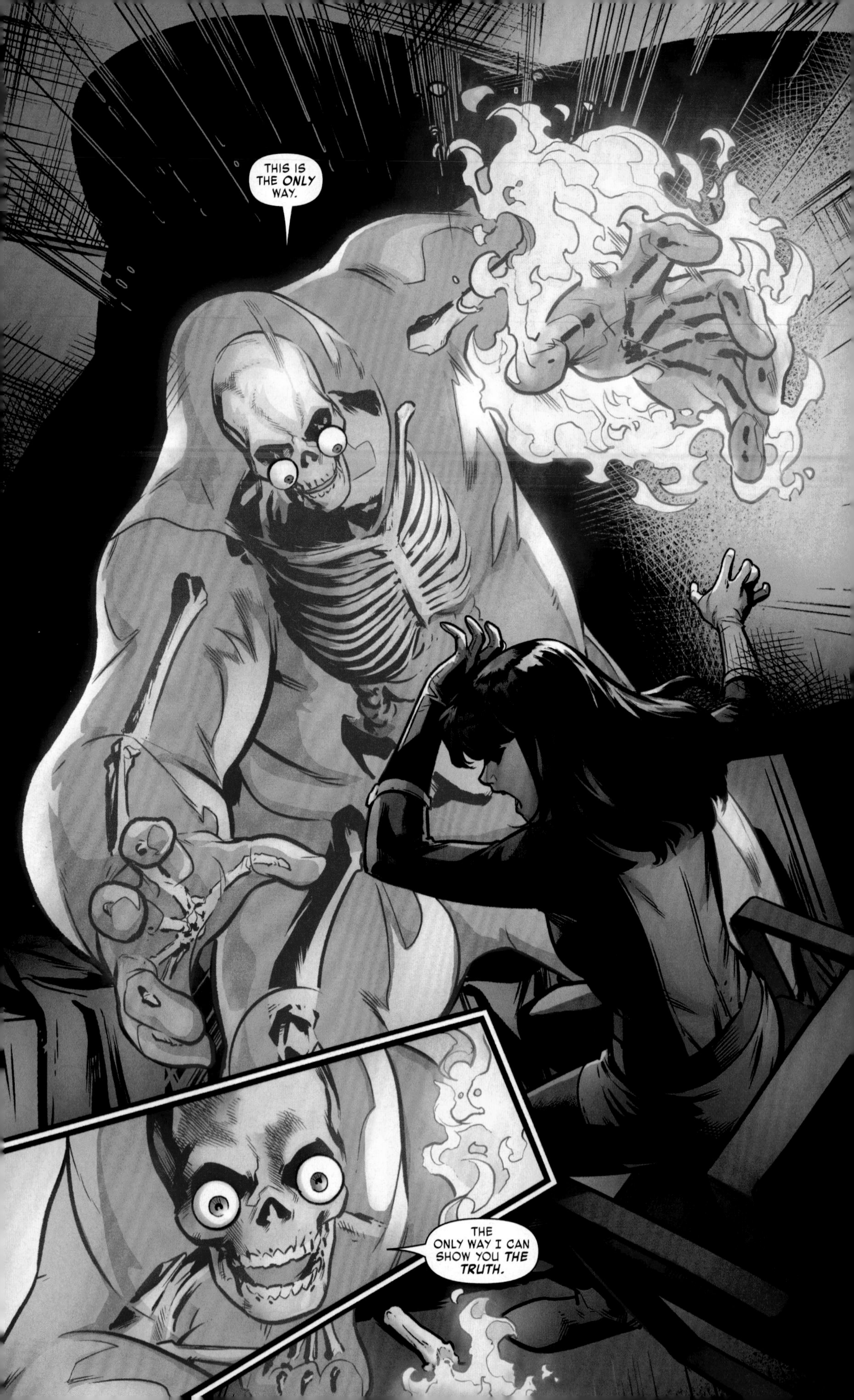
THIS IS THE ONLY WAY.
THE ONLY WAY I CAN SHOW YOU THE TRUTH.

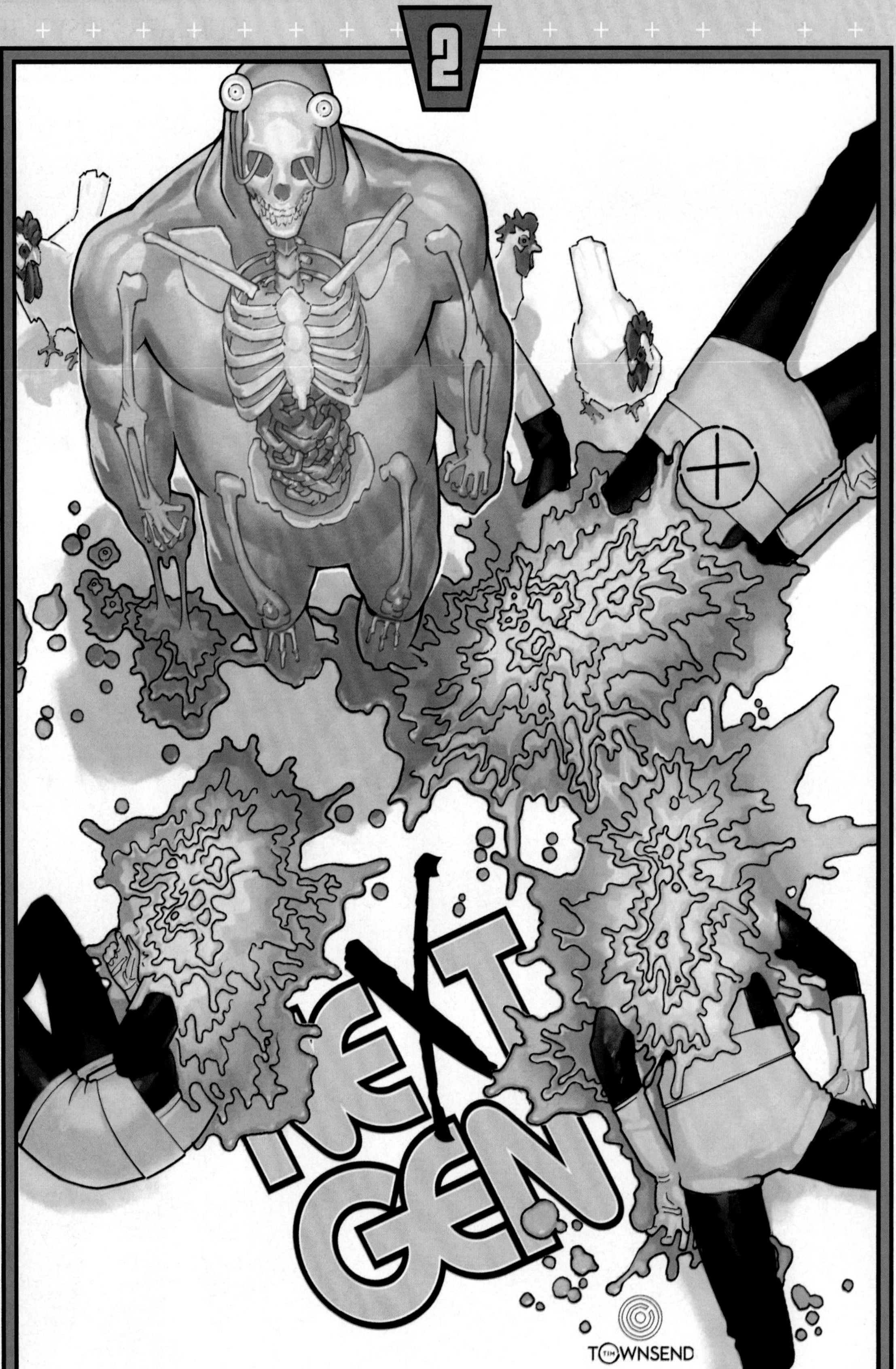
2
NEXT GEN
TOWNSEND

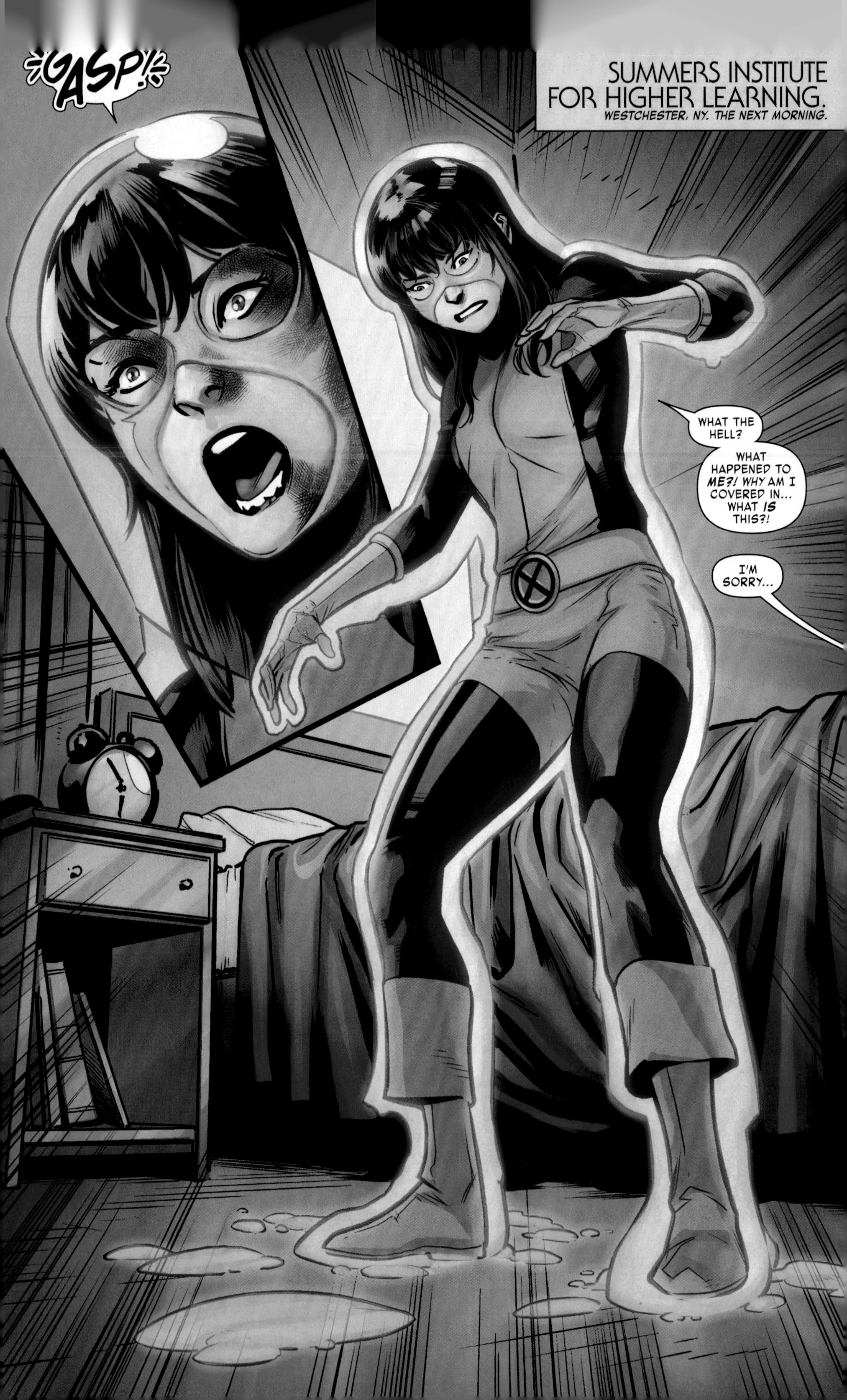
GASP!
SUMMERS INSTITUTE FOR HIGHER LEARNING.
WESTCHESTER, NY. THE NEXT MORNING.
WHAT THE HELL?
WHAT HAPPENED TO ME?! WHY AM I COVERED IN... WHAT IS THIS?!
I'M SORRY...

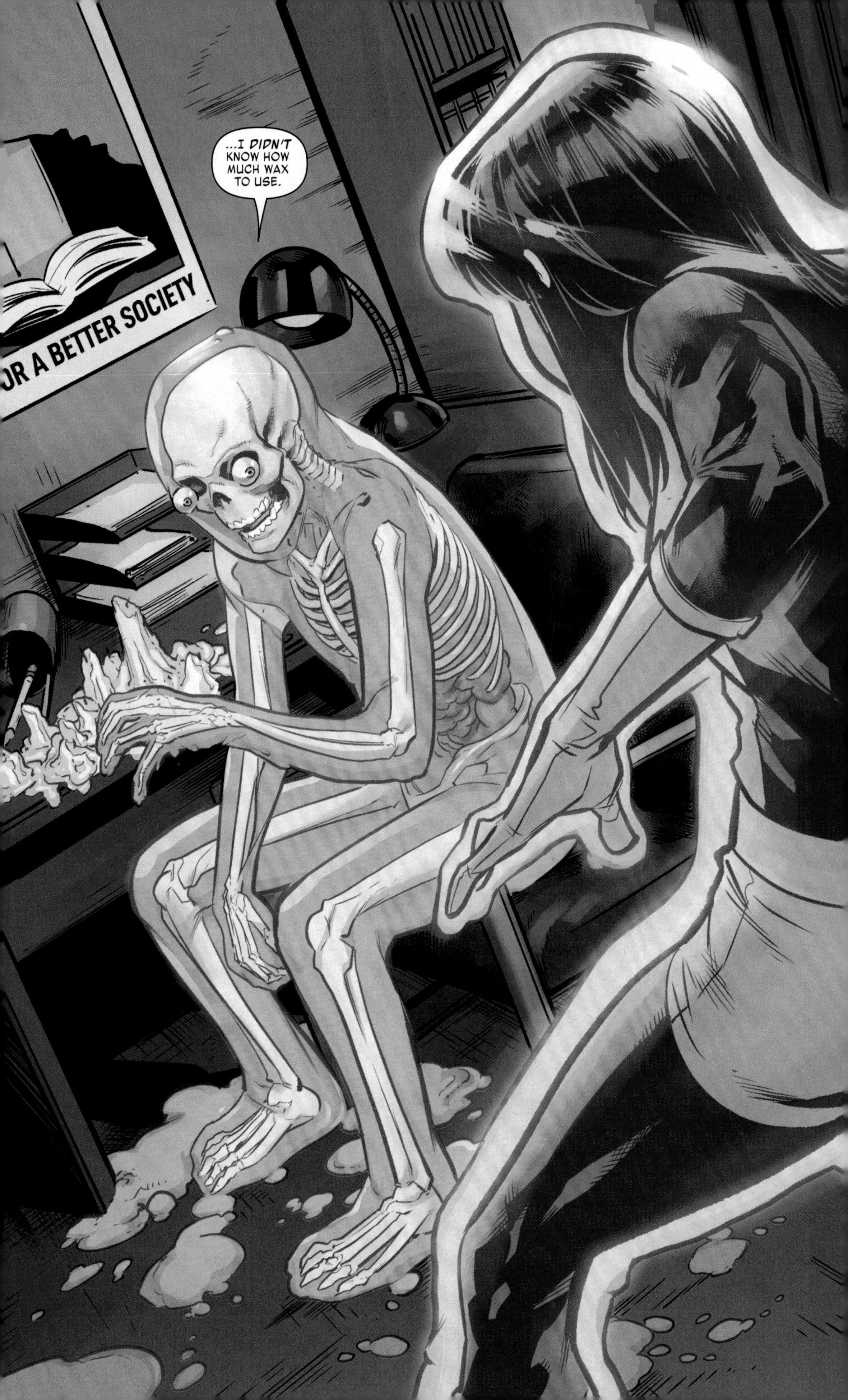

...I DIDN'T KNOW HOW MUCH WAX TO USE.
OR A BETTER SOCIETY

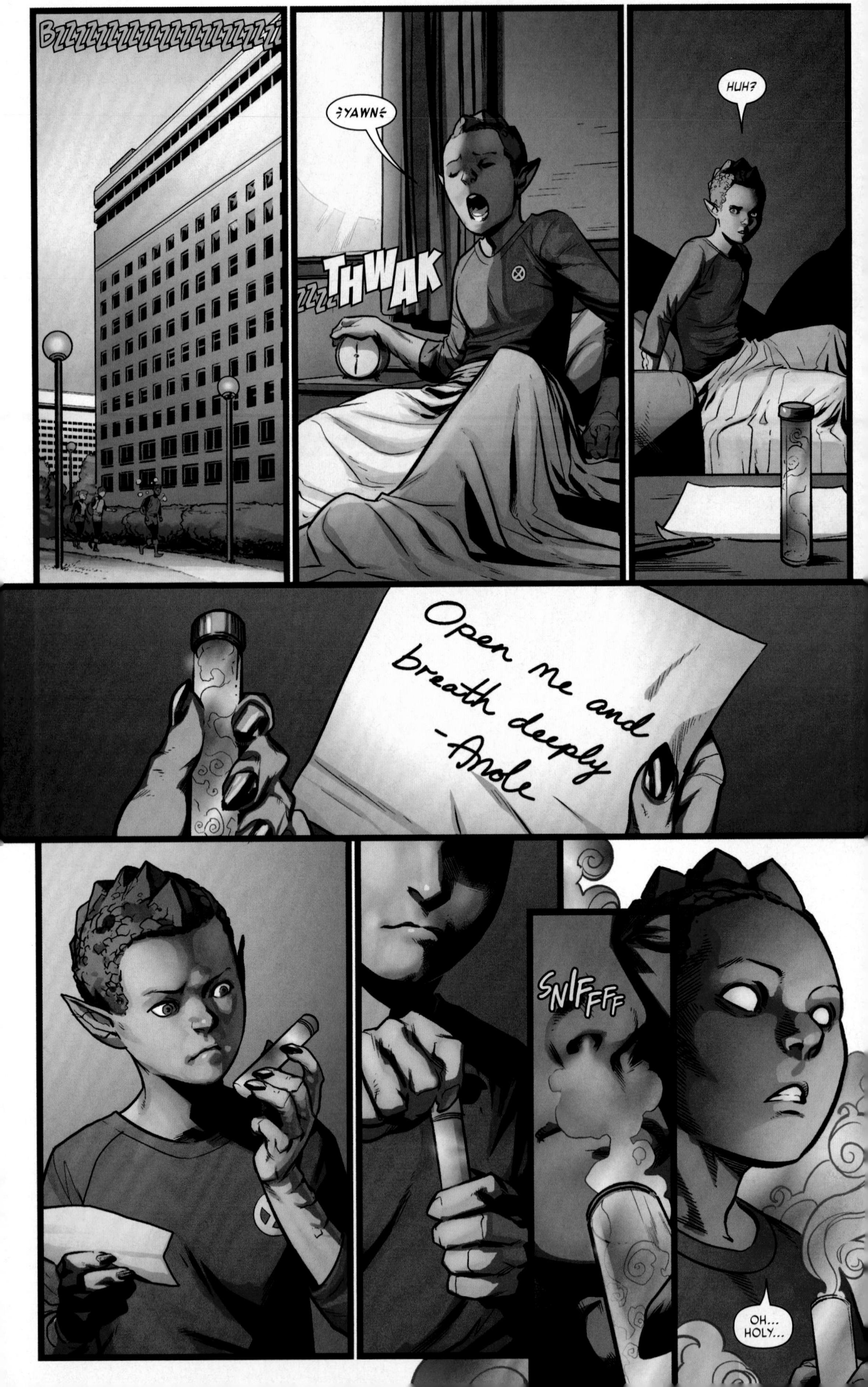
BZZZZZZZZZZZZZZZZZZZ
ZYAWNZ
ZZZ THWAK
HUH?
Open me and
breath deeply
-Anole
SNIFFFF
OH...
HOLY...

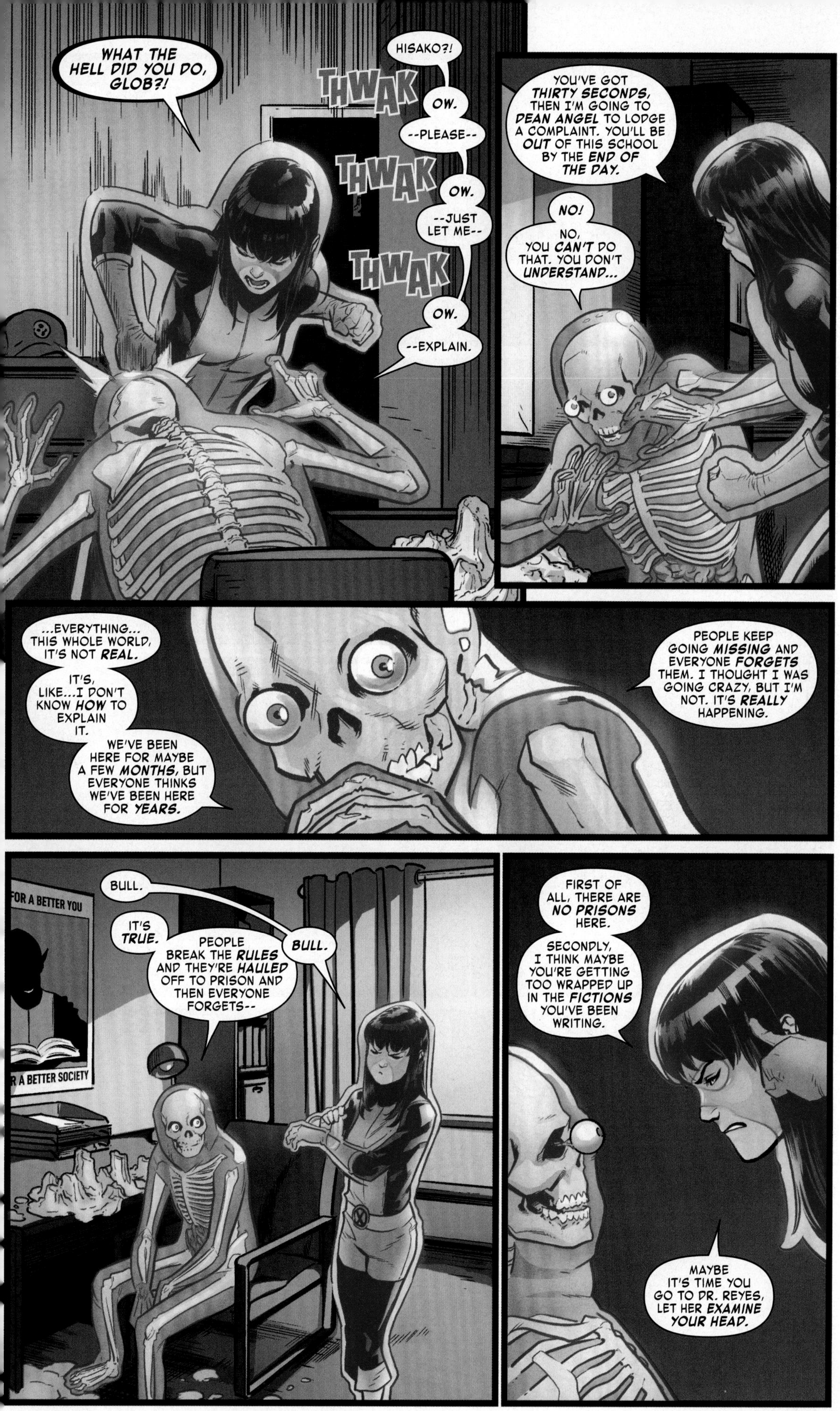
WHAT THE HELL DID YOU DO, GLOB?!
HISAKO?!
THWAK
OW.
--PLEASE--
THWAK
OW.
--JUST LET ME--
THWAK
OW.
--EXPLAIN.
YOU'VE GOT THIRTY SECONDS, THEN I'M GOING TO DEAN ANGEL TO LODGE A COMPLAINT. YOU'LL BE OUT OF THIS SCHOOL BY THE END OF THE DAY.
NO!
NO, YOU CAN'T DO THAT. YOU DON'T UNDERSTAND...
...EVERYTHING... THIS WHOLE WORLD, IT'S NOT REAL.
IT'S, LIKE...I DON'T KNOW HOW TO EXPLAIN IT.
WE'VE BEEN HERE FOR MAYBE A FEW MONTHS, BUT EVERYONE THINKS WE'VE BEEN HERE FOR YEARS.
PEOPLE KEEP GOING MISSING AND EVERYONE FORGETS THEM. I THOUGHT I WAS GOING CRAZY, BUT I'M NOT. IT'S REALLY HAPPENING.
FOR A BETTER YOU
R A BETTER SOCIETY
BULL.
IT'S TRUE.
PEOPLE BREAK THE RULES AND THEY'RE HAULED OFF TO PRISON AND THEN EVERYONE FORGETS--
BULL.
FIRST OF ALL, THERE ARE NO PRISONS HERE.
SECONDLY, I THINK MAYBE YOU'RE GETTING TOO WRAPPED UP IN THE FICTIONS YOU'VE BEEN WRITING.
MAYBE IT'S TIME YOU GO TO DR. REYES, LET HER EXAMINE YOUR HEAD.

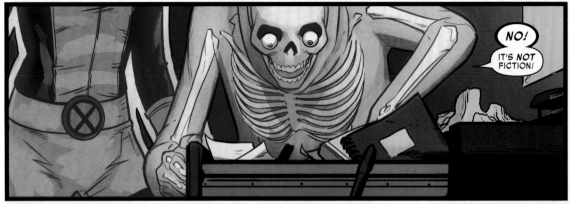

NO! IT'S *NOT* FICTION!

LOOK. IT'S...IT'S *EVERYTHING* I CAN REMEMBER FROM... FROM *BEFORE.*

BEFORE WE CAME HERE. *BEFORE* ALL OF THIS.

I'M WRITING IT ALL DOWN SO THAT THERE'S A RECORD OF IT.

I TOLD IARA IT WAS FAN FICTION BECAUSE I DIDN'T WANT THEM TO KNOW.

THEM *WHO?*

THEM!

THE *PEOPLE* WHO MAKE *PEOPLE* DISAPPEAR!

GET YOUR HANDS *OFF* OF ME!

I'M NOT BUYING INTO YOUR CONSPIRACY THEORIES, GLOB.

I'M NOT SURE *WHAT* I'M GOING TO DO.

I NEED SOME *TIME* TO THINK.

PLEASE *DON'T* TELL--

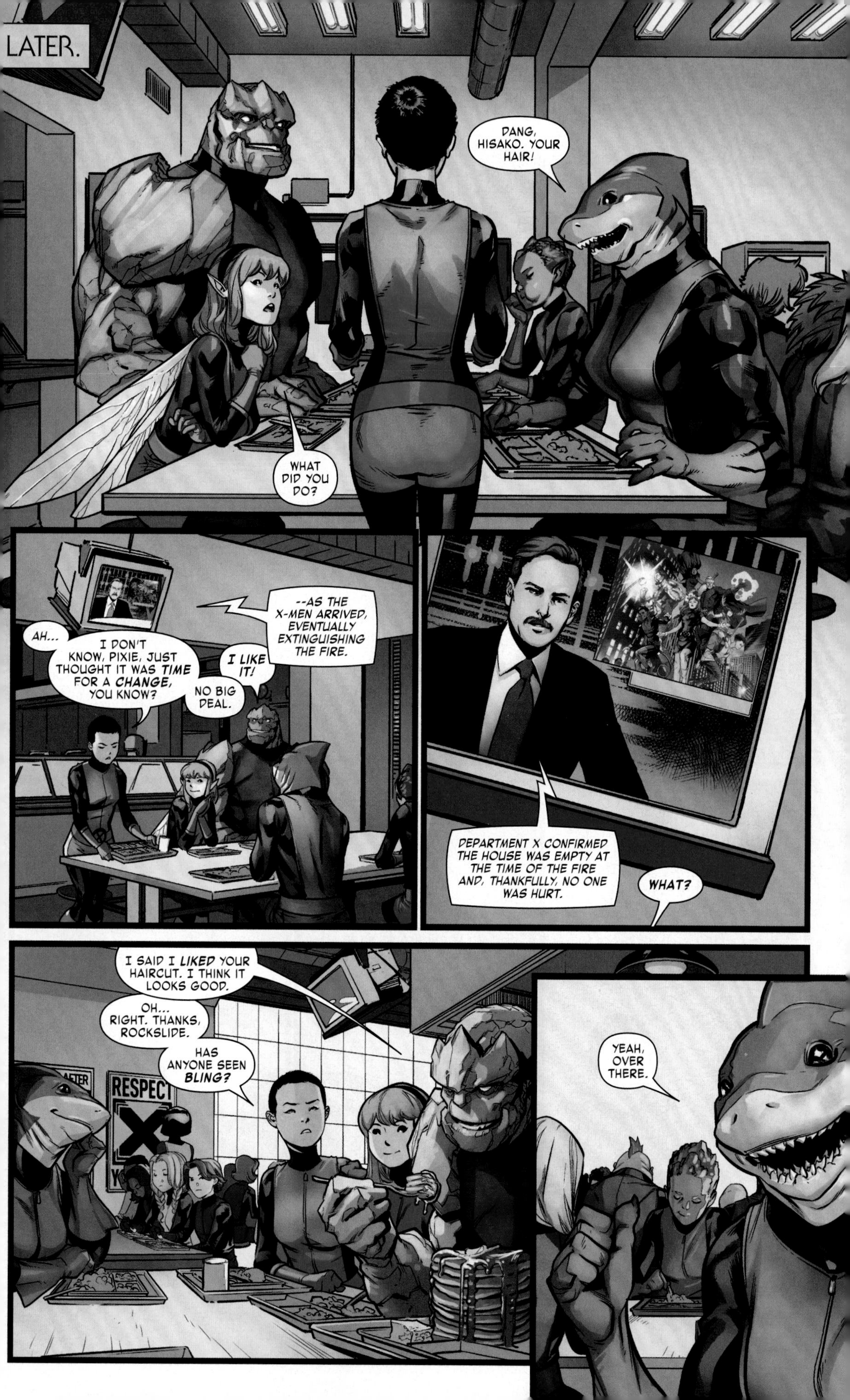
LATER.
DANG, HISAKO. YOUR HAIR!
WHAT DID YOU DO?
--AS THE X-MEN ARRIVED, EVENTUALLY EXTINGUISHING THE FIRE.
AH...
I DON'T KNOW, PIXIE, JUST THOUGHT IT WAS TIME FOR A CHANGE, YOU KNOW?
I LIKE IT!
NO BIG DEAL.
DEPARTMENT X CONFIRMED THE HOUSE WAS EMPTY AT THE TIME OF THE FIRE AND, THANKFULLY, NO ONE WAS HURT.
WHAT?
I SAID I LIKED YOUR HAIRCUT. I THINK IT LOOKS GOOD.
OH... RIGHT. THANKS, ROCKSLIDE.
HAS ANYONE SEEN BLING?
YEAH, OVER THERE.
RESPECT

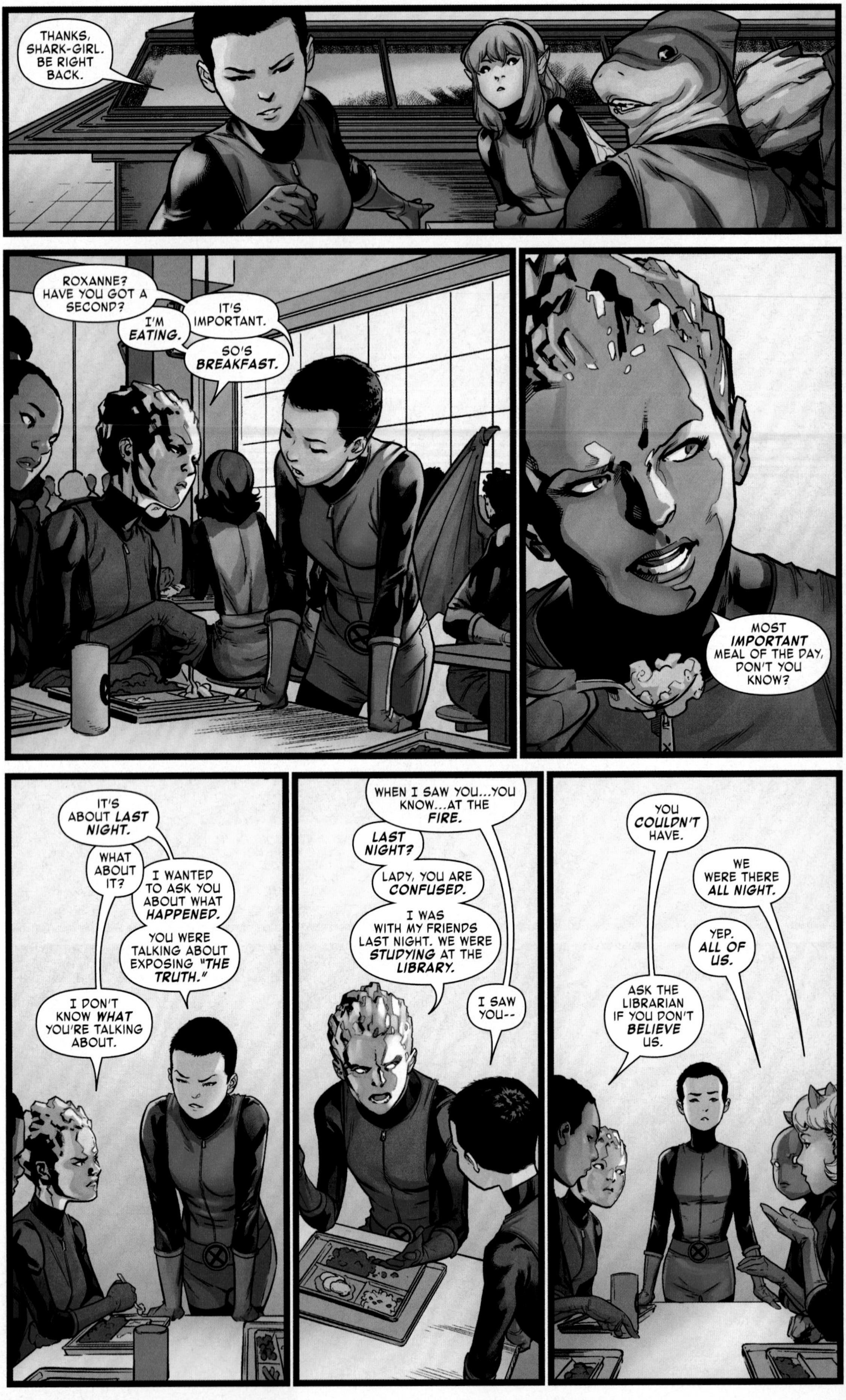
THANKS, SHARK-GIRL. BE RIGHT BACK.
ROXANNE? HAVE YOU GOT A SECOND?
I'M EATING.
IT'S IMPORTANT.
SO'S BREAKFAST.
MOST IMPORTANT MEAL OF THE DAY, DON'T YOU KNOW?
IT'S ABOUT LAST NIGHT.
WHAT ABOUT IT?
I WANTED TO ASK YOU ABOUT WHAT HAPPENED.
YOU WERE TALKING ABOUT EXPOSING "THE TRUTH."
I DON'T KNOW WHAT YOU'RE TALKING ABOUT.
WHEN I SAW YOU...YOU KNOW...AT THE FIRE.
LAST NIGHT?
LADY, YOU ARE CONFUSED.
I WAS WITH MY FRIENDS LAST NIGHT. WE WERE STUDYING AT THE LIBRARY.
I SAW YOU--
YOU COULDN'T HAVE.
WE WERE THERE ALL NIGHT.
YEP. ALL OF US.
ASK THE LIBRARIAN IF YOU DON'T BELIEVE US.

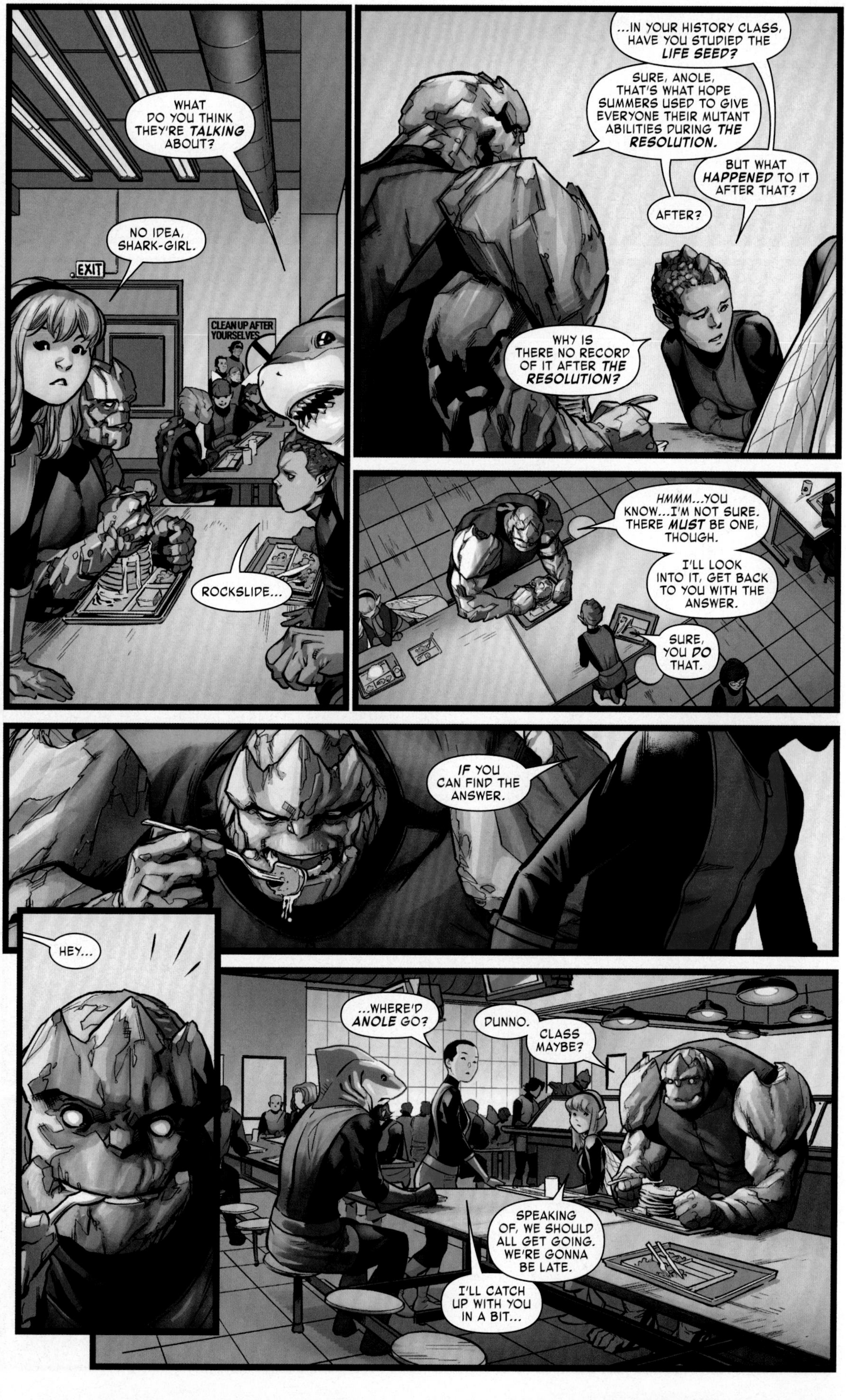

WHAT DO YOU THINK THEY'RE *TALKING* ABOUT?
NO IDEA, SHARK-GIRL.
EXIT
CLEAN UP AFTER YOURSELVES
ROCKSLIDE...
...IN YOUR HISTORY CLASS, HAVE YOU STUDIED THE *LIFE SEED?*
SURE, ANOLE, THAT'S WHAT HOPE SUMMERS USED TO GIVE EVERYONE THEIR MUTANT ABILITIES DURING *THE RESOLUTION.*
BUT WHAT *HAPPENED* TO IT AFTER THAT?
AFTER?
WHY IS THERE NO RECORD OF IT AFTER *THE RESOLUTION?*
HMMM...YOU KNOW...I'M NOT SURE. THERE *MUST* BE ONE, THOUGH.
I'LL LOOK INTO IT, GET BACK TO YOU WITH THE ANSWER.
SURE, YOU *DO* THAT.
IF YOU CAN FIND THE ANSWER.
HEY...
...WHERE'D *ANOLE* GO?
DUNNO.
CLASS MAYBE?
SPEAKING OF, WE SHOULD ALL GET GOING. WE'RE GONNA BE LATE.
I'LL CATCH UP WITH YOU IN A BIT...

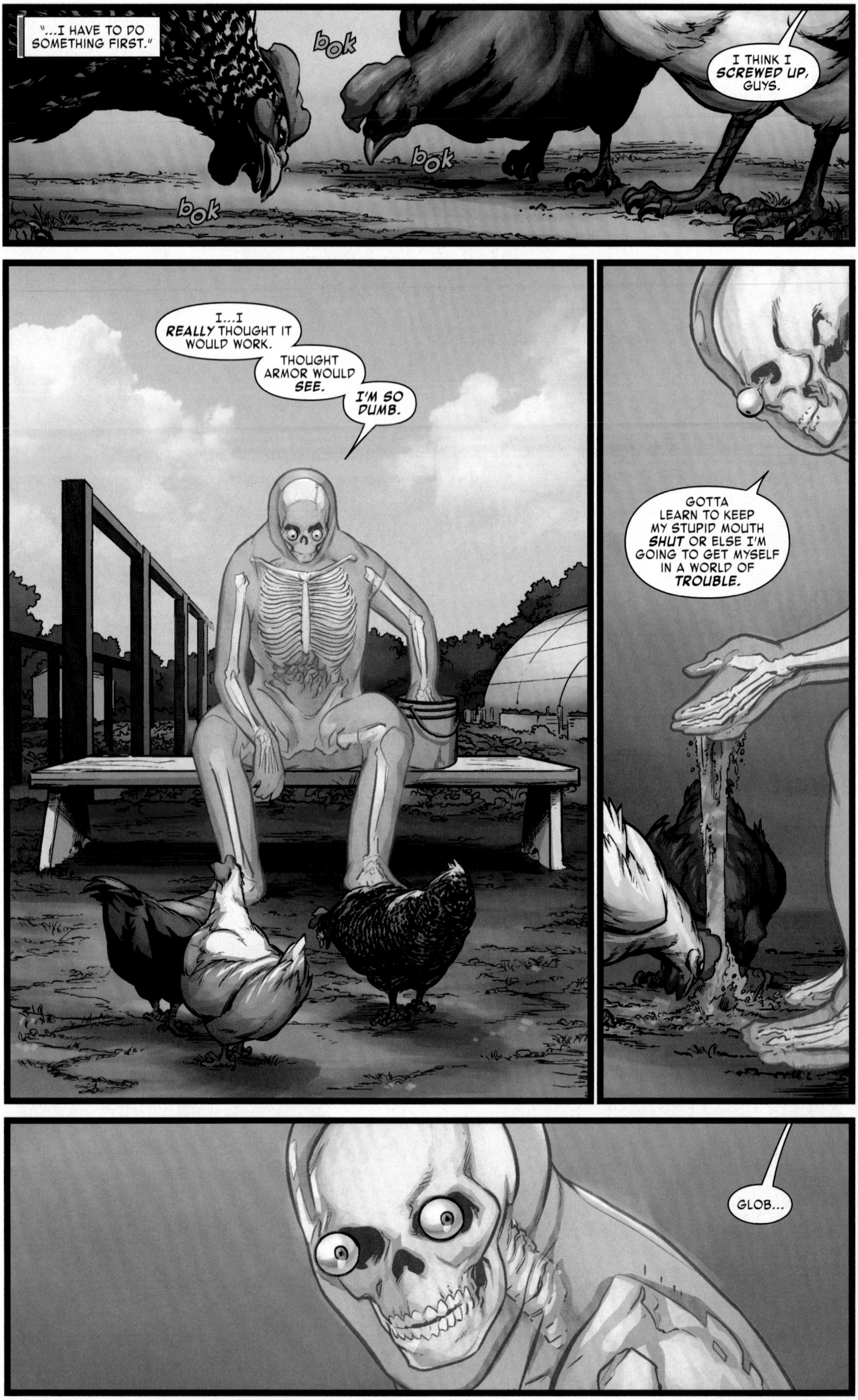
"...I HAVE TO DO SOMETHING FIRST."
bok
bok
bok
I THINK I SCREWED UP, GUYS.
I...I REALLY THOUGHT IT WOULD WORK.
THOUGHT ARMOR WOULD SEE.
I'M SO DUMB.
GOTTA LEARN TO KEEP MY STUPID MOUTH SHUT OR ELSE I'M GOING TO GET MYSELF IN A WORLD OF TROUBLE.
GLOB...

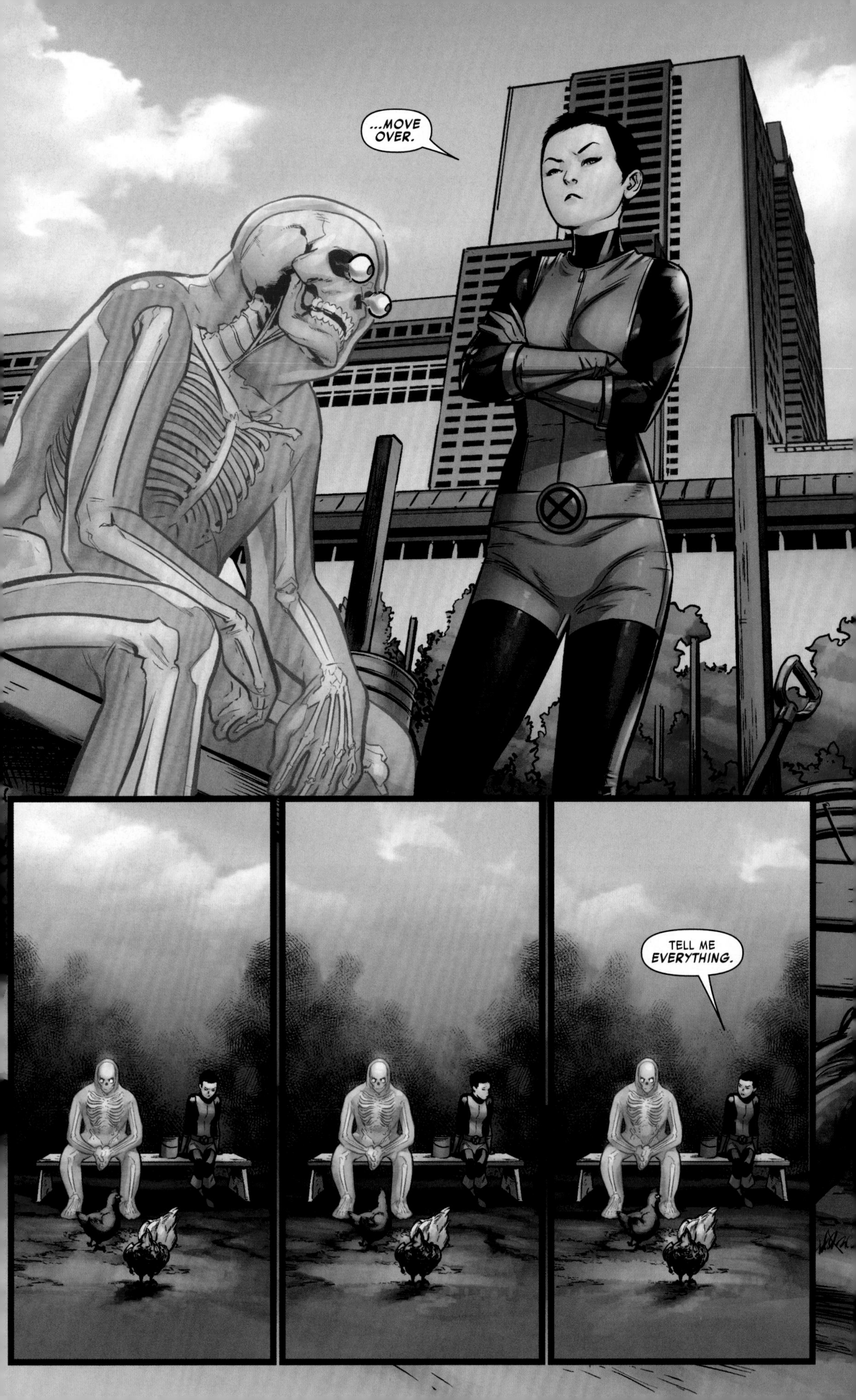
...MOVE OVER.
TELL ME EVERYTHING.

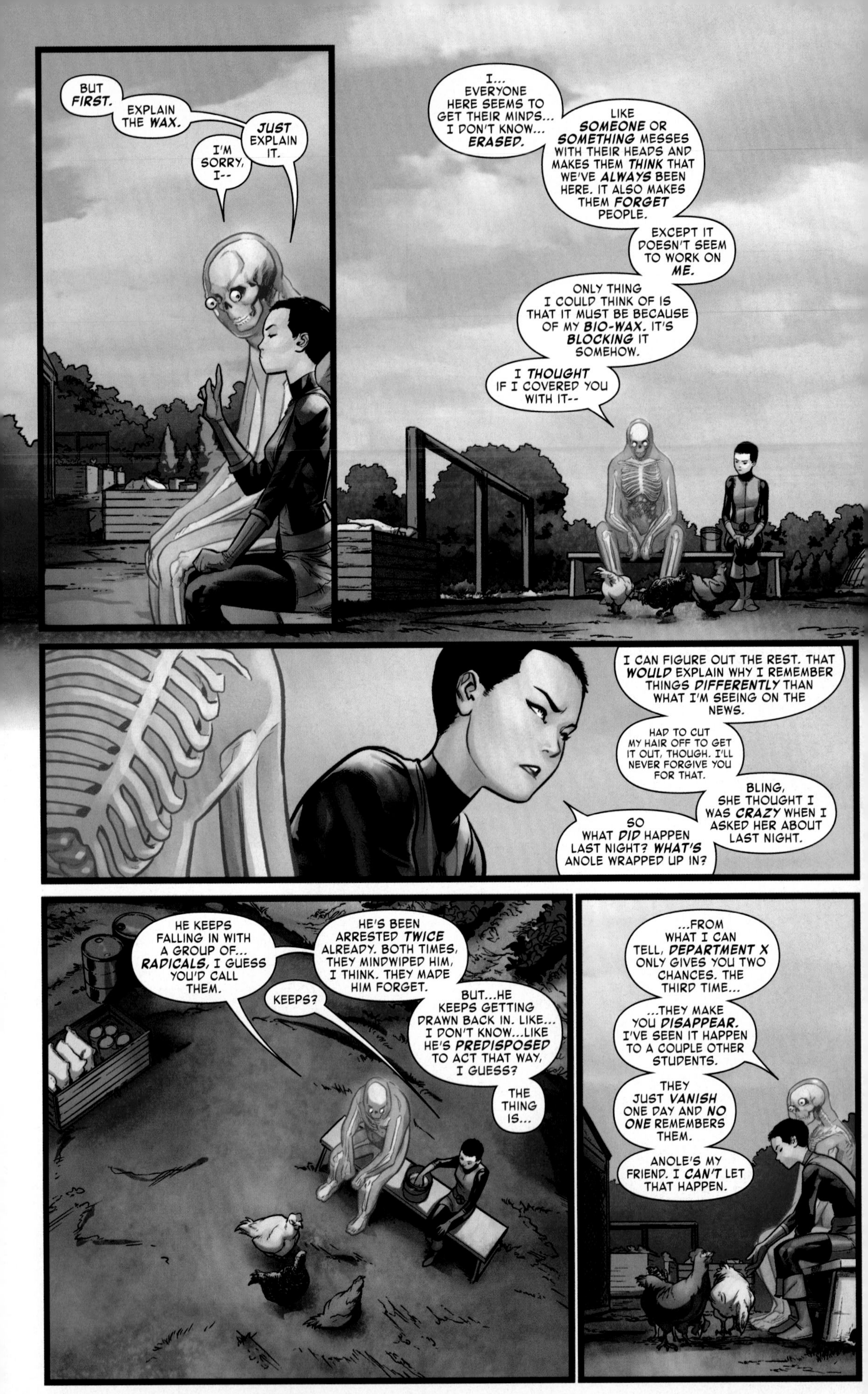

BUT FIRST.
EXPLAIN THE WAX.
JUST EXPLAIN IT.
I'M SORRY, I--
I... EVERYONE HERE SEEMS TO GET THEIR MINDS... I DON'T KNOW... ERASED.
LIKE SOMEONE OR SOMETHING MESSES WITH THEIR HEADS AND MAKES THEM THINK THAT WE'VE ALWAYS BEEN HERE. IT ALSO MAKES THEM FORGET PEOPLE.
EXCEPT IT DOESN'T SEEM TO WORK ON ME.
ONLY THING I COULD THINK OF IS THAT IT MUST BE BECAUSE OF MY BIO-WAX. IT'S BLOCKING IT SOMEHOW.
I THOUGHT IF I COVERED YOU WITH IT--
I CAN FIGURE OUT THE REST. THAT WOULD EXPLAIN WHY I REMEMBER THINGS DIFFERENTLY THAN WHAT I'M SEEING ON THE NEWS.
HAD TO CUT MY HAIR OFF TO GET IT OUT, THOUGH. I'LL NEVER FORGIVE YOU FOR THAT.
BLING, SHE THOUGHT I WAS CRAZY WHEN I ASKED HER ABOUT LAST NIGHT.
SO WHAT DID HAPPEN LAST NIGHT? WHAT'S ANOLE WRAPPED UP IN?
HE KEEPS FALLING IN WITH A GROUP OF... RADICALS, I GUESS YOU'D CALL THEM.
KEEPS?
HE'S BEEN ARRESTED TWICE ALREADY. BOTH TIMES, THEY MINDWIPED HIM, I THINK. THEY MADE HIM FORGET.
BUT...HE KEEPS GETTING DRAWN BACK IN. LIKE... I DON'T KNOW...LIKE HE'S PREDISPOSED TO ACT THAT WAY, I GUESS?
THE THING IS...
...FROM WHAT I CAN TELL, DEPARTMENT X ONLY GIVES YOU TWO CHANCES. THE THIRD TIME...
...THEY MAKE YOU DISAPPEAR. I'VE SEEN IT HAPPEN TO A COUPLE OTHER STUDENTS.
THEY JUST VANISH ONE DAY AND NO ONE REMEMBERS THEM.
ANOLE'S MY FRIEND. I CAN'T LET THAT HAPPEN.

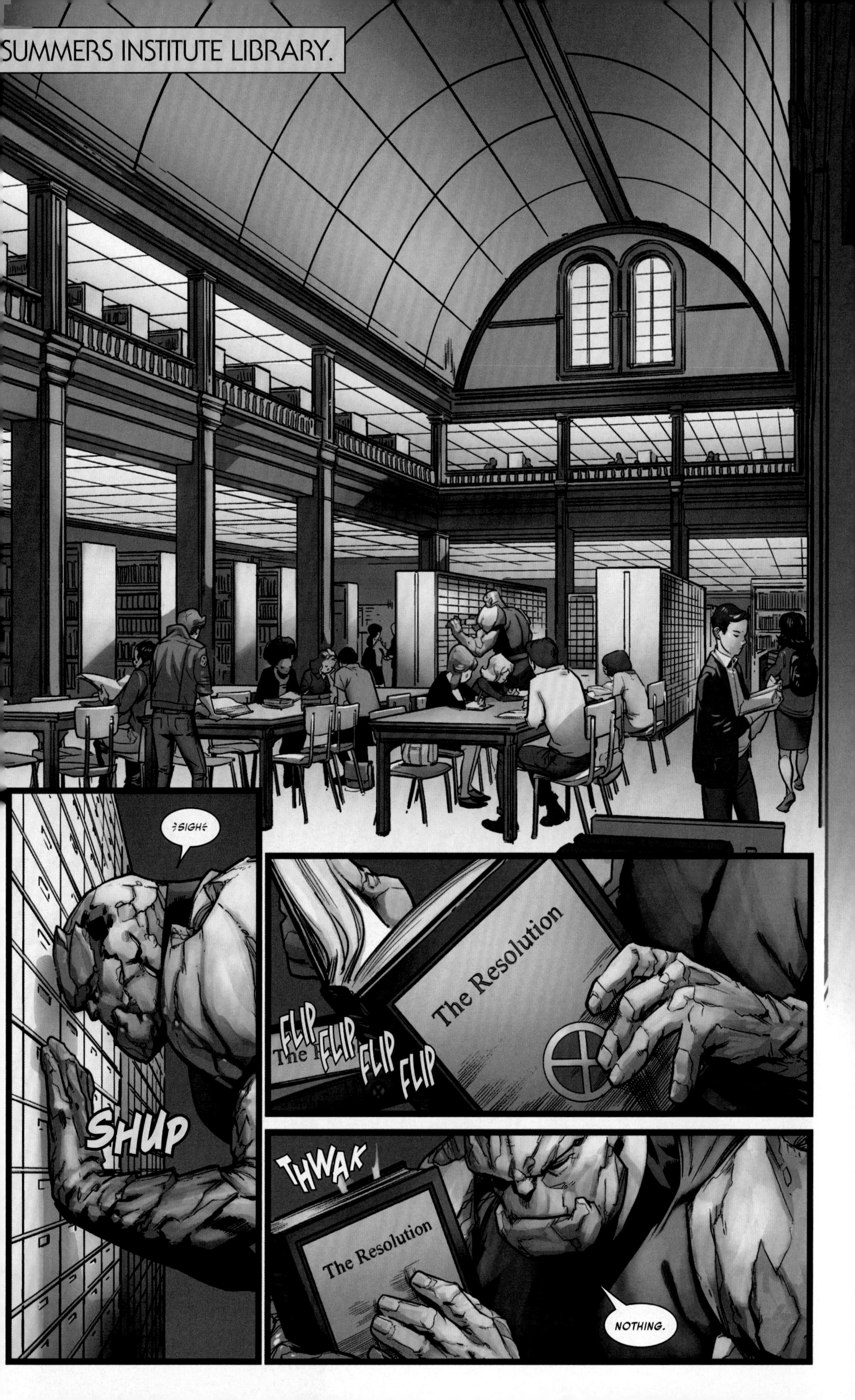
SUMMERS INSTITUTE LIBRARY.
SIGH
SHUP
FLIP FLIP FLIP FLIP
The Resolution
THWAK
The Resolution
NOTHING.

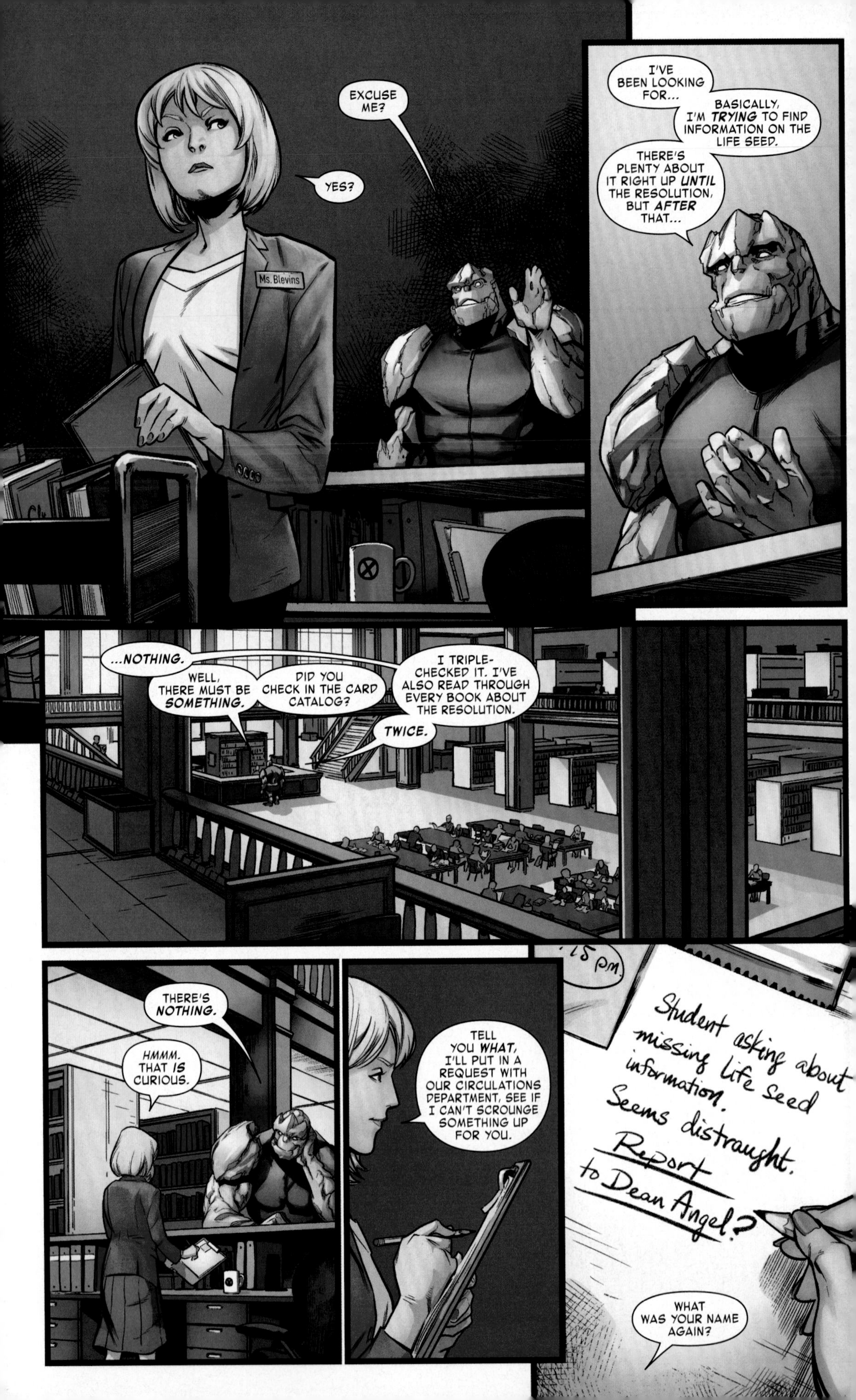

EXCUSE ME?
YES?
Ms. Blevins
I'VE BEEN LOOKING FOR...
BASICALLY, I'M TRYING TO FIND INFORMATION ON THE LIFE SEED.
THERE'S PLENTY ABOUT IT RIGHT UP UNTIL THE RESOLUTION, BUT AFTER THAT...
...NOTHING.
WELL, THERE MUST BE SOMETHING.
DID YOU CHECK IN THE CARD CATALOG?
I TRIPLE-CHECKED IT. I'VE ALSO READ THROUGH EVERY BOOK ABOUT THE RESOLUTION.
TWICE.
THERE'S NOTHING.
HMMM. THAT IS CURIOUS.
TELL YOU WHAT, I'LL PUT IN A REQUEST WITH OUR CIRCULATIONS DEPARTMENT, SEE IF I CAN'T SCROUNGE SOMETHING UP FOR YOU.
Student asking about missing Life Seed information. Seems distraught. Report to Dean Angel?
WHAT WAS YOUR NAME AGAIN?

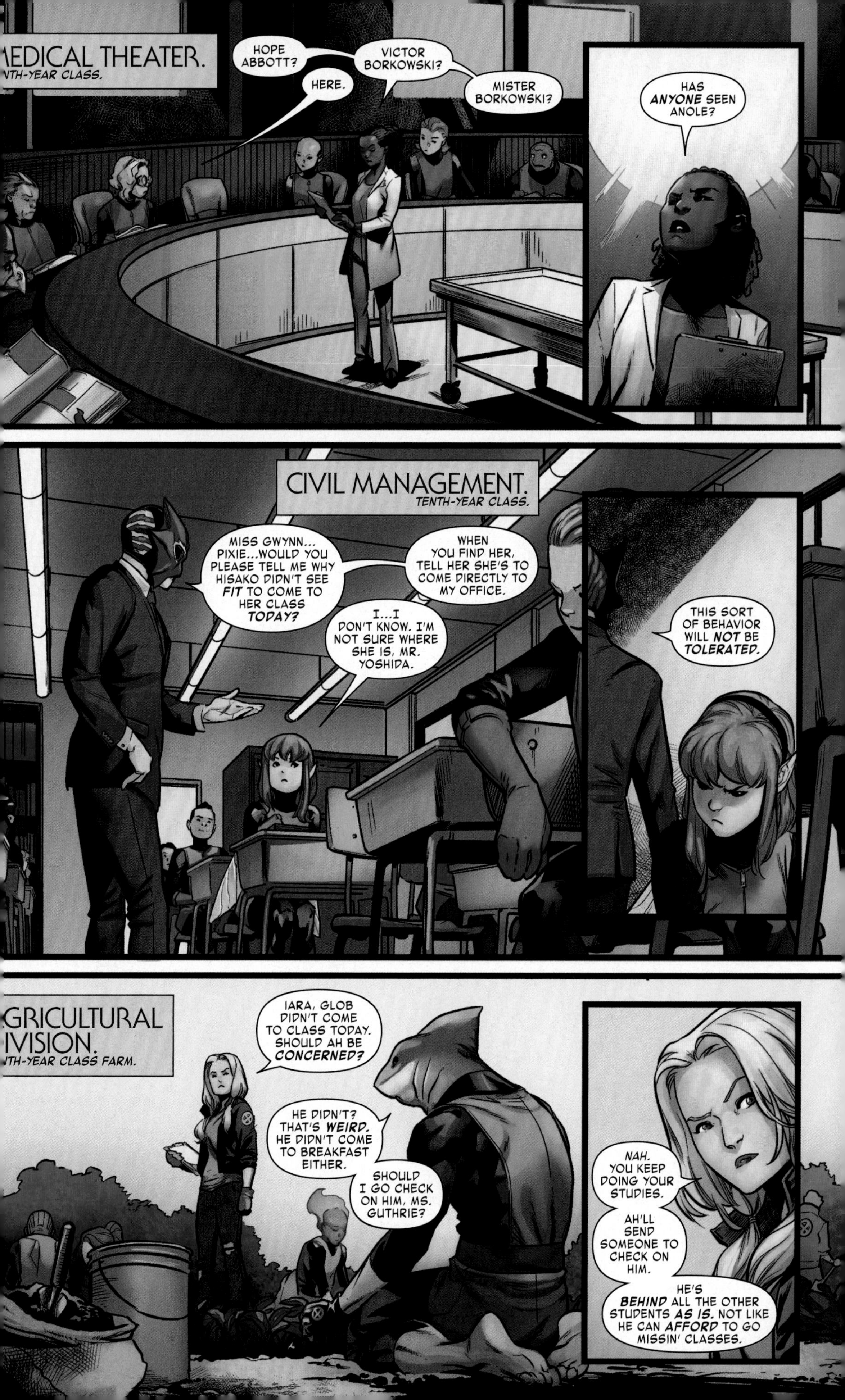

MEDICAL THEATER.
NTH-YEAR CLASS.
HOPE ABBOTT?
HERE.
VICTOR BORKOWSKI?
MISTER BORKOWSKI?
HAS ANYONE SEEN ANOLE?
CIVIL MANAGEMENT.
TENTH-YEAR CLASS.
MISS GWYNN... PIXIE...WOULD YOU PLEASE TELL ME WHY HISAKO DIDN'T SEE FIT TO COME TO HER CLASS TODAY?
I...I DON'T KNOW. I'M NOT SURE WHERE SHE IS, MR. YOSHIDA.
WHEN YOU FIND HER, TELL HER SHE'S TO COME DIRECTLY TO MY OFFICE.
THIS SORT OF BEHAVIOR WILL NOT BE TOLERATED.
GRICULTURAL IVISION.
NTH-YEAR CLASS FARM.
IARA, GLOB DIDN'T COME TO CLASS TODAY. SHOULD AH BE CONCERNED?
HE DIDN'T? THAT'S WEIRD. HE DIDN'T COME TO BREAKFAST EITHER.
SHOULD I GO CHECK ON HIM, MS. GUTHRIE?
NAH. YOU KEEP DOING YOUR STUDIES.
AH'LL SEND SOMEONE TO CHECK ON HIM.
HE'S BEHIND ALL THE OTHER STUDENTS AS IS. NOT LIKE HE CAN AFFORD TO GO MISSIN' CLASSES.

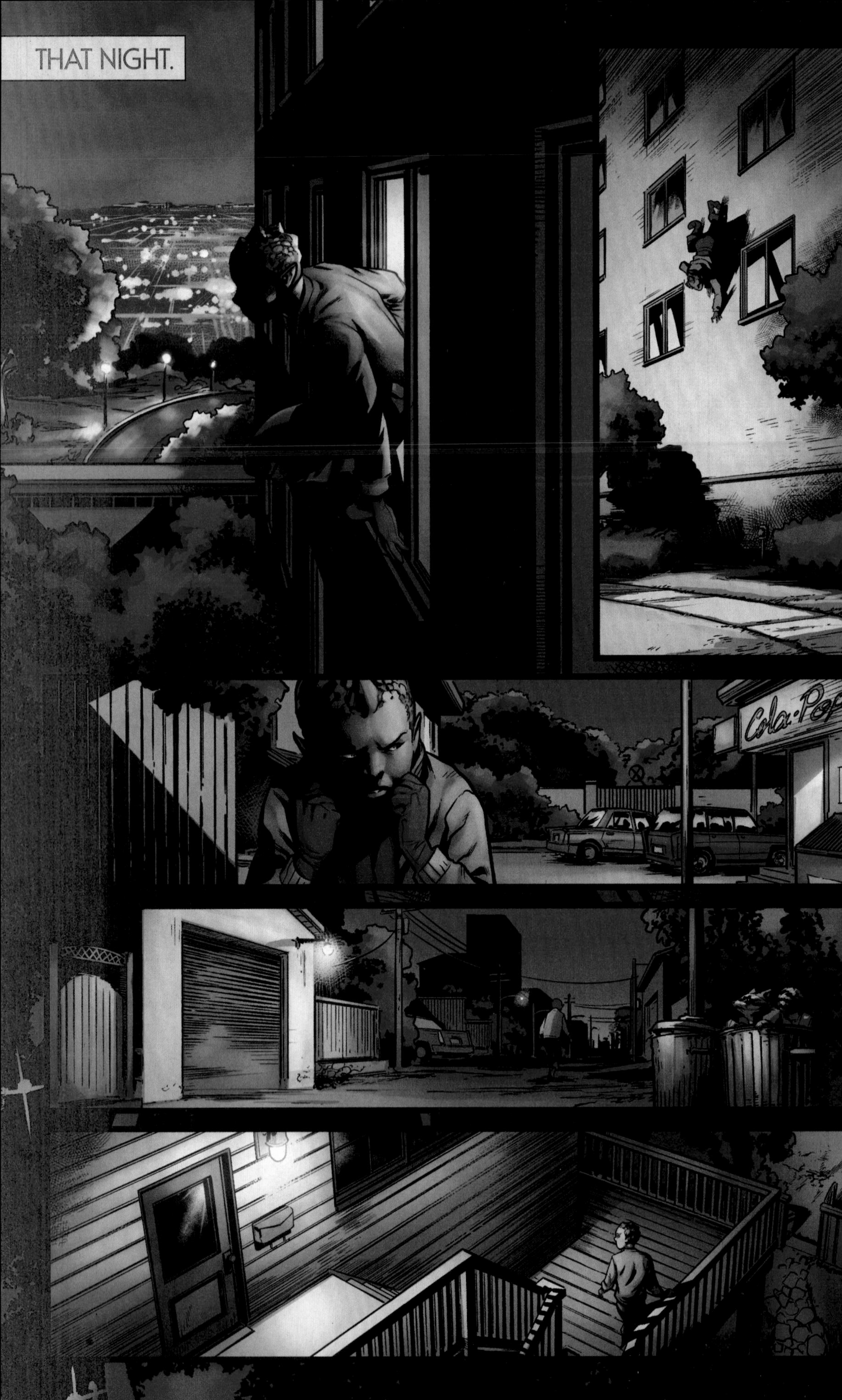
THAT NIGHT.
Cola·Pop

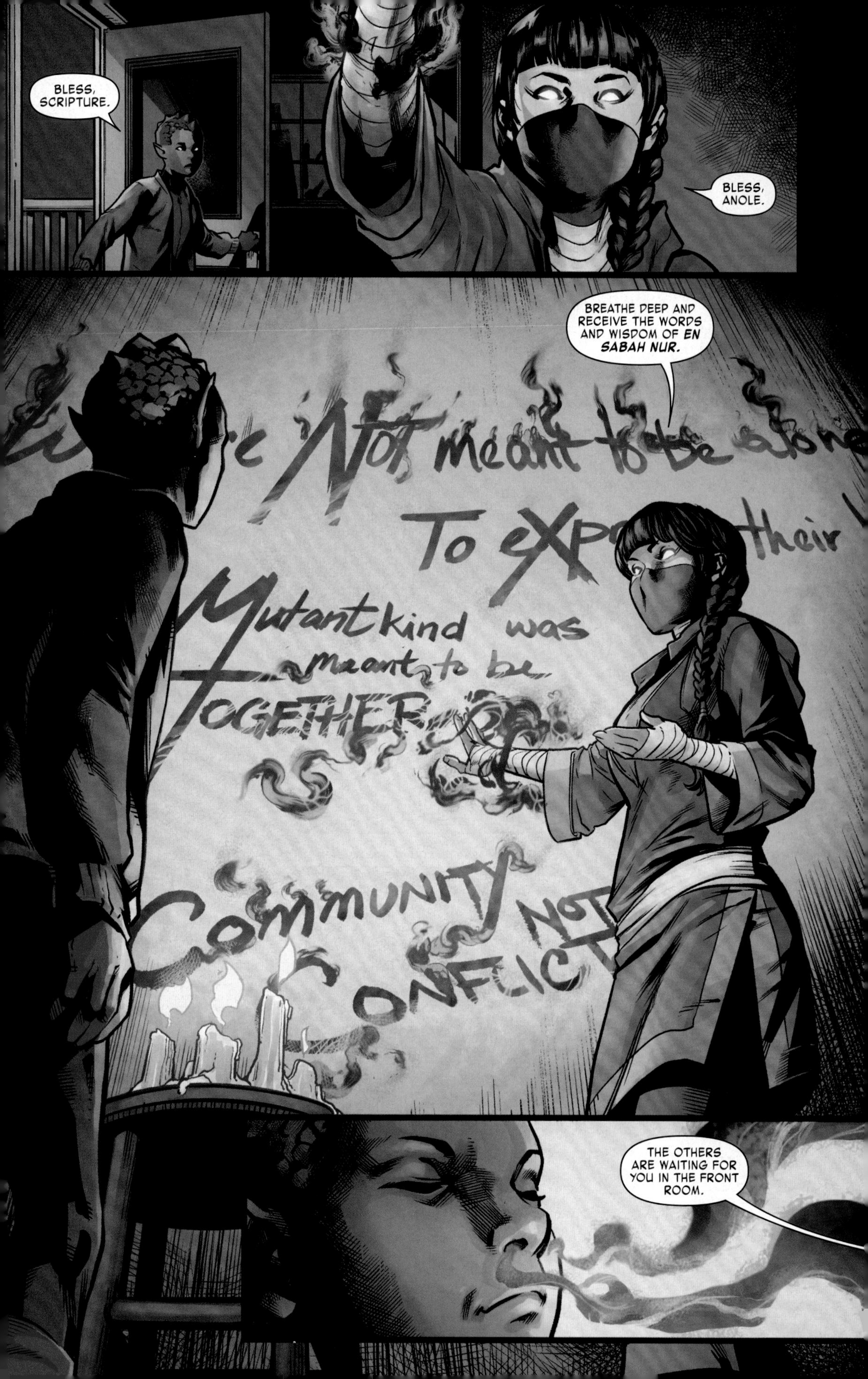

BLESS, SCRIPTURE.
BLESS, ANOLE.
BREATHE DEEP AND RECEIVE THE WORDS AND WISDOM OF *EN SABAH NUR.*
Not meant to be
their
Mutantkind was
meant to be
TOGETHER
COMMUNITY NOT
ONFLICT
THE OTHERS ARE WAITING FOR YOU IN THE FRONT ROOM.

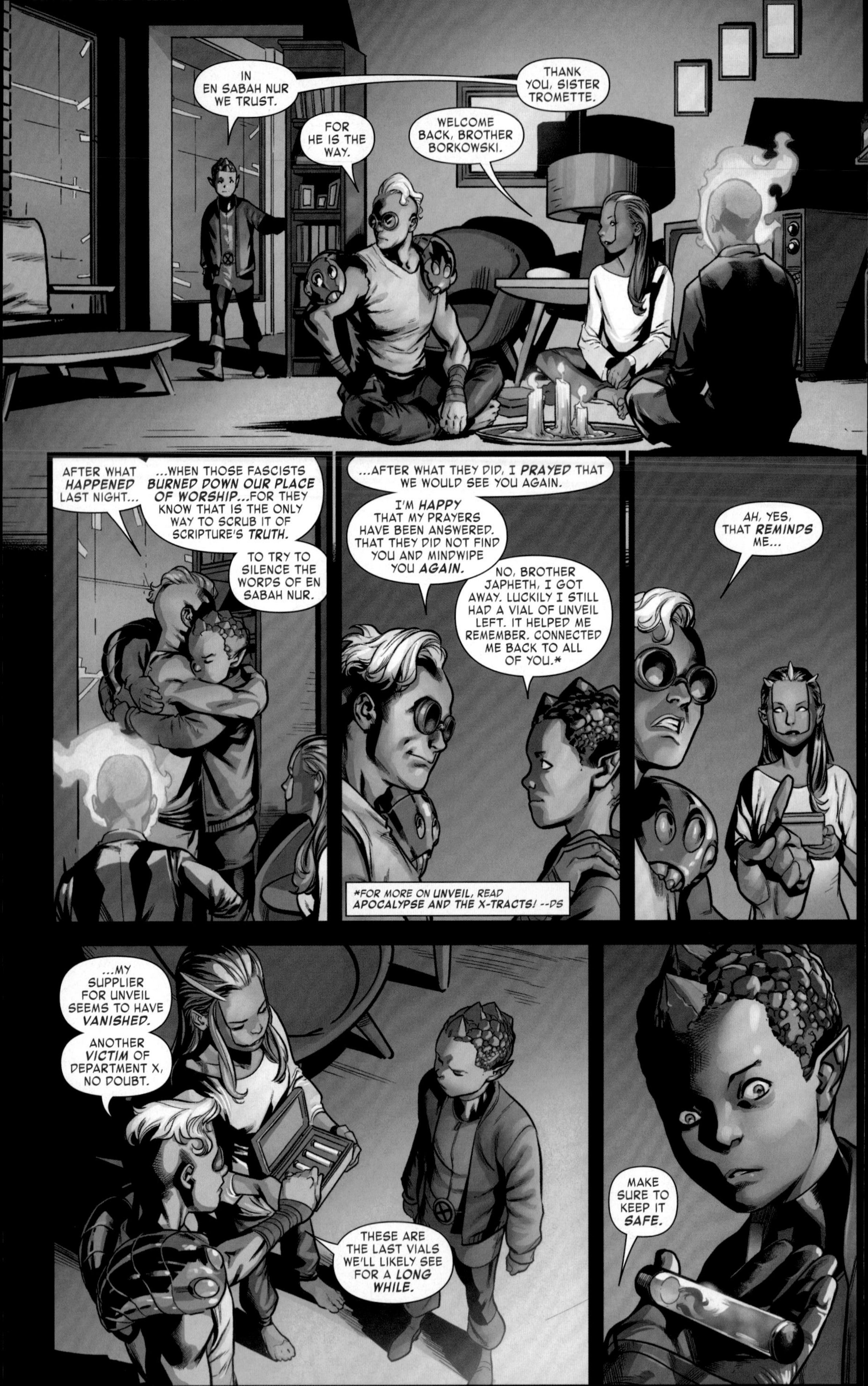

IN EN SABAH NUR WE TRUST.
THANK YOU, SISTER TROMETTE.
FOR HE IS THE WAY.
WELCOME BACK, BROTHER BORKOWSKI.
AFTER WHAT *HAPPENED* LAST NIGHT...
...WHEN THOSE FASCISTS *BURNED DOWN OUR PLACE OF WORSHIP*...FOR THEY KNOW THAT IS THE ONLY WAY TO SCRUB IT OF SCRIPTURE'S *TRUTH.*
TO TRY TO SILENCE THE WORDS OF EN SABAH NUR.
...AFTER WHAT THEY DID, I *PRAYED* THAT WE WOULD SEE YOU AGAIN.
I'M *HAPPY* THAT MY PRAYERS HAVE BEEN ANSWERED. THAT THEY DID NOT FIND YOU AND MINDWIPE YOU *AGAIN.*
NO, BROTHER JAPHETH, I GOT AWAY. LUCKILY I STILL HAD A VIAL OF UNVEIL LEFT. IT HELPED ME REMEMBER. CONNECTED ME BACK TO ALL OF YOU.*
*FOR MORE ON UNVEIL, READ APOCALYPSE AND THE X-TRACTS! --DS
AH, YES, THAT *REMINDS* ME...
...MY SUPPLIER FOR UNVEIL SEEMS TO HAVE *VANISHED.*
ANOTHER *VICTIM* OF DEPARTMENT X, NO DOUBT.
THESE ARE THE LAST VIALS WE'LL LIKELY SEE FOR A *LONG WHILE.*
MAKE SURE TO KEEP IT *SAFE.*

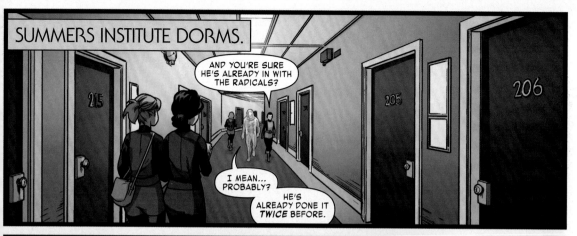

SUMMERS INSTITUTE DORMS.
AND YOU'RE SURE HE'S ALREADY IN WITH THE RADICALS?
I MEAN... PROBABLY?
HE'S ALREADY DONE IT TWICE BEFORE.
205
NOK NOK NOK
ANOLE?
SCREW THIS, WE'RE GOING IN.
ARMOR, WE CAN'T JUST BREAK INTO ANOLE'S ROOM!
IF HE'S IN TROUBLE, MAYBE HE LEFT BEHIND SOME SORT OF CLUE AS TO WHERE HE WENT.
OH NO.
WHAT?
WE MIGHT BE TOO LATE. THIS IS A VIAL OF UNVEIL. IF HE'S TAKEN IT THEN HE'S REMEMBERED AND...

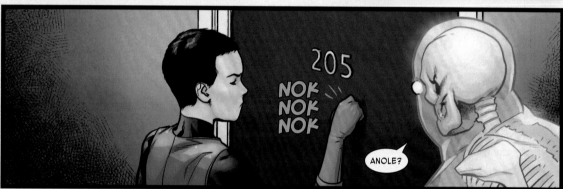

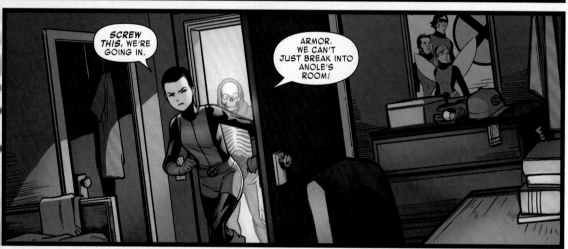

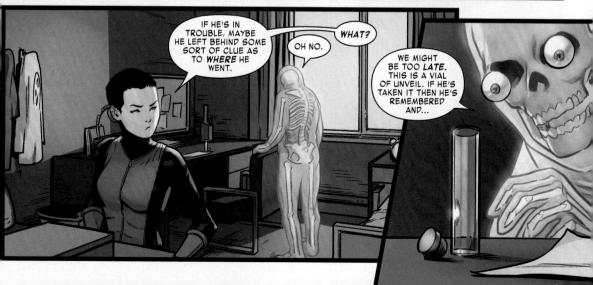

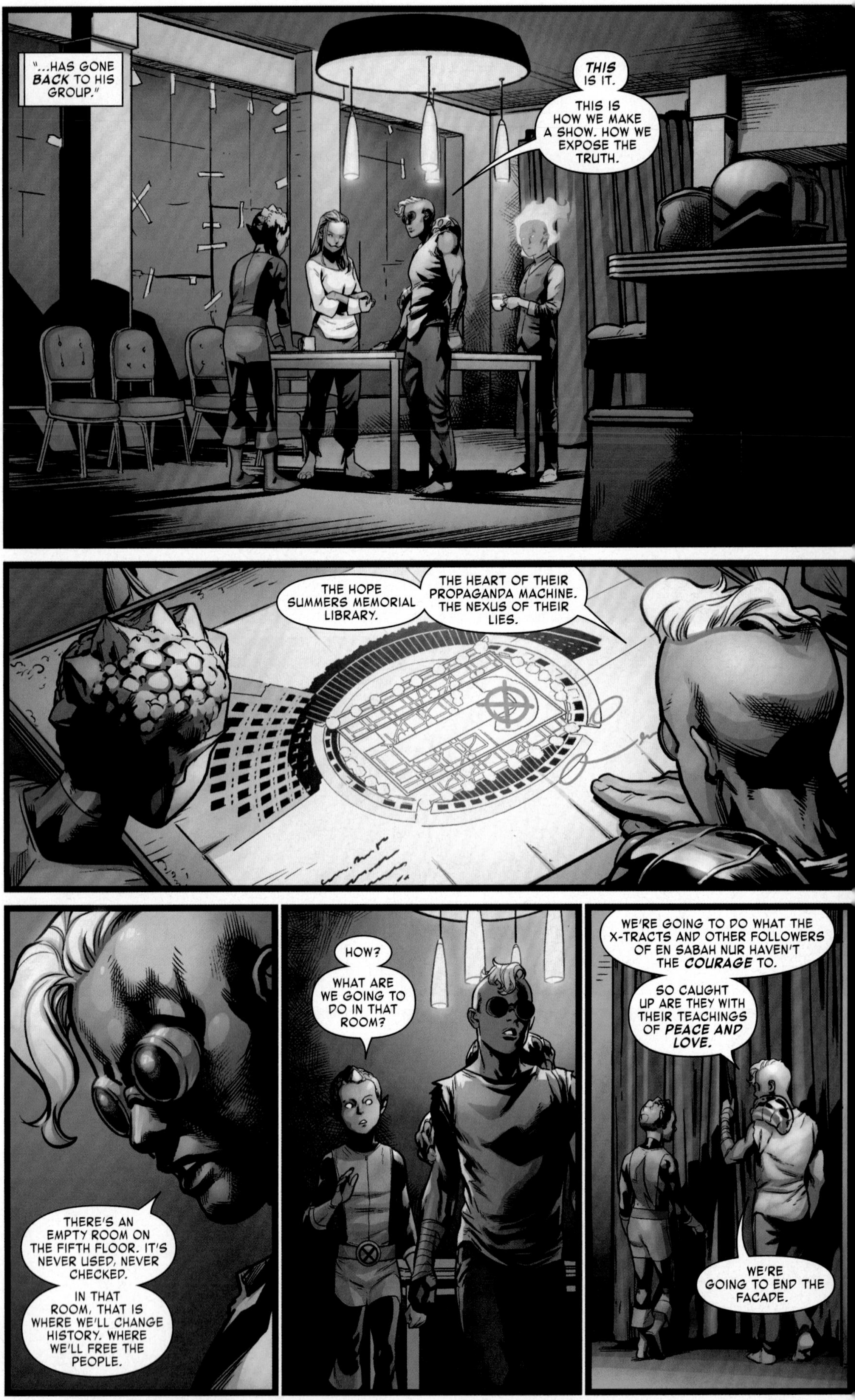
"...HAS GONE BACK TO HIS GROUP."
THIS IS IT.
THIS IS HOW WE MAKE A SHOW. HOW WE EXPOSE THE TRUTH.
THE HOPE SUMMERS MEMORIAL LIBRARY.
THE HEART OF THEIR PROPAGANDA MACHINE. THE NEXUS OF THEIR LIES.
THERE'S AN EMPTY ROOM ON THE FIFTH FLOOR. IT'S NEVER USED, NEVER CHECKED.
IN THAT ROOM, THAT IS WHERE WE'LL CHANGE HISTORY. WHERE WE'LL FREE THE PEOPLE.
HOW?
WHAT ARE WE GOING TO DO IN THAT ROOM?
WE'RE GOING TO DO WHAT THE X-TRACTS AND OTHER FOLLOWERS OF EN SABAH NUR HAVEN'T THE COURAGE TO.
SO CAUGHT UP ARE THEY WITH THEIR TEACHINGS OF PEACE AND LOVE.
WE'RE GOING TO END THE FACADE.

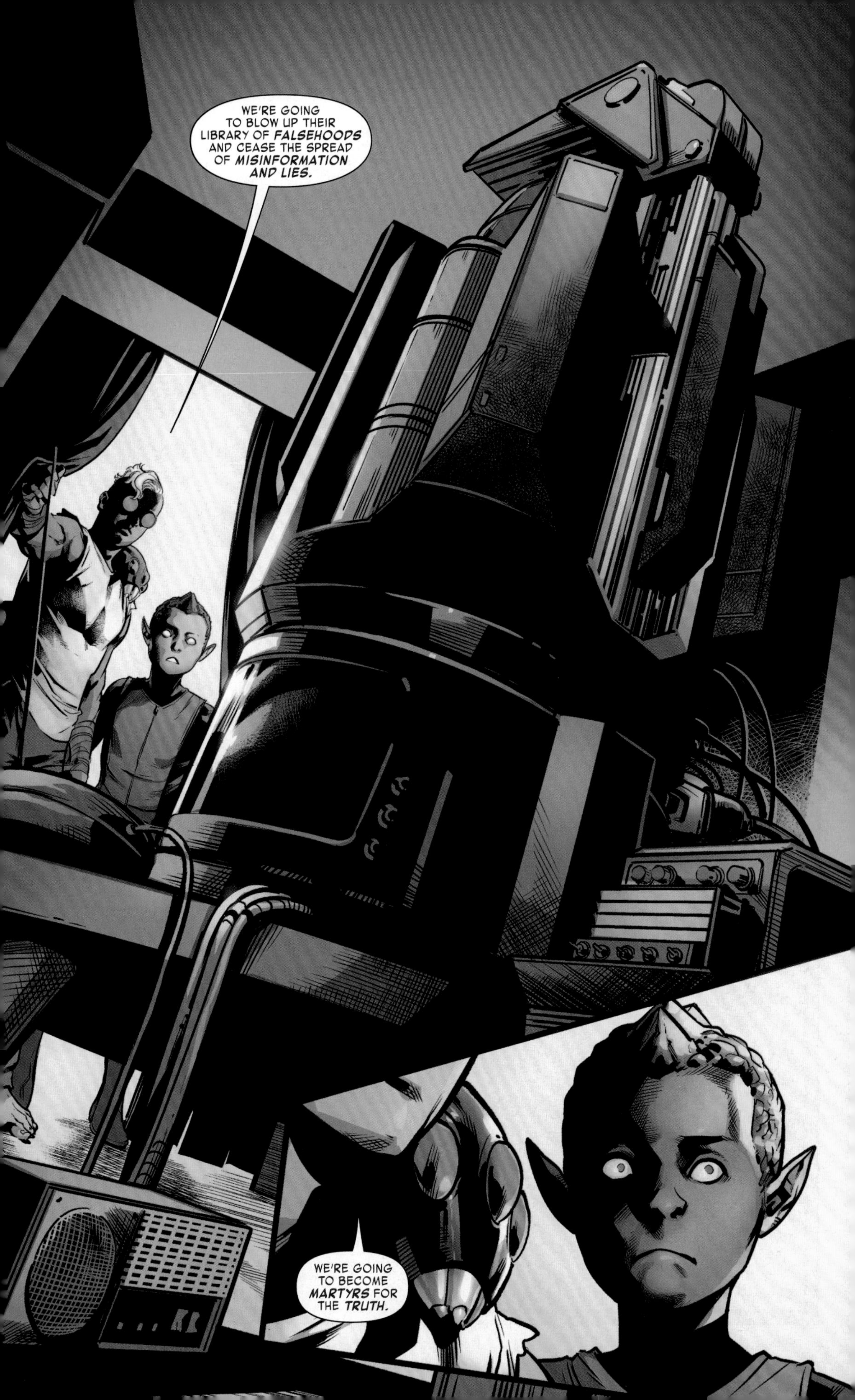
WE'RE GOING TO BLOW UP THEIR LIBRARY OF FALSEHOODS AND CEASE THE SPREAD OF MISINFORMATION AND LIES.
WE'RE GOING TO BECOME MARTYRS FOR THE TRUTH.

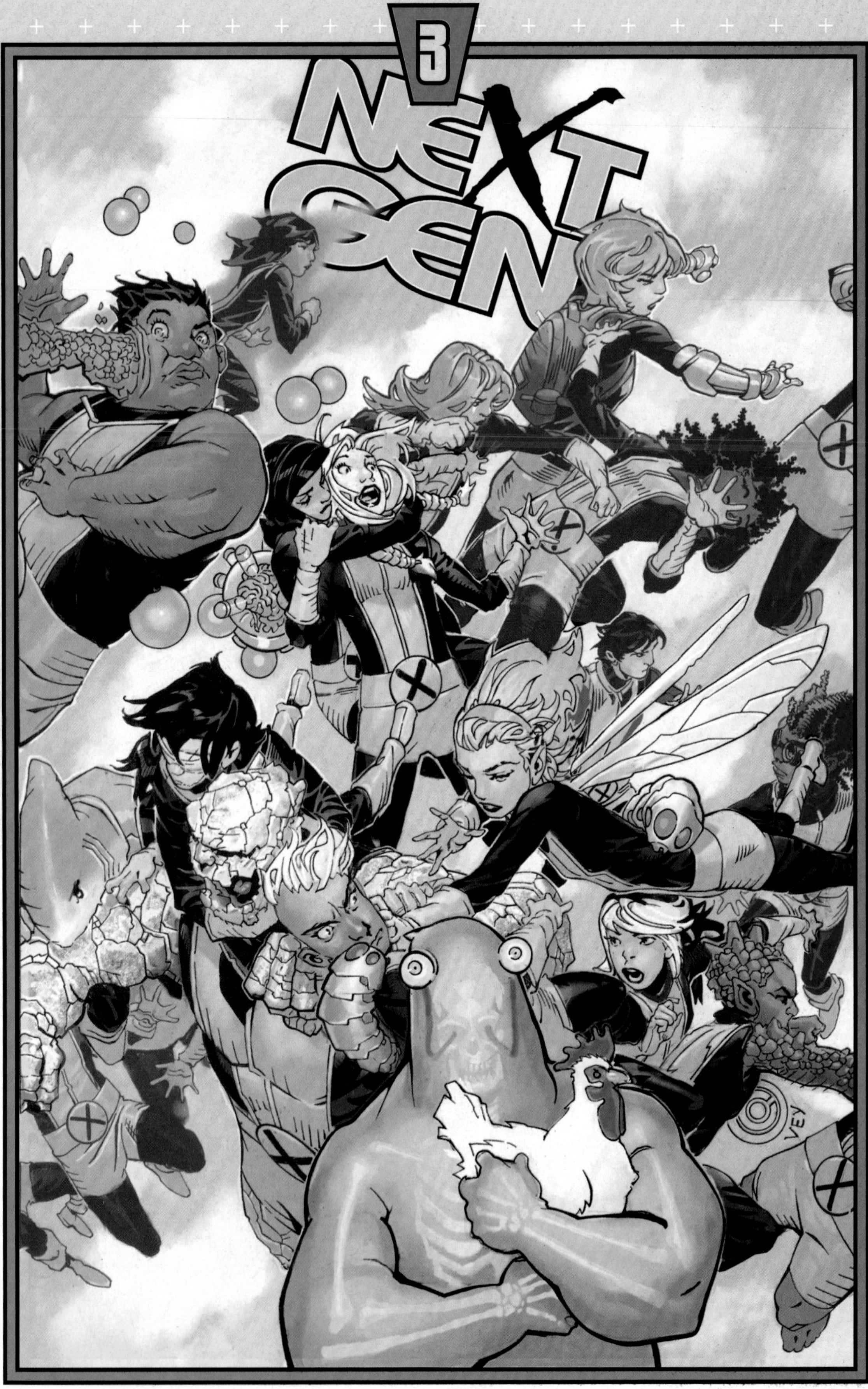
3
NEXT GEN
VEY

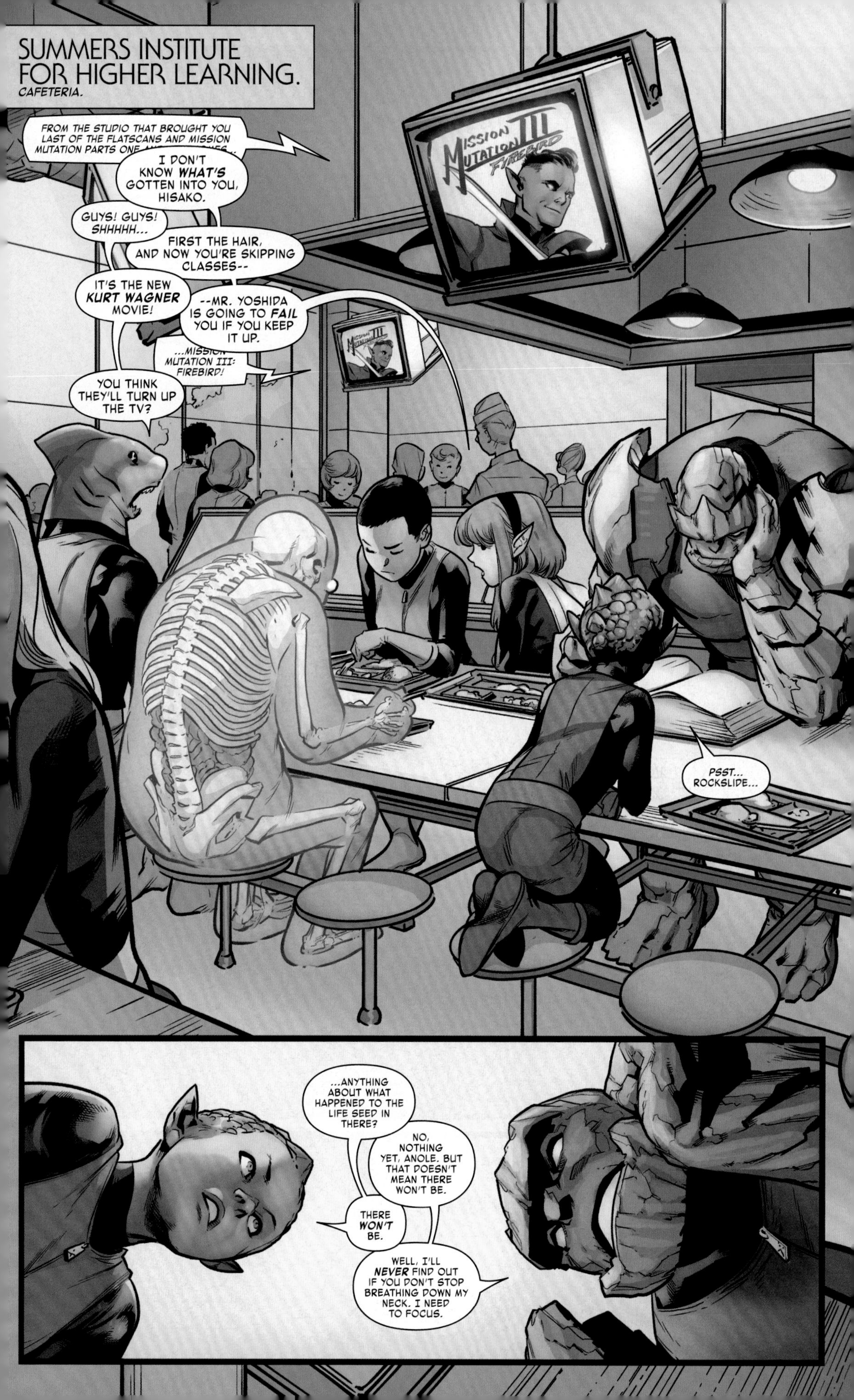
SUMMERS INSTITUTE FOR HIGHER LEARNING.
CAFETERIA.
FROM THE STUDIO THAT BROUGHT YOU LAST OF THE FLATSCANS AND MISSION MUTATION PARTS ONE
I DON'T KNOW WHAT'S GOTTEN INTO YOU, HISAKO.
MISSION MUTATION III FIREBIRD
GUYS! GUYS! SHHHHH...
FIRST THE HAIR, AND NOW YOU'RE SKIPPING CLASSES--
IT'S THE NEW KURT WAGNER MOVIE!
--MR. YOSHIDA IS GOING TO FAIL YOU IF YOU KEEP IT UP.
...MISSION MUTATION III: FIREBIRD!
YOU THINK THEY'LL TURN UP THE TV?
PSST... ROCKSLIDE...
...ANYTHING ABOUT WHAT HAPPENED TO THE LIFE SEED IN THERE?
NO, NOTHING YET, ANOLE. BUT THAT DOESN'T MEAN THERE WON'T BE.
THERE WON'T BE.
WELL, I'LL NEVER FIND OUT IF YOU DON'T STOP BREATHING DOWN MY NECK. I NEED TO FOCUS.

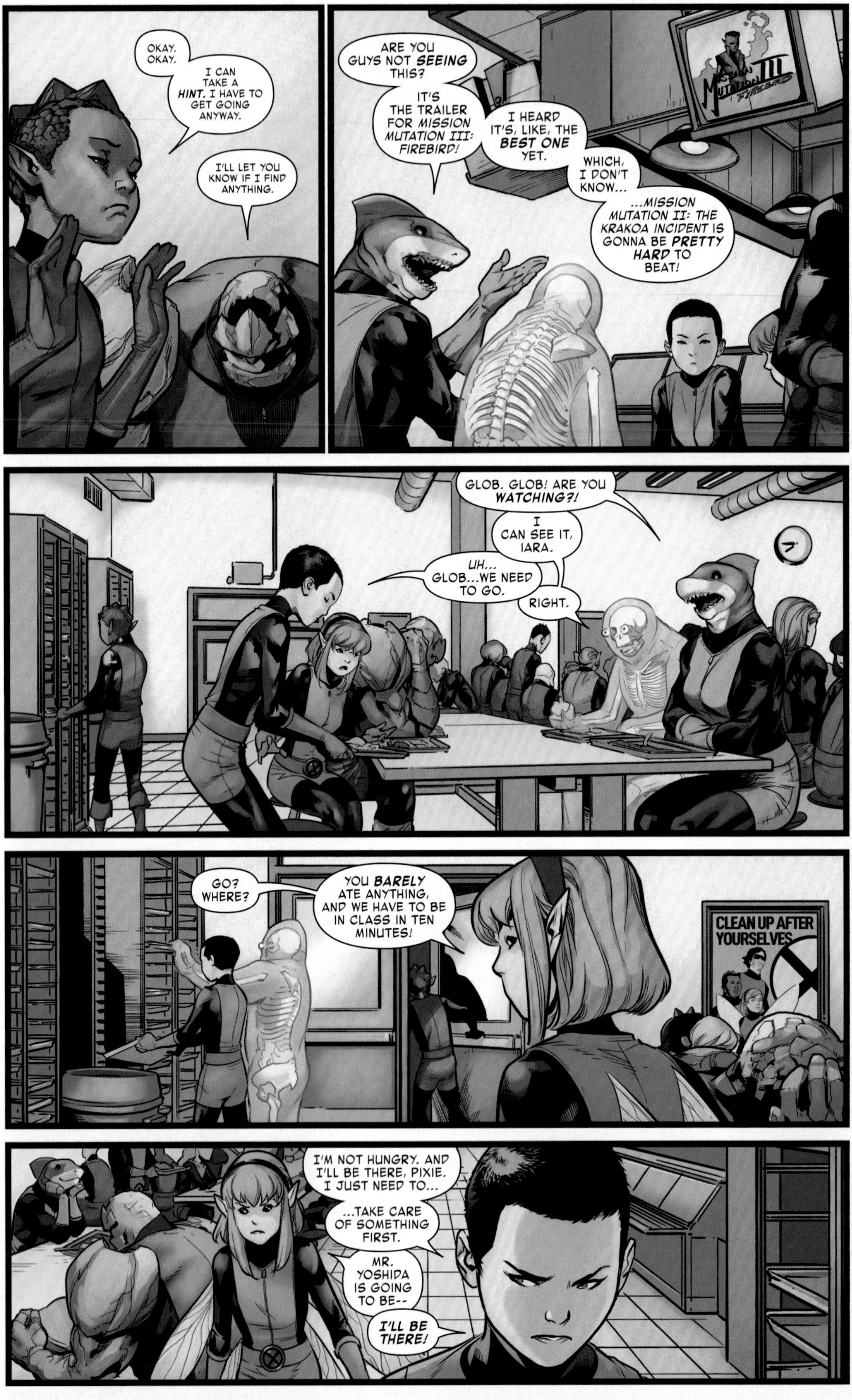

OKAY. OKAY.
I CAN TAKE A HINT. I HAVE TO GET GOING ANYWAY.
I'LL LET YOU KNOW IF I FIND ANYTHING.
ARE YOU GUYS NOT SEEING THIS?
IT'S THE TRAILER FOR MISSION MUTATION III: FIREBIRD!
I HEARD IT'S, LIKE, THE BEST ONE YET.
WHICH, I DON'T KNOW...
...MISSION MUTATION II: THE KRAKOA INCIDENT IS GONNA BE PRETTY HARD TO BEAT!
GLOB. GLOB! ARE YOU WATCHING?!
I CAN SEE IT, IARA.
UH... GLOB...WE NEED TO GO.
RIGHT.
GO? WHERE?
YOU BARELY ATE ANYTHING, AND WE HAVE TO BE IN CLASS IN TEN MINUTES!
CLEAN UP AFTER YOURSELVES
I'M NOT HUNGRY. AND I'LL BE THERE, PIXIE. I JUST NEED TO...
...TAKE CARE OF SOMETHING FIRST.
MR. YOSHIDA IS GOING TO BE--
I'LL BE THERE!

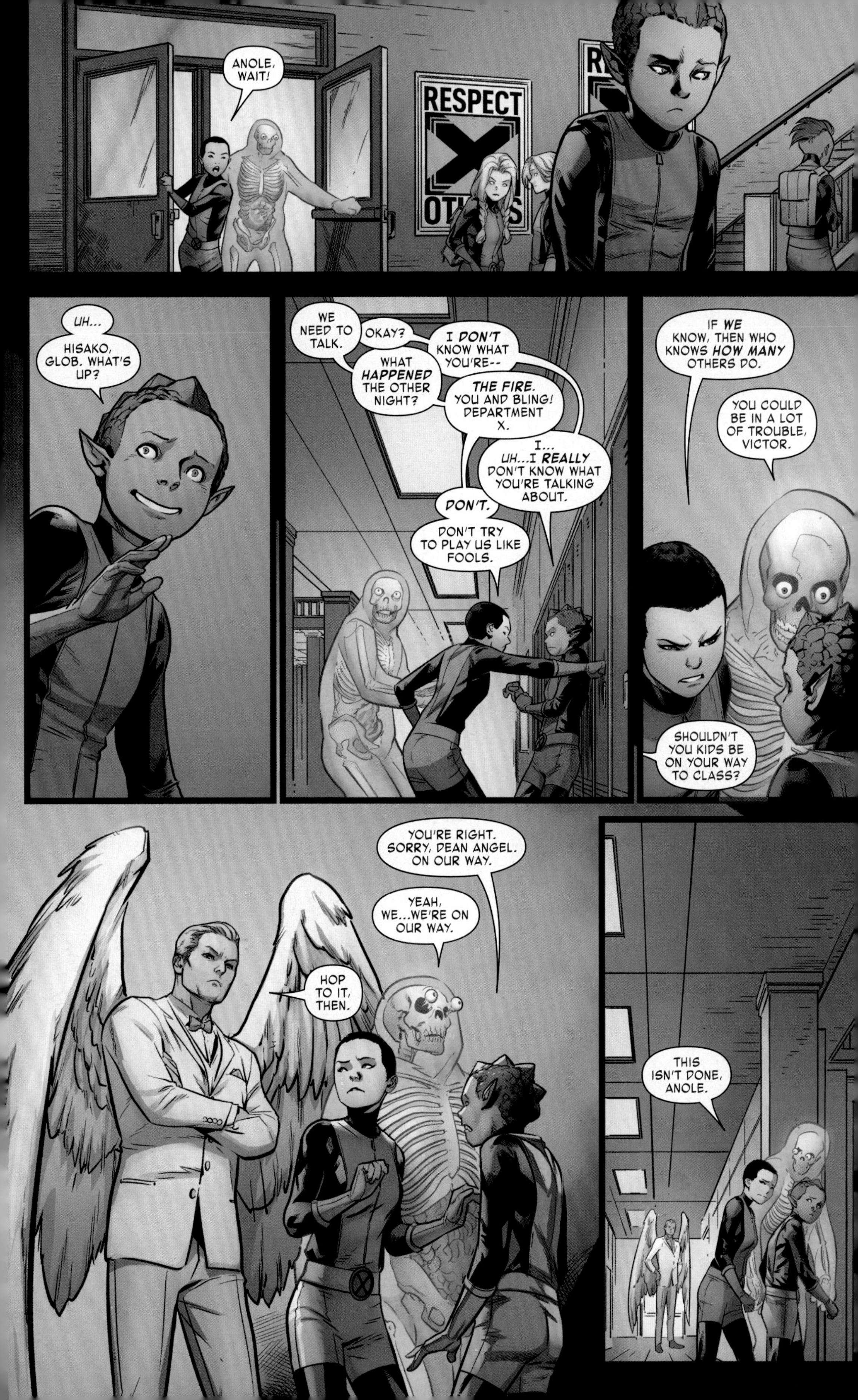

ANOLE, WAIT!
RESPECT OTHERS
UH...
HISAKO, GLOB. WHAT'S UP?
WE NEED TO TALK.
OKAY?
I DON'T KNOW WHAT YOU'RE--
WHAT HAPPENED THE OTHER NIGHT?
THE FIRE. YOU AND BLING! DEPARTMENT X.
I... UH...I REALLY DON'T KNOW WHAT YOU'RE TALKING ABOUT.
DON'T.
DON'T TRY TO PLAY US LIKE FOOLS.
IF WE KNOW, THEN WHO KNOWS HOW MANY OTHERS DO.
YOU COULD BE IN A LOT OF TROUBLE, VICTOR.
SHOULDN'T YOU KIDS BE ON YOUR WAY TO CLASS?
YOU'RE RIGHT. SORRY, DEAN ANGEL. ON OUR WAY.
YEAH, WE...WE'RE ON OUR WAY.
HOP TO IT, THEN.
THIS ISN'T DONE, ANOLE.

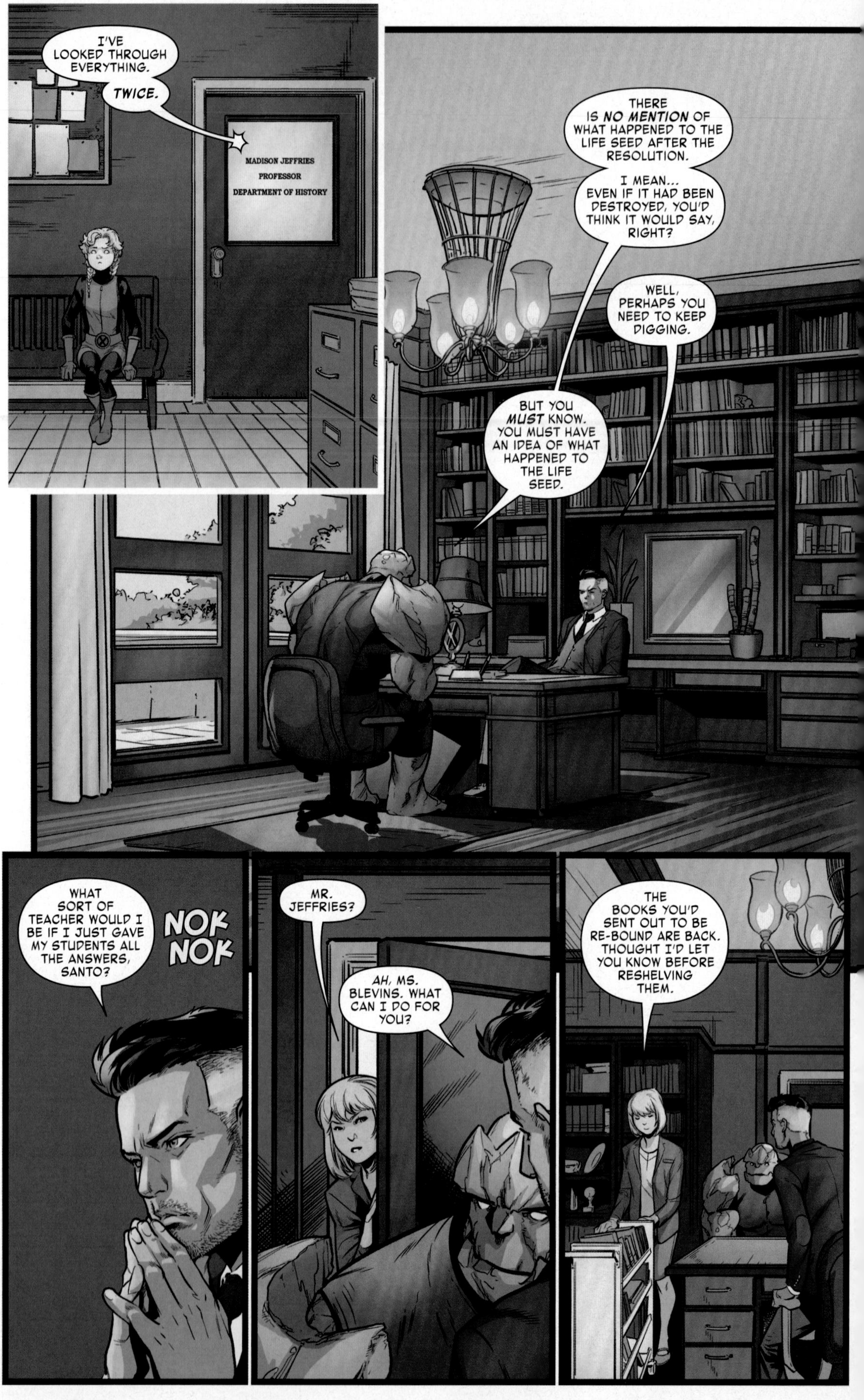
I'VE LOOKED THROUGH EVERYTHING.
TWICE.
MADISON JEFFRIES
PROFESSOR
DEPARTMENT OF HISTORY
THERE IS NO MENTION OF WHAT HAPPENED TO THE LIFE SEED AFTER THE RESOLUTION.
I MEAN... EVEN IF IT HAD BEEN DESTROYED, YOU'D THINK IT WOULD SAY, RIGHT?
WELL, PERHAPS YOU NEED TO KEEP DIGGING.
BUT YOU MUST KNOW. YOU MUST HAVE AN IDEA OF WHAT HAPPENED TO THE LIFE SEED.
WHAT SORT OF TEACHER WOULD I BE IF I JUST GAVE MY STUDENTS ALL THE ANSWERS, SANTO?
NOK NOK
MR. JEFFRIES?
AH, MS. BLEVINS. WHAT CAN I DO FOR YOU?
THE BOOKS YOU'D SENT OUT TO BE RE-BOUND ARE BACK. THOUGHT I'D LET YOU KNOW BEFORE RESHELVING THEM.

WELL, LOOK AT *THAT*.

I SUSPECT THAT YOU'LL FIND WHAT YOU'RE LOOKING FOR IN HERE.

THANK YOU, MS. BLEVINS. YOU CAN LEAVE THESE BOOKS WITH ME FOR NOW.

HAPPY TO BE OF SERVICE.

BUT...

...I CHECKED ALL THE LIBRARY CARDS. ALL THE RECORDS. THERE WAS *NOTHING* ABOUT THIS BOOK ON FILE.

YOU PROBABLY JUST MISSED IT.

HAPPENS TO THE BEST OF US.

BUT I TRIPLE-CHECKED. I--

SANTO...

Quest For the Life Seed

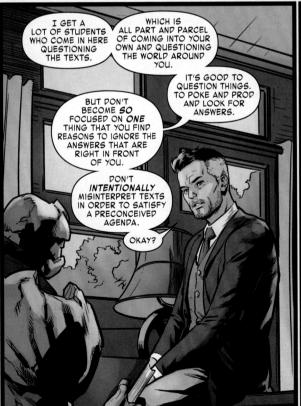

I GET A LOT OF STUDENTS WHO COME IN HERE QUESTIONING THE TEXTS.

WHICH IS ALL PART AND PARCEL OF COMING INTO YOUR OWN AND QUESTIONING THE WORLD AROUND YOU.

IT'S GOOD TO QUESTION THINGS. TO POKE AND PROD AND LOOK FOR ANSWERS.

BUT DON'T BECOME *SO* FOCUSED ON *ONE* THING THAT YOU FIND REASONS TO IGNORE THE ANSWERS THAT ARE RIGHT IN FRONT OF YOU.

DON'T *INTENTIONALLY* MISINTERPRET TEXTS IN ORDER TO SATISFY A PRECONCEIVED AGENDA.

OKAY?

OKAY.

CIVIL MANAGEMENT.
TENTH-YEAR CLASS.

OKAY, CLASS...

...THERE IS AN *EPIDEMIC* SWEEPING OUR WORLD, AND AS THE NEXT GENERATION OF DEPARTMENT X OFFICERS, IT IS UP TO *YOU* TO BE EXTRA VIGILANT AND KEEP AN EYE OUT FOR IT.

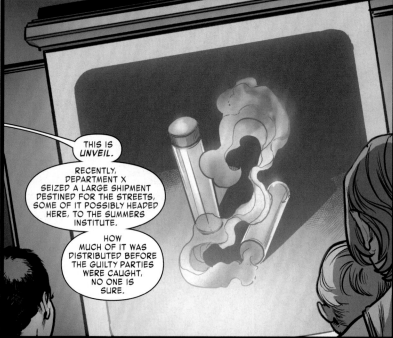

THIS IS *UNVEIL.*

RECENTLY, DEPARTMENT X SEIZED A LARGE SHIPMENT DESTINED FOR THE STREETS, SOME OF IT POSSIBLY HEADED HERE, TO THE SUMMERS INSTITUTE.

HOW MUCH OF IT WAS DISTRIBUTED BEFORE THE GUILTY PARTIES WERE CAUGHT, NO ONE IS SURE.

SOME PEOPLE TAKE UNVEIL BECAUSE THEY BELIEVE IT WILL MAKE THEM FEEL BETTER. THEY THINK THAT IT WILL OPEN THEIR MINDS.

BUT INSTEAD, THEY FIND THEMSELVES ADDICTED. DESPERATE AND READY TO DO ANYTHING TO GET ANOTHER DOSE.

MANY WILL TAKE TOO MUCH AND *DIE.*

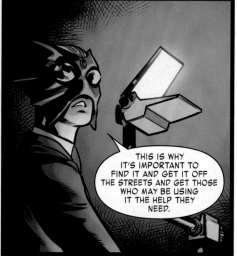

THIS IS WHY IT'S IMPORTANT TO FIND IT AND GET IT OFF THE STREETS AND GET THOSE WHO MAY BE USING IT THE HELP THEY NEED.

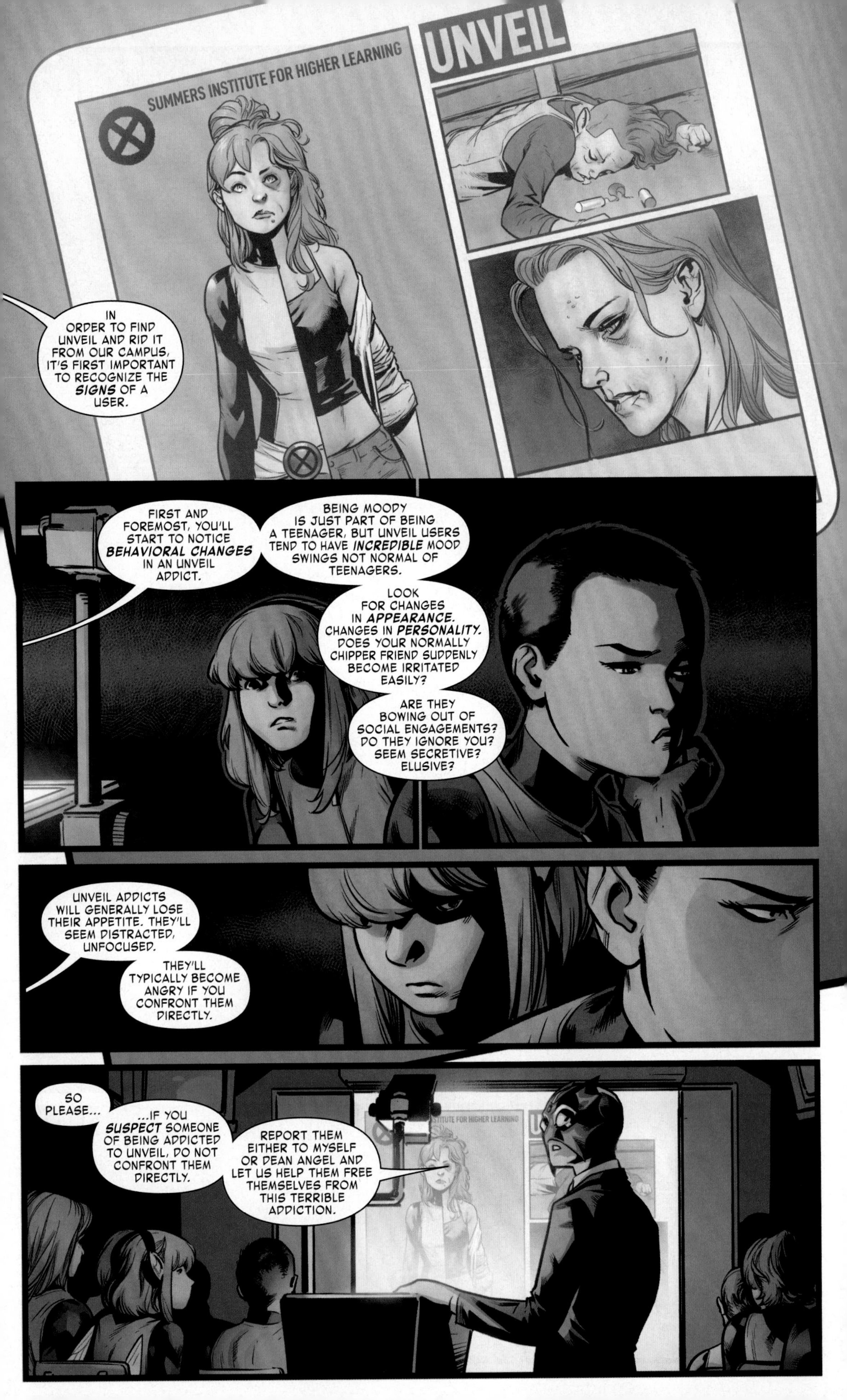
UNVEIL
SUMMERS INSTITUTE FOR HIGHER LEARNING
IN ORDER TO FIND UNVEIL AND RID IT FROM OUR CAMPUS, IT'S FIRST IMPORTANT TO RECOGNIZE THE SIGNS OF A USER.
FIRST AND FOREMOST, YOU'LL START TO NOTICE BEHAVIORAL CHANGES IN AN UNVEIL ADDICT.
BEING MOODY IS JUST PART OF BEING A TEENAGER, BUT UNVEIL USERS TEND TO HAVE INCREDIBLE MOOD SWINGS NOT NORMAL OF TEENAGERS.
LOOK FOR CHANGES IN APPEARANCE. CHANGES IN PERSONALITY. DOES YOUR NORMALLY CHIPPER FRIEND SUDDENLY BECOME IRRITATED EASILY?
ARE THEY BOWING OUT OF SOCIAL ENGAGEMENTS? DO THEY IGNORE YOU? SEEM SECRETIVE? ELUSIVE?
UNVEIL ADDICTS WILL GENERALLY LOSE THEIR APPETITE. THEY'LL SEEM DISTRACTED, UNFOCUSED.
THEY'LL TYPICALLY BECOME ANGRY IF YOU CONFRONT THEM DIRECTLY.
SO PLEASE...
...IF YOU SUSPECT SOMEONE OF BEING ADDICTED TO UNVEIL, DO NOT CONFRONT THEM DIRECTLY.
REPORT THEM EITHER TO MYSELF OR DEAN ANGEL AND LET US HELP THEM FREE THEMSELVES FROM THIS TERRIBLE ADDICTION.

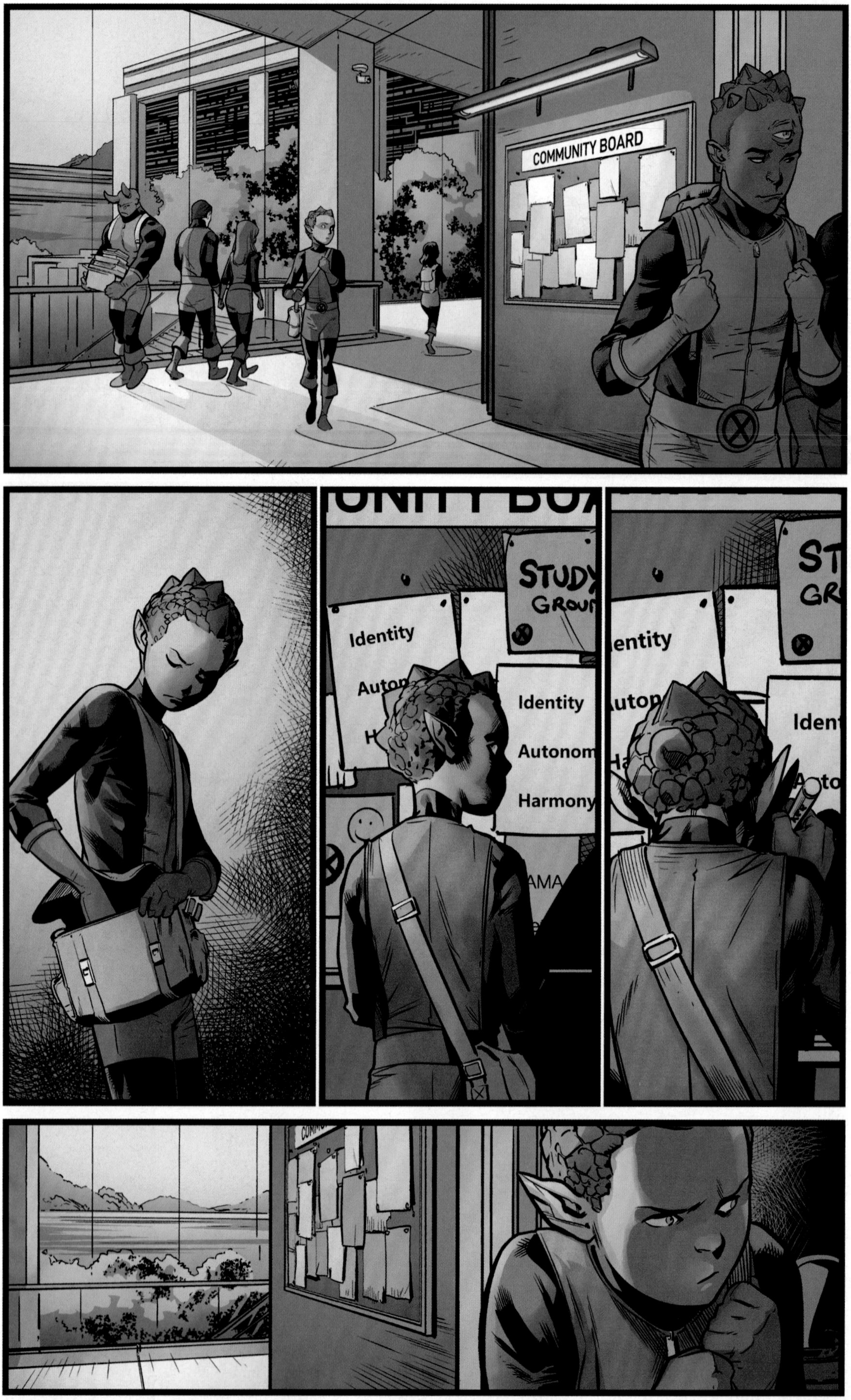

COMMUNITY BOARD
Identity
Identity
Harmony

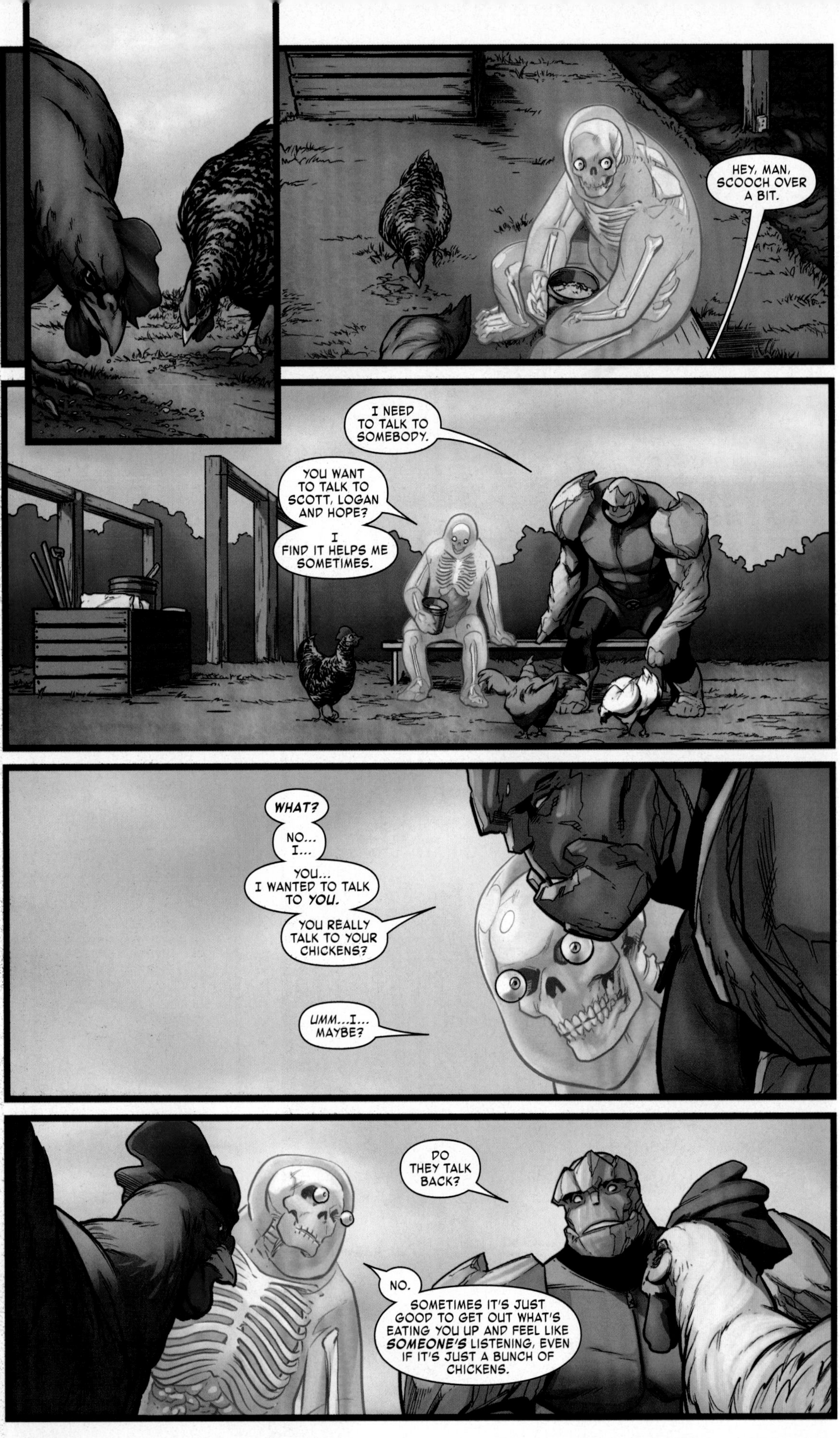
HEY, MAN, SCOOCH OVER A BIT.
I NEED TO TALK TO SOMEBODY.
YOU WANT TO TALK TO SCOTT, LOGAN AND HOPE?
I FIND IT HELPS ME SOMETIMES.
WHAT?
NO... I...
YOU... I WANTED TO TALK TO YOU.
YOU REALLY TALK TO YOUR CHICKENS?
UMM...I... MAYBE?
DO THEY TALK BACK?
NO.
SOMETIMES IT'S JUST GOOD TO GET OUT WHAT'S EATING YOU UP AND FEEL LIKE SOMEONE'S LISTENING, EVEN IF IT'S JUST A BUNCH OF CHICKENS.

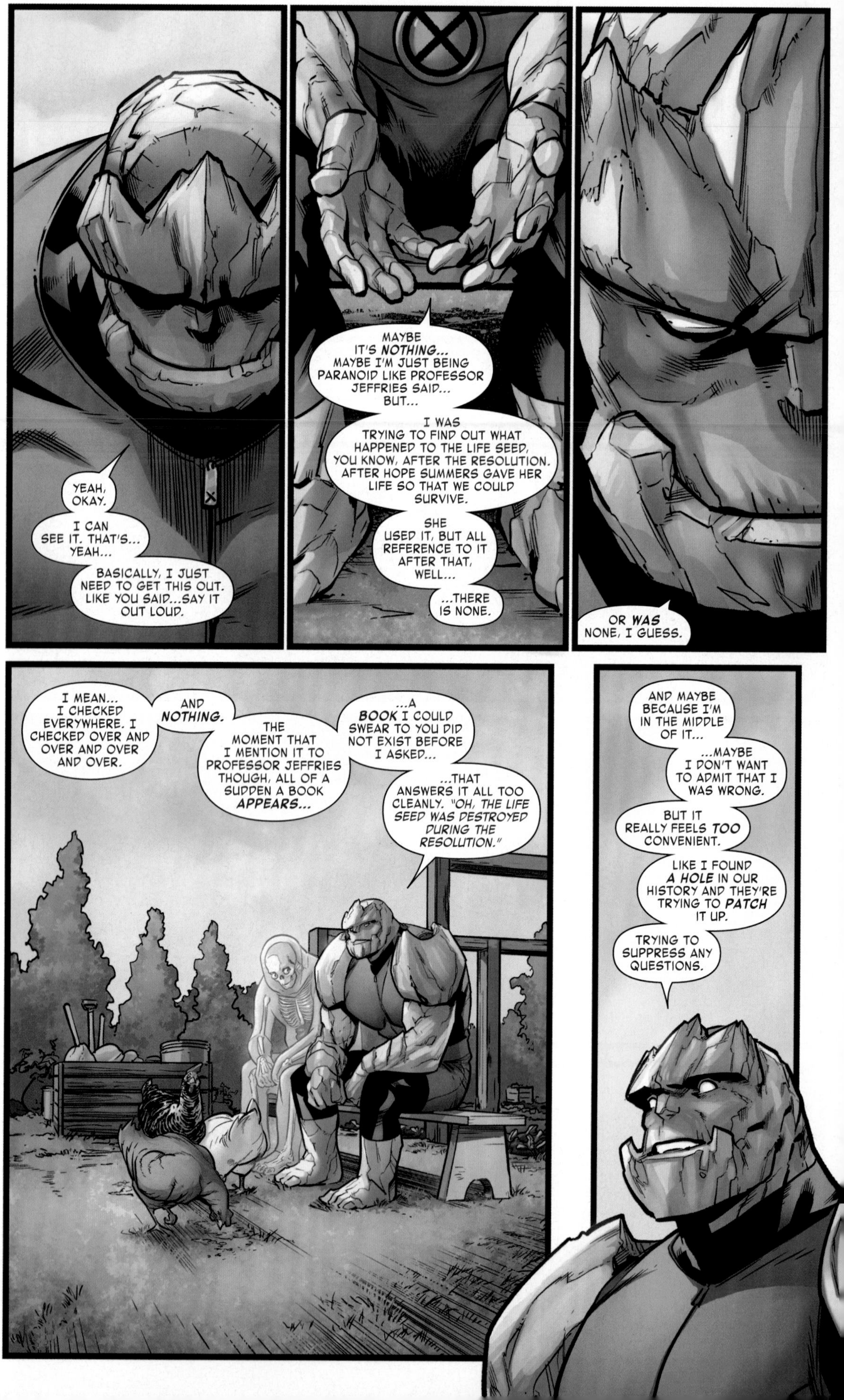
YEAH, OKAY.
I CAN SEE IT. THAT'S... YEAH...
BASICALLY, I JUST NEED TO GET THIS OUT. LIKE YOU SAID...SAY IT OUT LOUD.
MAYBE IT'S NOTHING... MAYBE I'M JUST BEING PARANOID LIKE PROFESSOR JEFFRIES SAID... BUT...
I WAS TRYING TO FIND OUT WHAT HAPPENED TO THE LIFE SEED, YOU KNOW, AFTER THE RESOLUTION. AFTER HOPE SUMMERS GAVE HER LIFE SO THAT WE COULD SURVIVE.
SHE USED IT, BUT ALL REFERENCE TO IT AFTER THAT, WELL...
...THERE IS NONE.
OR WAS NONE, I GUESS.
I MEAN... I CHECKED EVERYWHERE. I CHECKED OVER AND OVER AND OVER AND OVER.
AND NOTHING.
THE MOMENT THAT I MENTION IT TO PROFESSOR JEFFRIES THOUGH, ALL OF A SUDDEN A BOOK APPEARS...
...A BOOK I COULD SWEAR TO YOU DID NOT EXIST BEFORE I ASKED...
...THAT ANSWERS IT ALL TOO CLEANLY. "OH, THE LIFE SEED WAS DESTROYED DURING THE RESOLUTION."
AND MAYBE BECAUSE I'M IN THE MIDDLE OF IT...
...MAYBE I DON'T WANT TO ADMIT THAT I WAS WRONG.
BUT IT REALLY FEELS TOO CONVENIENT.
LIKE I FOUND A HOLE IN OUR HISTORY AND THEY'RE TRYING TO PATCH IT UP.
TRYING TO SUPPRESS ANY QUESTIONS.

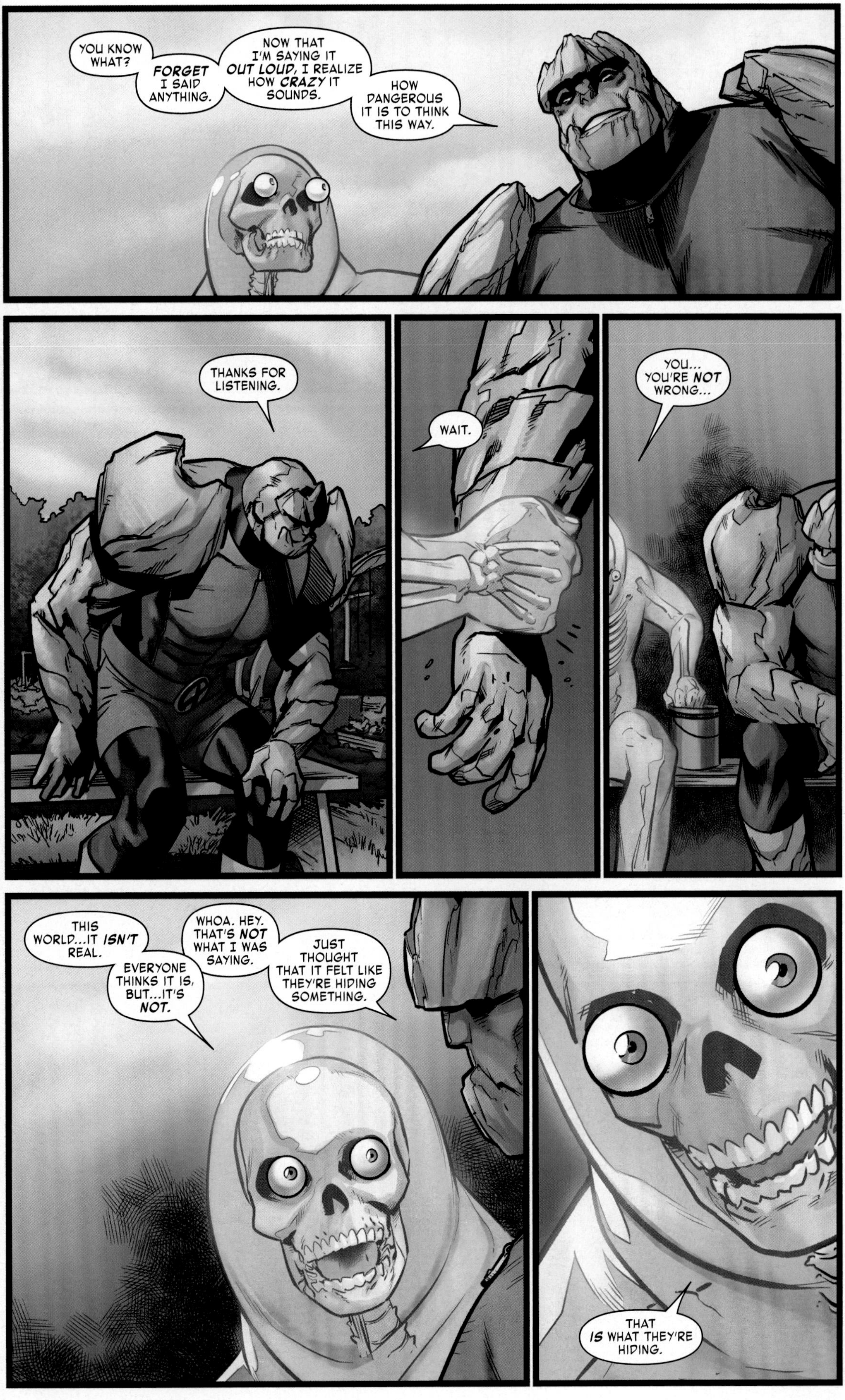

YOU KNOW WHAT?
FORGET I SAID ANYTHING.
NOW THAT I'M SAYING IT OUT LOUD, I REALIZE HOW CRAZY IT SOUNDS.
HOW DANGEROUS IT IS TO THINK THIS WAY.
THANKS FOR LISTENING.
WAIT.
YOU... YOU'RE NOT WRONG...
THIS WORLD...IT ISN'T REAL.
EVERYONE THINKS IT IS, BUT...IT'S NOT.
WHOA. HEY. THAT'S NOT WHAT I WAS SAYING.
JUST THOUGHT THAT IT FELT LIKE THEY'RE HIDING SOMETHING.
THAT IS WHAT THEY'RE HIDING.

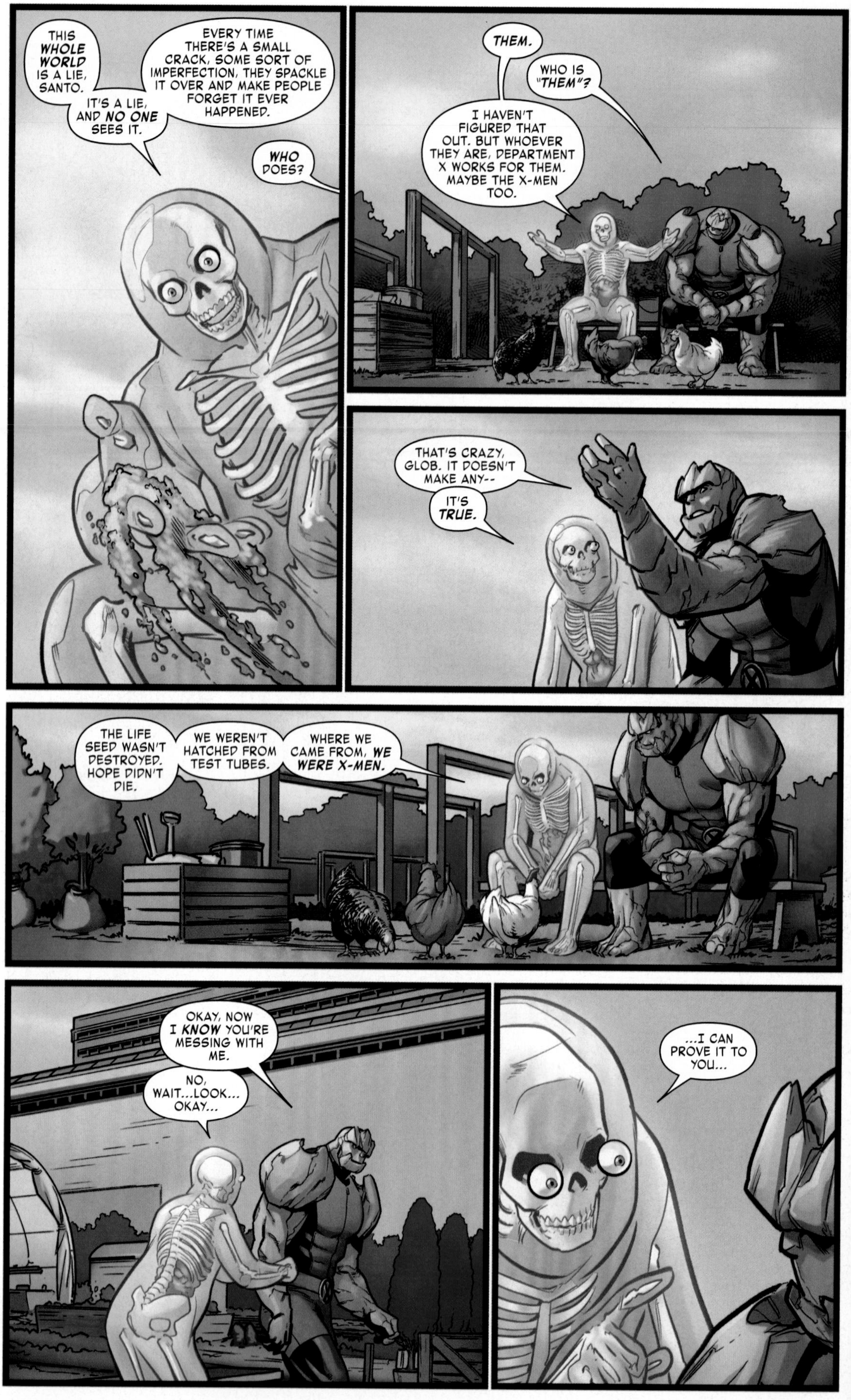
THIS WHOLE WORLD IS A LIE, SANTO.
IT'S A LIE, AND NO ONE SEES IT.
EVERY TIME THERE'S A SMALL CRACK, SOME SORT OF IMPERFECTION, THEY SPACKLE IT OVER AND MAKE PEOPLE FORGET IT EVER HAPPENED.
WHO DOES?
THEM.
WHO IS "THEM"?
I HAVEN'T FIGURED THAT OUT. BUT WHOEVER THEY ARE, DEPARTMENT X WORKS FOR THEM. MAYBE THE X-MEN TOO.
THAT'S CRAZY, GLOB. IT DOESN'T MAKE ANY--
IT'S TRUE.
THE LIFE SEED WASN'T DESTROYED. HOPE DIDN'T DIE.
WE WEREN'T HATCHED FROM TEST TUBES.
WHERE WE CAME FROM, WE WERE X-MEN.
OKAY, NOW I KNOW YOU'RE MESSING WITH ME.
NO, WAIT...LOOK... OKAY...
...I CAN PROVE IT TO YOU...

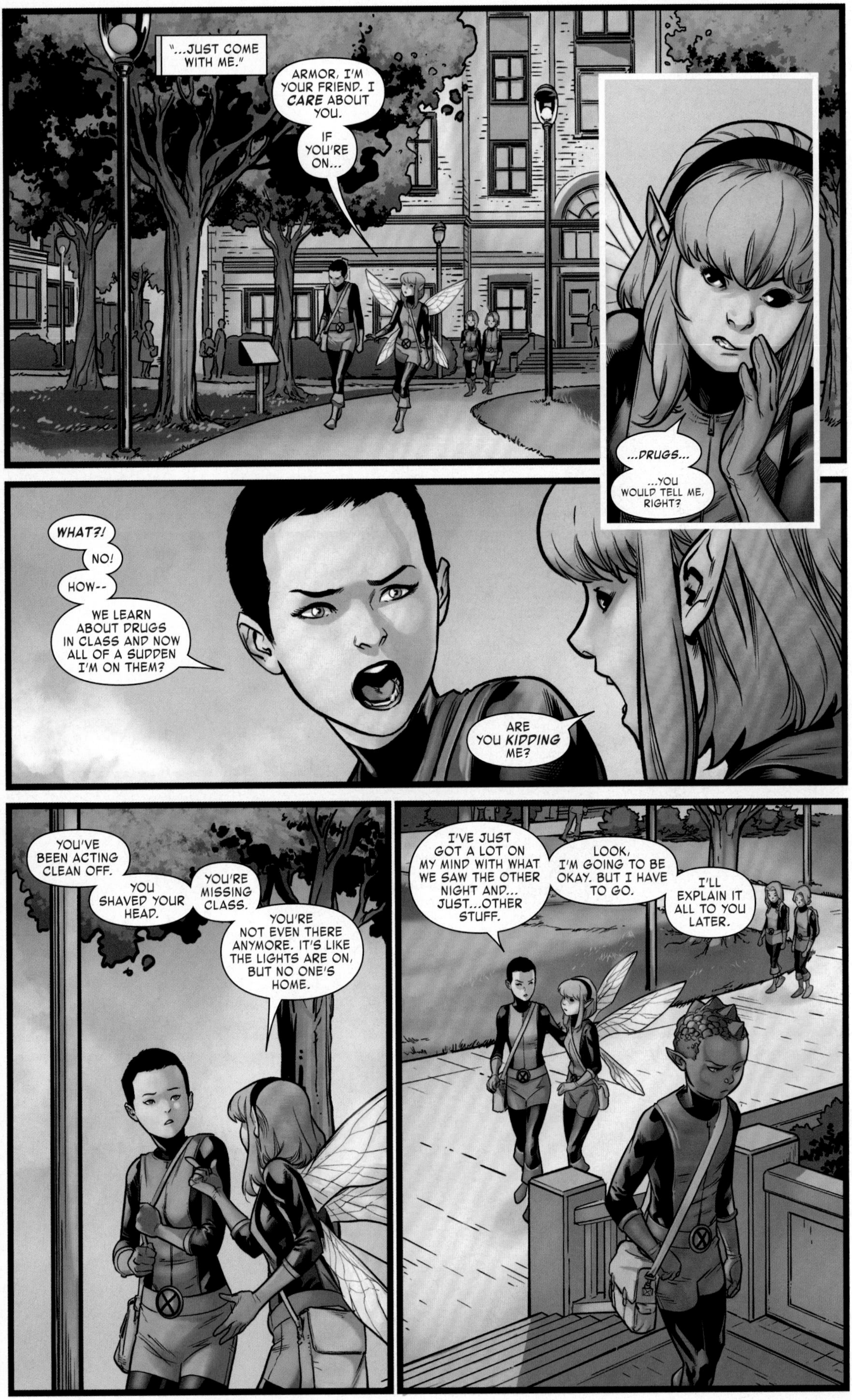
"...JUST COME WITH ME."
ARMOR, I'M YOUR FRIEND. I CARE ABOUT YOU.
IF YOU'RE ON...
...DRUGS...
...YOU WOULD TELL ME, RIGHT?
WHAT?!
NO!
HOW--
WE LEARN ABOUT DRUGS IN CLASS AND NOW ALL OF A SUDDEN I'M ON THEM?
ARE YOU KIDDING ME?
YOU'VE BEEN ACTING CLEAN OFF.
YOU SHAVED YOUR HEAD.
YOU'RE MISSING CLASS.
YOU'RE NOT EVEN THERE ANYMORE. IT'S LIKE THE LIGHTS ARE ON, BUT NO ONE'S HOME.
I'VE JUST GOT A LOT ON MY MIND WITH WHAT WE SAW THE OTHER NIGHT AND... JUST...OTHER STUFF.
LOOK, I'M GOING TO BE OKAY. BUT I HAVE TO GO.
I'LL EXPLAIN IT ALL TO YOU LATER.

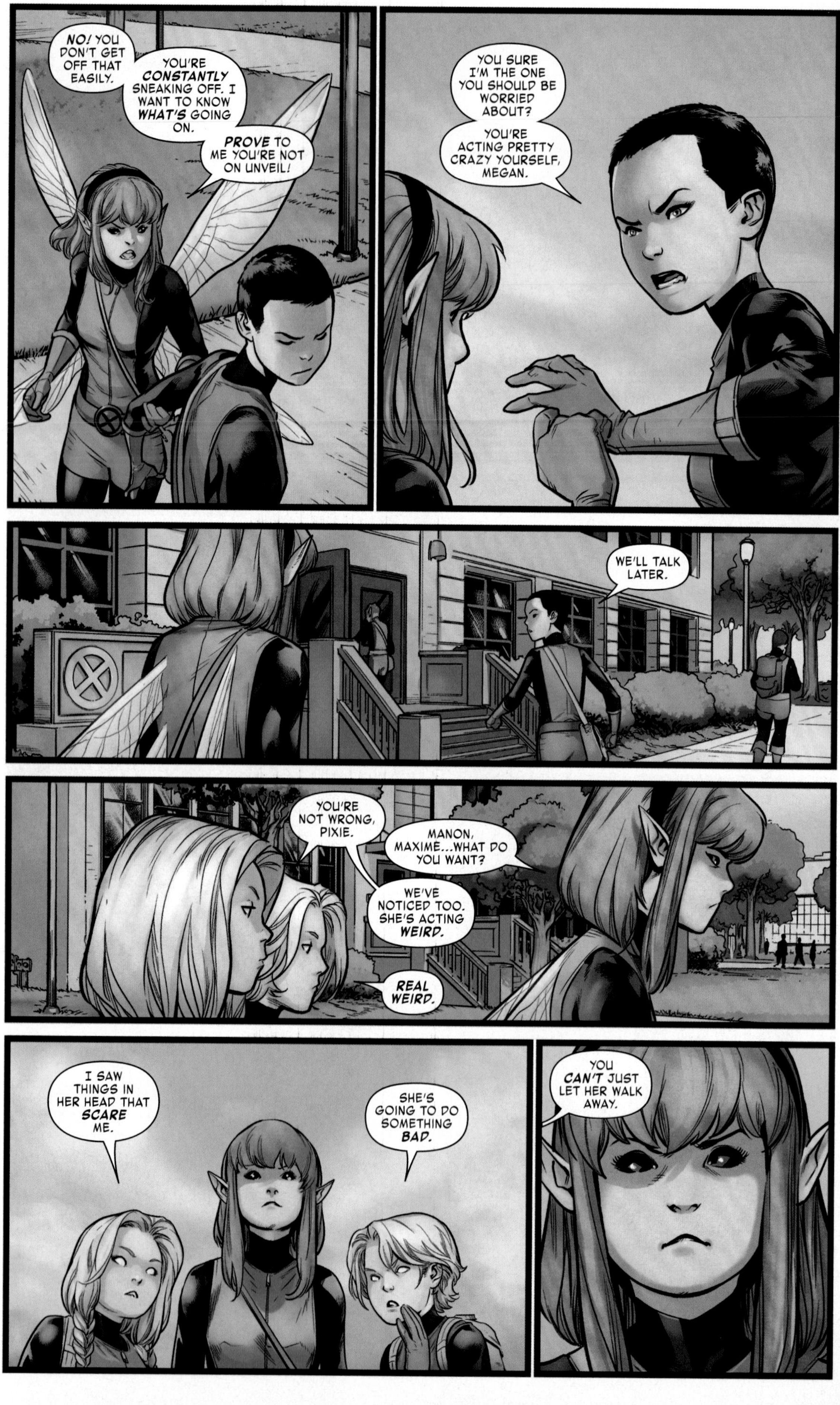
NO! YOU DON'T GET OFF THAT EASILY.
YOU'RE CONSTANTLY SNEAKING OFF. I WANT TO KNOW WHAT'S GOING ON.
PROVE TO ME YOU'RE NOT ON UNVEIL!
YOU SURE I'M THE ONE YOU SHOULD BE WORRIED ABOUT?
YOU'RE ACTING PRETTY CRAZY YOURSELF, MEGAN.
WE'LL TALK LATER.
YOU'RE NOT WRONG, PIXIE.
MANON, MAXIME...WHAT DO YOU WANT?
WE'VE NOTICED TOO. SHE'S ACTING WEIRD.
REAL WEIRD.
I SAW THINGS IN HER HEAD THAT SCARE ME.
SHE'S GOING TO DO SOMETHING BAD.
YOU CAN'T JUST LET HER WALK AWAY.

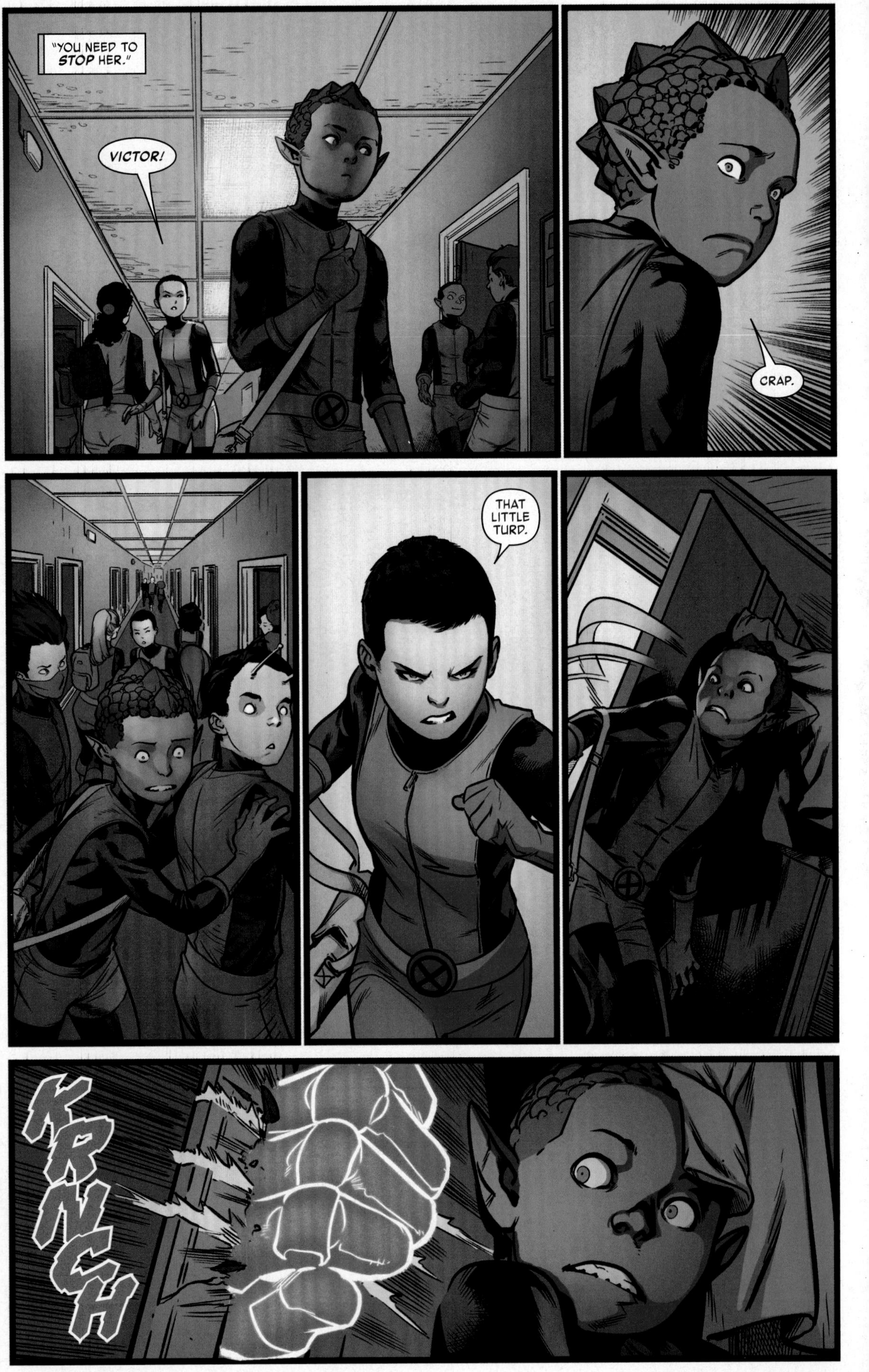

"YOU NEED TO STOP HER."
VICTOR!
CRAP.
THAT LITTLE TURD.
KRNCH

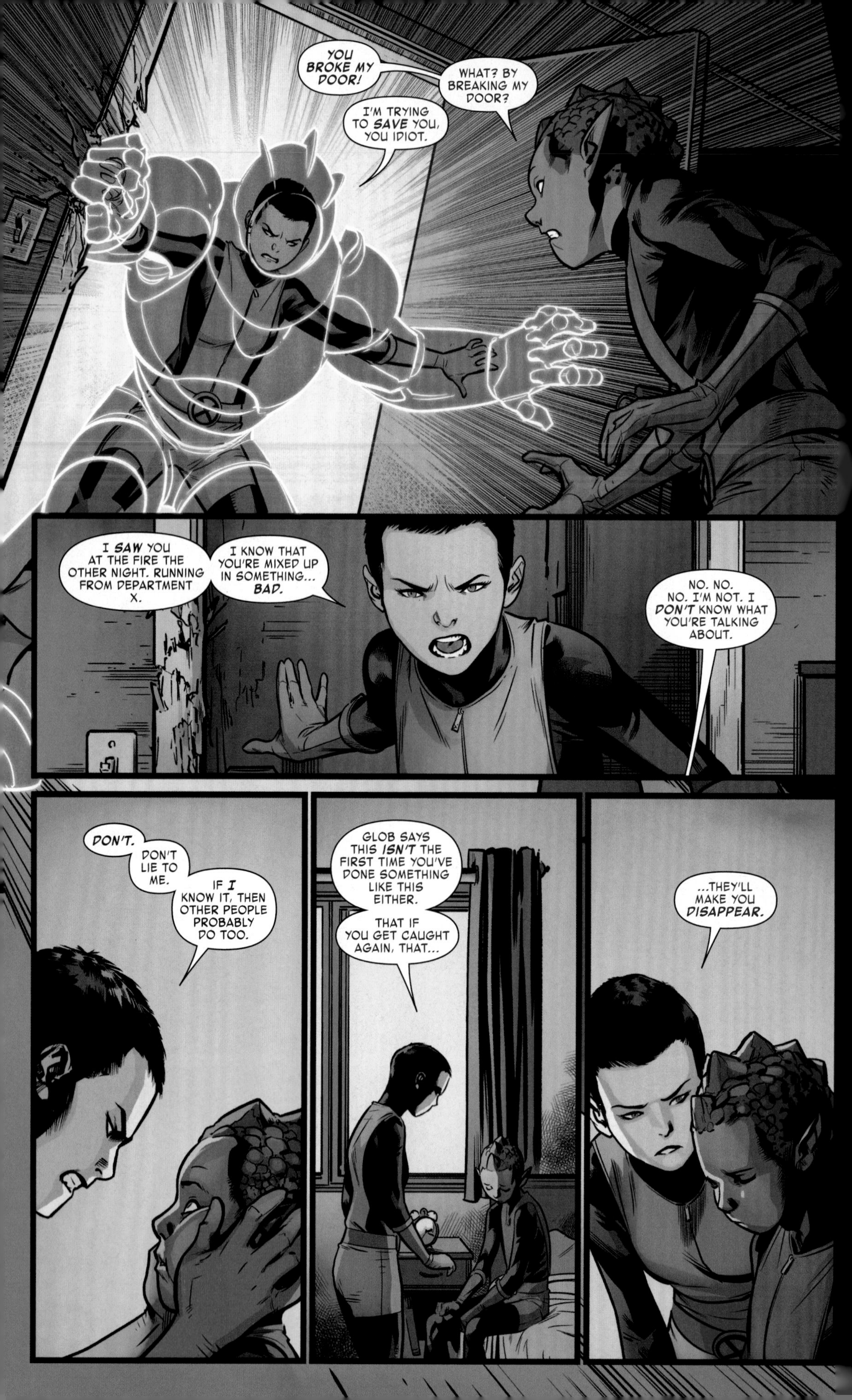
YOU BROKE MY DOOR!
I'M TRYING TO SAVE YOU, YOU IDIOT.
WHAT? BY BREAKING MY DOOR?
I SAW YOU AT THE FIRE THE OTHER NIGHT. RUNNING FROM DEPARTMENT X.
I KNOW THAT YOU'RE MIXED UP IN SOMETHING... BAD.
NO. NO. NO. I'M NOT. I DON'T KNOW WHAT YOU'RE TALKING ABOUT.
DON'T.
DON'T LIE TO ME.
IF I KNOW IT, THEN OTHER PEOPLE PROBABLY DO TOO.
GLOB SAYS THIS ISN'T THE FIRST TIME YOU'VE DONE SOMETHING LIKE THIS EITHER.
THAT IF YOU GET CAUGHT AGAIN, THAT...
...THEY'LL MAKE YOU DISAPPEAR.

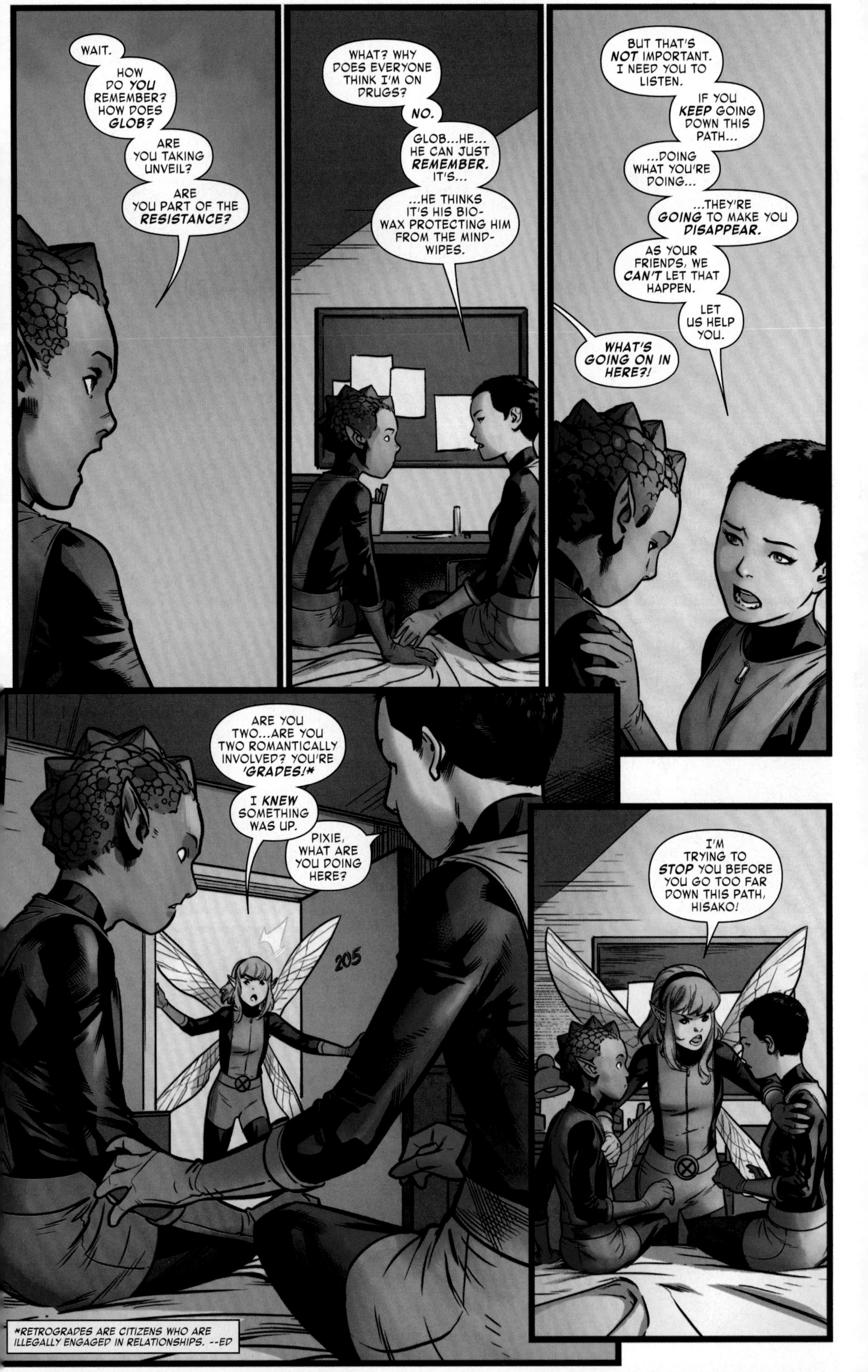
WAIT.
HOW DO YOU REMEMBER? HOW DOES GLOB?
ARE YOU TAKING UNVEIL?
ARE YOU PART OF THE RESISTANCE?
WHAT? WHY DOES EVERYONE THINK I'M ON DRUGS?
NO.
GLOB...HE... HE CAN JUST REMEMBER. IT'S...
...HE THINKS IT'S HIS BIO-WAX PROTECTING HIM FROM THE MIND-WIPES.
BUT THAT'S NOT IMPORTANT. I NEED YOU TO LISTEN.
IF YOU KEEP GOING DOWN THIS PATH...
...DOING WHAT YOU'RE DOING...
...THEY'RE GOING TO MAKE YOU DISAPPEAR.
AS YOUR FRIENDS, WE CAN'T LET THAT HAPPEN.
LET US HELP YOU.
WHAT'S GOING ON IN HERE?!
ARE YOU TWO...ARE YOU TWO ROMANTICALLY INVOLVED? YOU'RE 'GRADES!*
I KNEW SOMETHING WAS UP.
PIXIE, WHAT ARE YOU DOING HERE?
205
*RETROGRADES ARE CITIZENS WHO ARE ILLEGALLY ENGAGED IN RELATIONSHIPS. --ED
I'M TRYING TO STOP YOU BEFORE YOU GO TOO FAR DOWN THIS PATH, HISAKO!

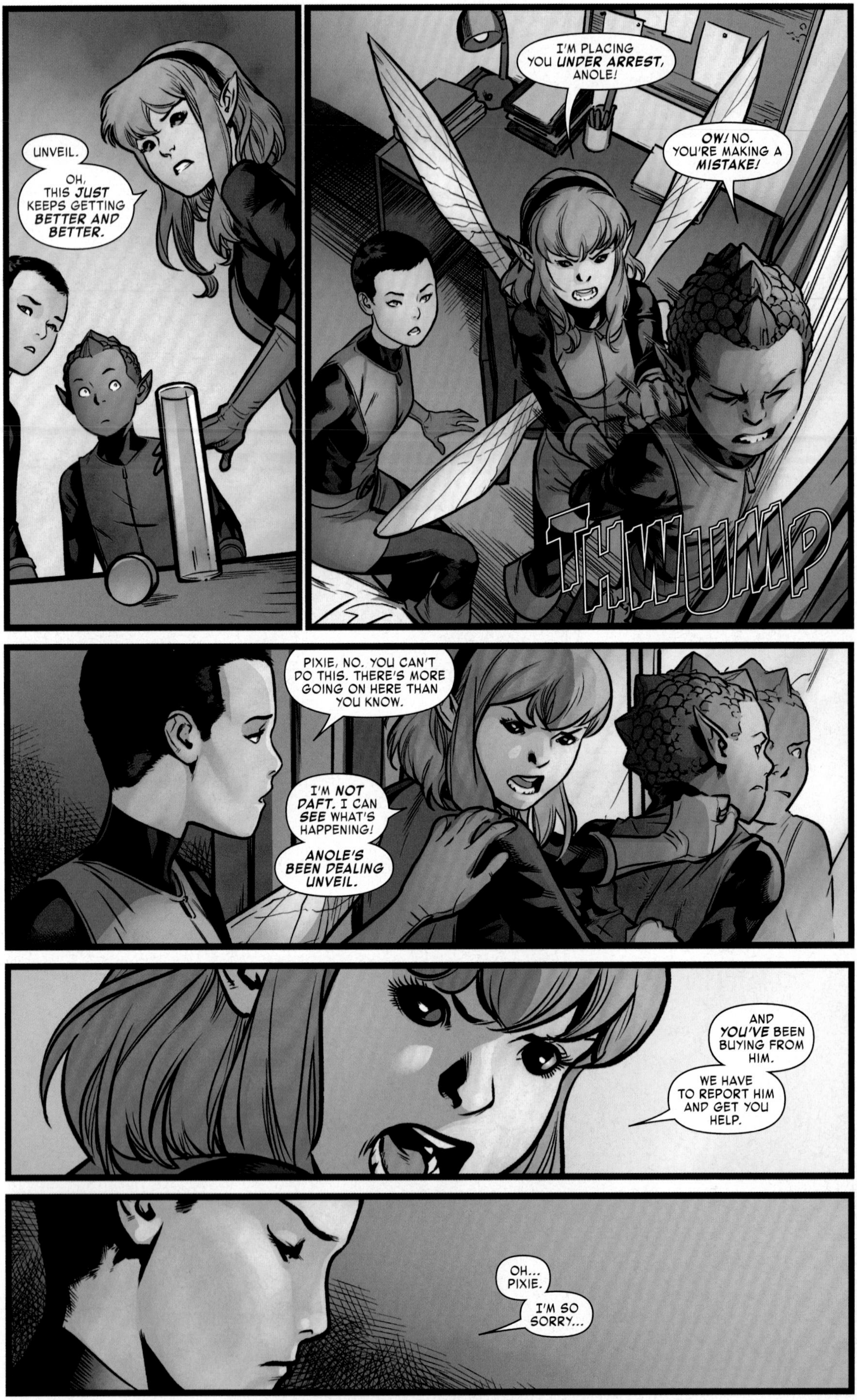
UNVEIL.
OH, THIS JUST KEEPS GETTING BETTER AND BETTER.
I'M PLACING YOU UNDER ARREST, ANOLE!
OW! NO. YOU'RE MAKING A MISTAKE!
THWUMP
PIXIE, NO. YOU CAN'T DO THIS. THERE'S MORE GOING ON HERE THAN YOU KNOW.
I'M NOT DAFT. I CAN SEE WHAT'S HAPPENING!
ANOLE'S BEEN DEALING UNVEIL.
AND YOU'VE BEEN BUYING FROM HIM.
WE HAVE TO REPORT HIM AND GET YOU HELP.
OH... PIXIE.
I'M SO SORRY...

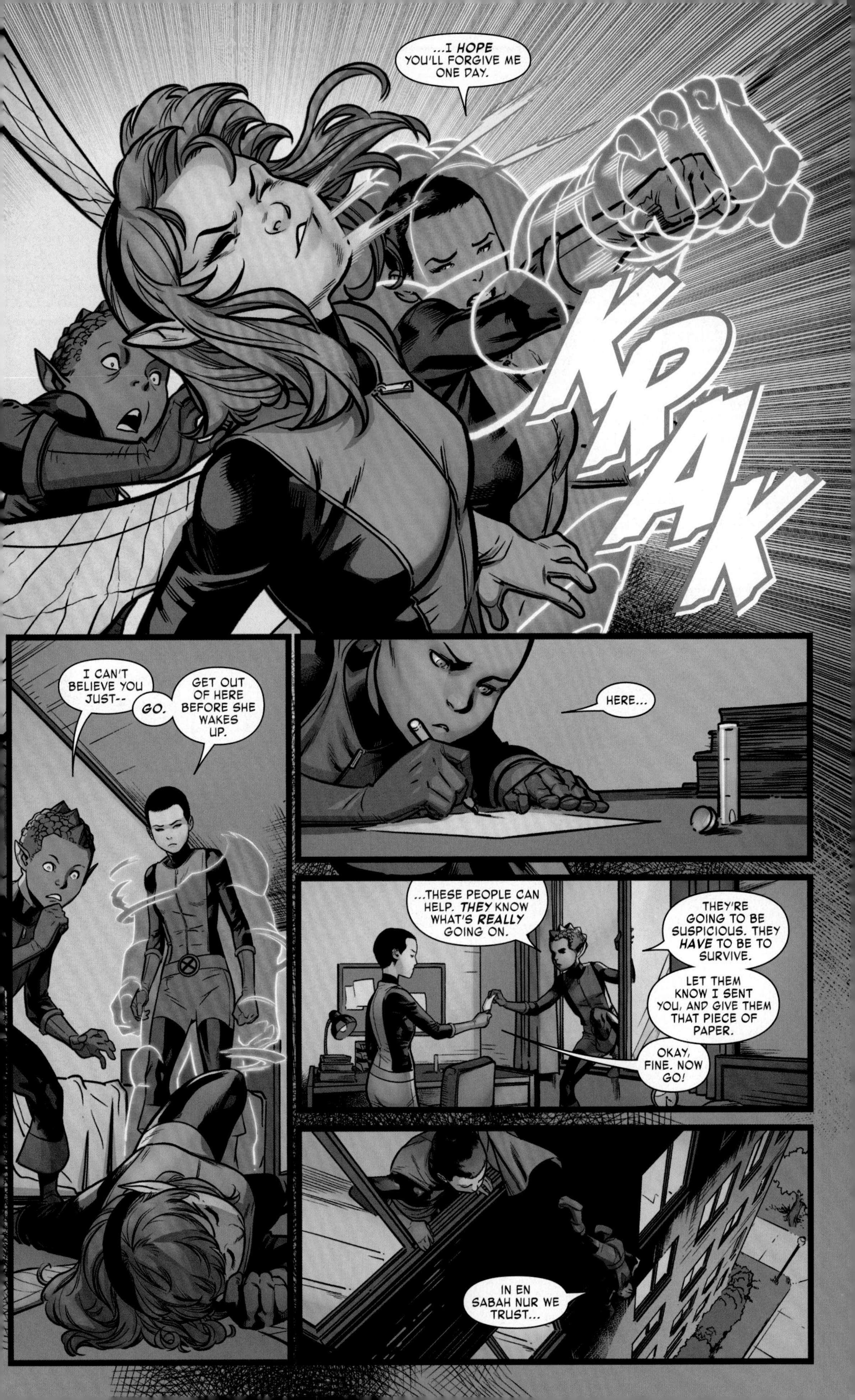

...I HOPE YOU'LL FORGIVE ME ONE DAY.
KRAK
I CAN'T BELIEVE YOU JUST--
GO.
GET OUT OF HERE BEFORE SHE WAKES UP.
HERE...
...THESE PEOPLE CAN HELP. THEY KNOW WHAT'S REALLY GOING ON.
THEY'RE GOING TO BE SUSPICIOUS. THEY HAVE TO BE TO SURVIVE.
LET THEM KNOW I SENT YOU, AND GIVE THEM THAT PIECE OF PAPER.
OKAY, FINE. NOW GO!
IN EN SABAH NUR WE TRUST...

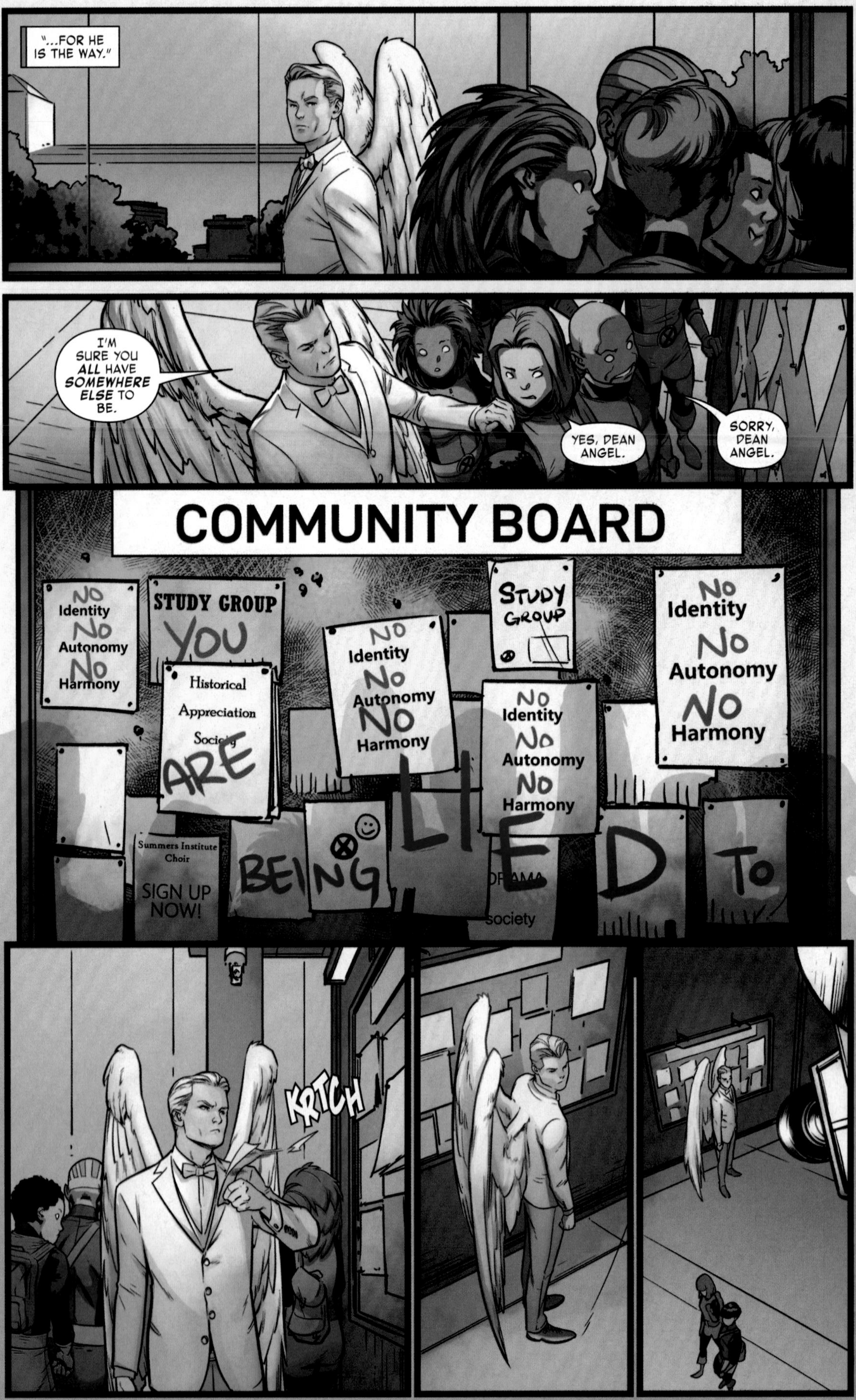
"...FOR HE IS THE WAY."
I'M SURE YOU ALL HAVE SOMEWHERE ELSE TO BE.
YES, DEAN ANGEL.
SORRY, DEAN ANGEL.
COMMUNITY BOARD
NO Identity NO Autonomy NO Harmony
STUDY GROUP
YOU
Historical Appreciation Society
ARE
NO Identity NO Autonomy NO Harmony
STUDY GROUP
NO Identity NO Autonomy NO Harmony
NO Identity NO Autonomy NO Harmony
Summers Institute Choir
SIGN UP NOW!
BEING
LIED
TO
society
KRTCH

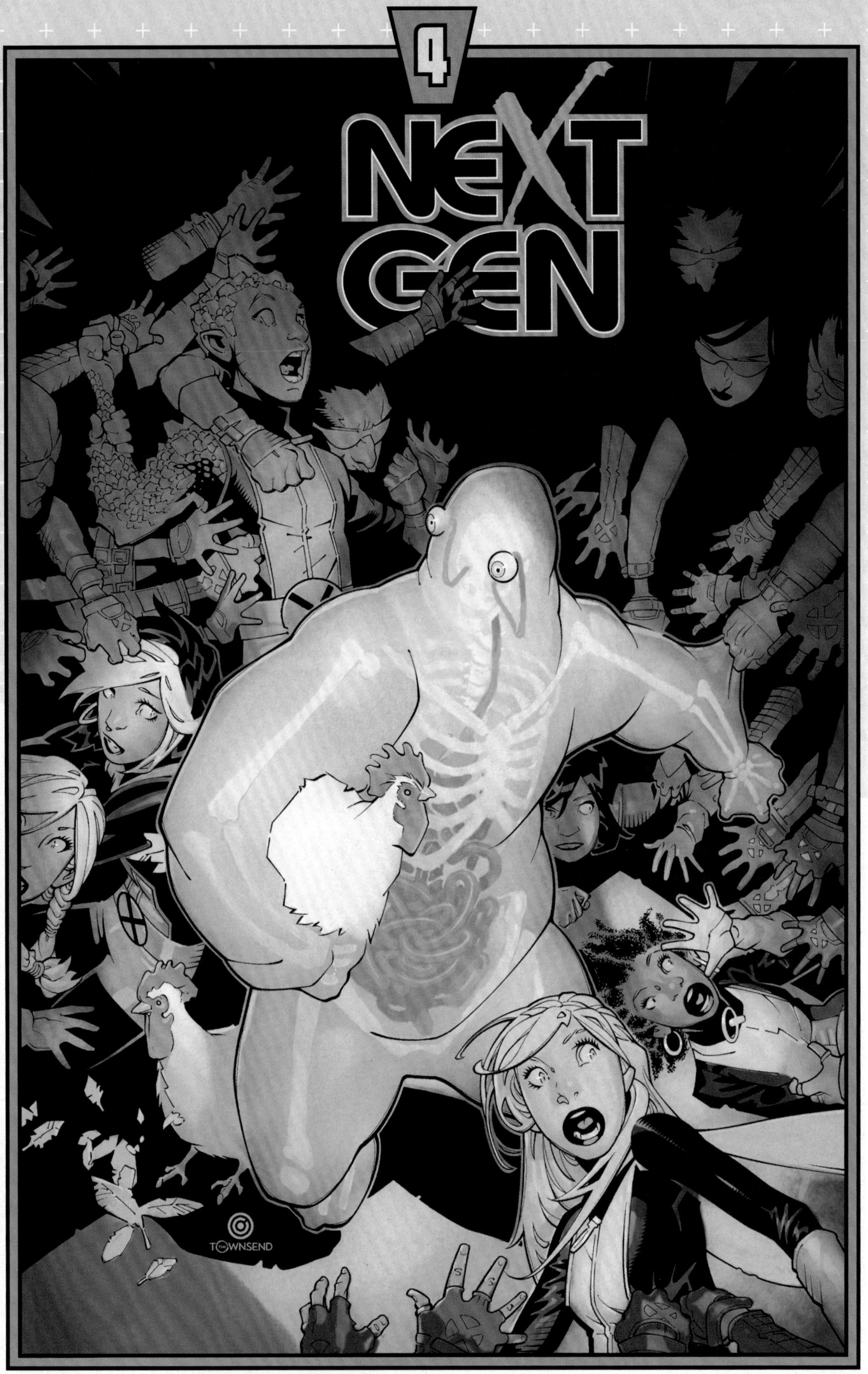
4
NEXT GEN
TOWNSEND

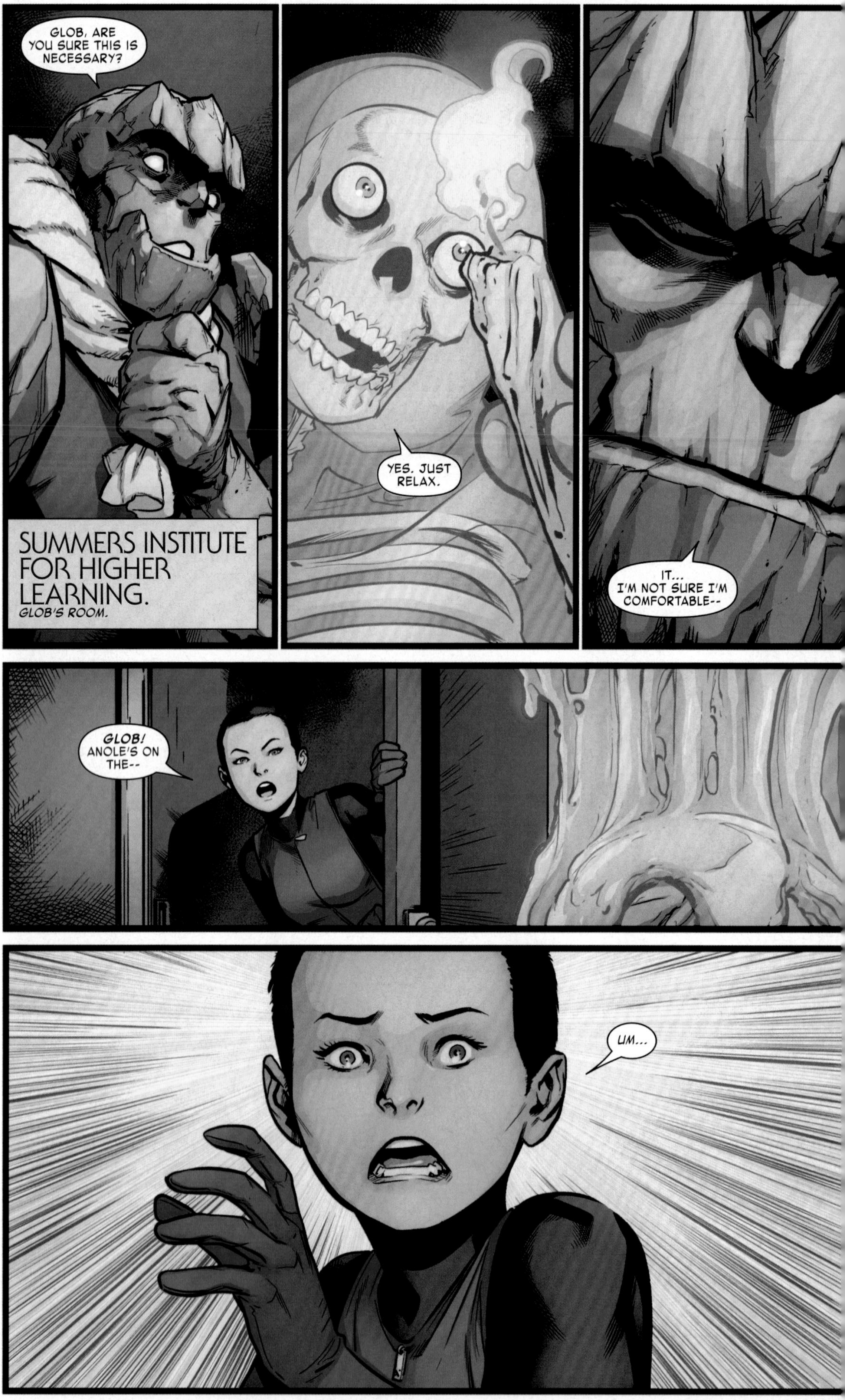
GLOB, ARE YOU SURE THIS IS NECESSARY?
SUMMERS INSTITUTE FOR HIGHER LEARNING.
GLOB'S ROOM.
YES. JUST RELAX.
IT... I'M NOT SURE I'M COMFORTABLE--
GLOB! ANOLE'S ON THE--
UM...

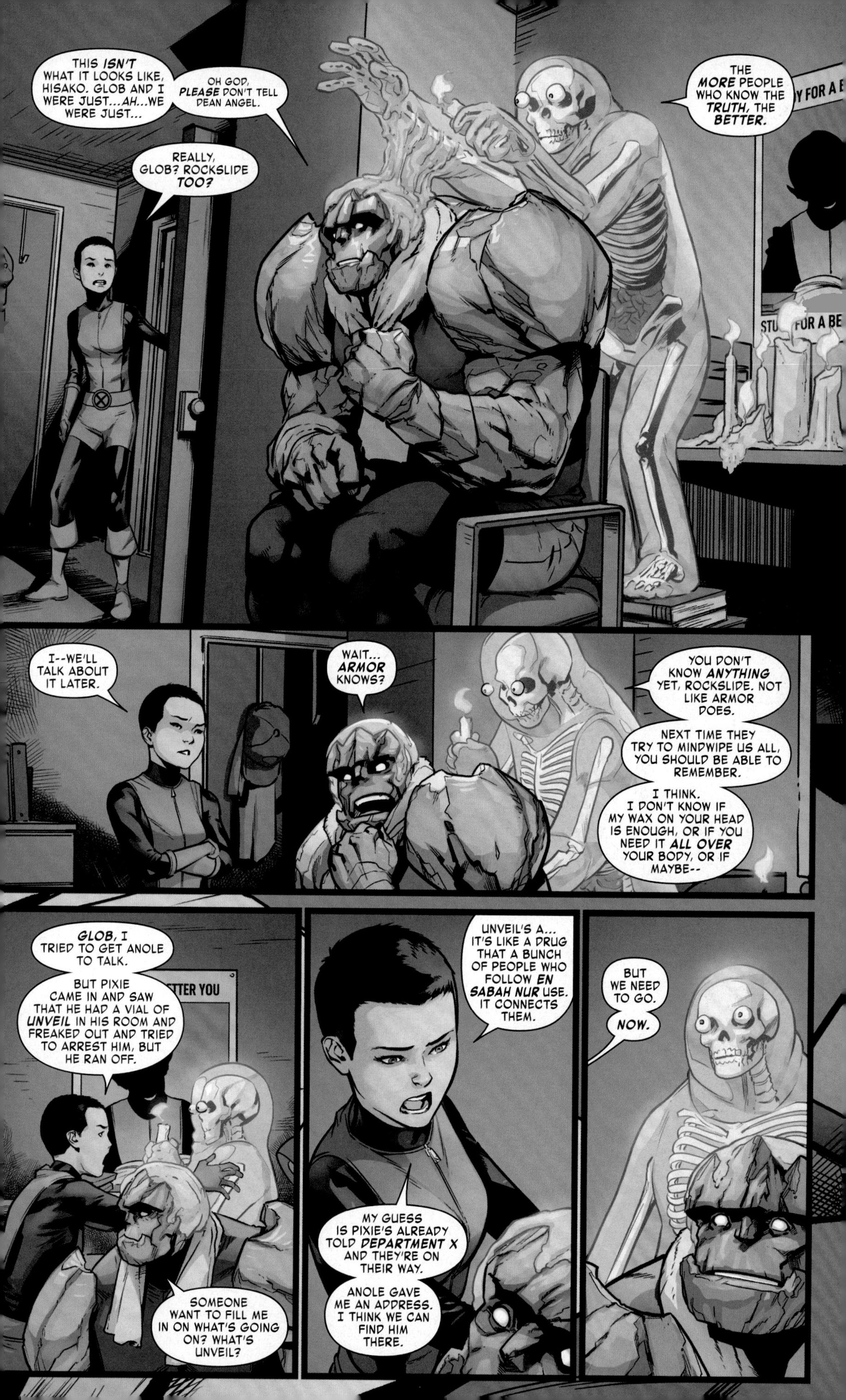
THIS ISN'T WHAT IT LOOKS LIKE, HISAKO. GLOB AND I WERE JUST...AH...WE WERE JUST...
OH GOD, PLEASE DON'T TELL DEAN ANGEL.
REALLY, GLOB? ROCKSLIDE TOO?
THE MORE PEOPLE WHO KNOW THE TRUTH, THE BETTER.
I--WE'LL TALK ABOUT IT LATER.
WAIT... ARMOR KNOWS?
YOU DON'T KNOW ANYTHING YET, ROCKSLIDE. NOT LIKE ARMOR DOES.
NEXT TIME THEY TRY TO MINDWIPE US ALL, YOU SHOULD BE ABLE TO REMEMBER.
I THINK. I DON'T KNOW IF MY WAX ON YOUR HEAD IS ENOUGH, OR IF YOU NEED IT ALL OVER YOUR BODY, OR IF MAYBE--
GLOB, I TRIED TO GET ANOLE TO TALK.
BUT PIXIE CAME IN AND SAW THAT HE HAD A VIAL OF UNVEIL IN HIS ROOM AND FREAKED OUT AND TRIED TO ARREST HIM, BUT HE RAN OFF.
SOMEONE WANT TO FILL ME IN ON WHAT'S GOING ON? WHAT'S UNVEIL?
UNVEIL'S A... IT'S LIKE A DRUG THAT A BUNCH OF PEOPLE WHO FOLLOW EN SABAH NUR USE. IT CONNECTS THEM.
MY GUESS IS PIXIE'S ALREADY TOLD DEPARTMENT X AND THEY'RE ON THEIR WAY.
ANOLE GAVE ME AN ADDRESS. I THINK WE CAN FIND HIM THERE.
BUT WE NEED TO GO.
NOW.

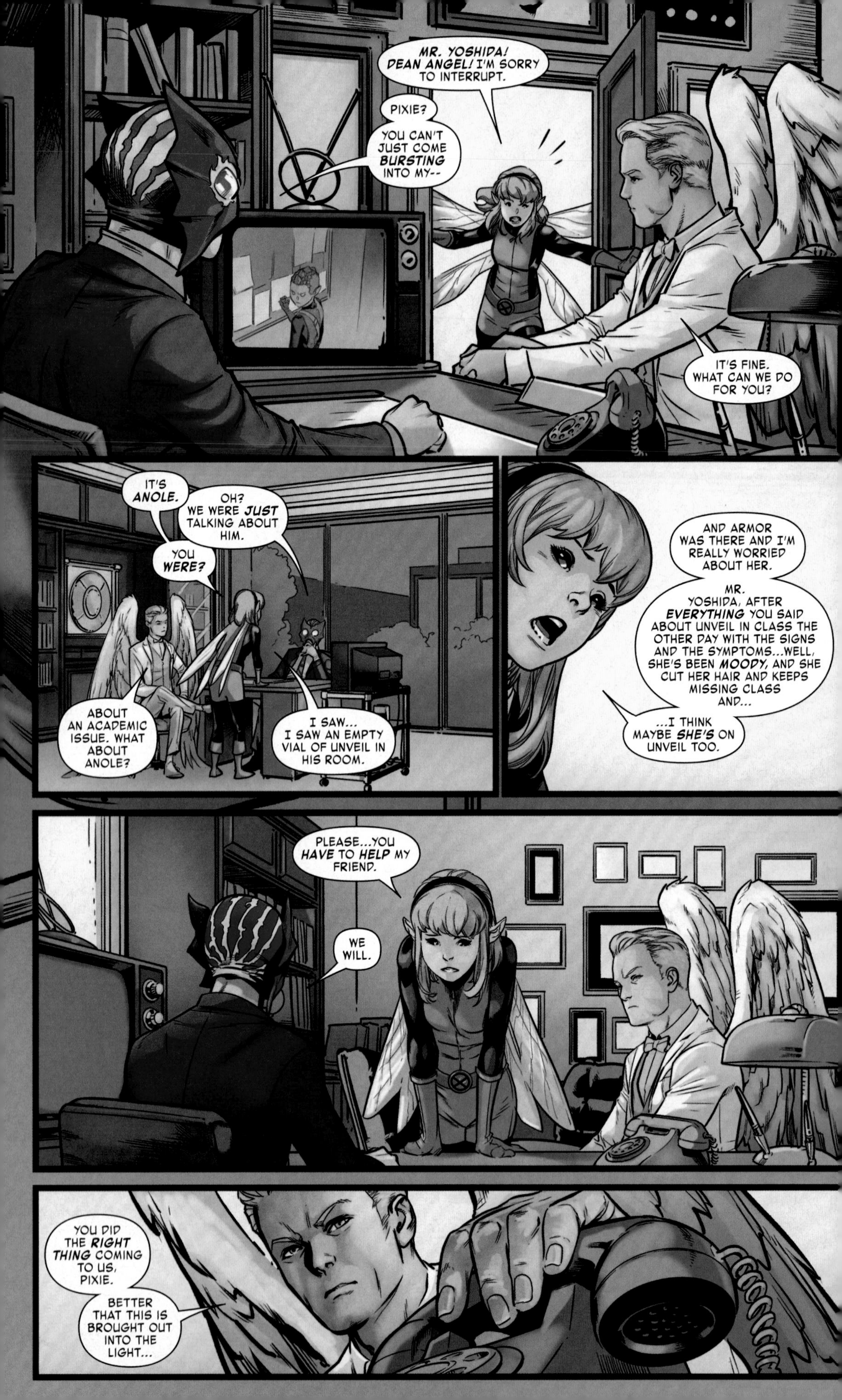
MR. YOSHIDA! DEAN ANGEL! I'M SORRY TO INTERRUPT.
PIXIE?
YOU CAN'T JUST COME BURSTING INTO MY--
IT'S FINE. WHAT CAN WE DO FOR YOU?
IT'S ANOLE.
OH? WE WERE JUST TALKING ABOUT HIM.
YOU WERE?
ABOUT AN ACADEMIC ISSUE. WHAT ABOUT ANOLE?
I SAW... I SAW AN EMPTY VIAL OF UNVEIL IN HIS ROOM.
AND ARMOR WAS THERE AND I'M REALLY WORRIED ABOUT HER.
MR. YOSHIDA, AFTER EVERYTHING YOU SAID ABOUT UNVEIL IN CLASS THE OTHER DAY WITH THE SIGNS AND THE SYMPTOMS...WELL, SHE'S BEEN MOODY, AND SHE CUT HER HAIR AND KEEPS MISSING CLASS AND...
...I THINK MAYBE SHE'S ON UNVEIL TOO.
PLEASE...YOU HAVE TO HELP MY FRIEND.
WE WILL.
YOU DID THE RIGHT THING COMING TO US, PIXIE.
BETTER THAT THIS IS BROUGHT OUT INTO THE LIGHT...

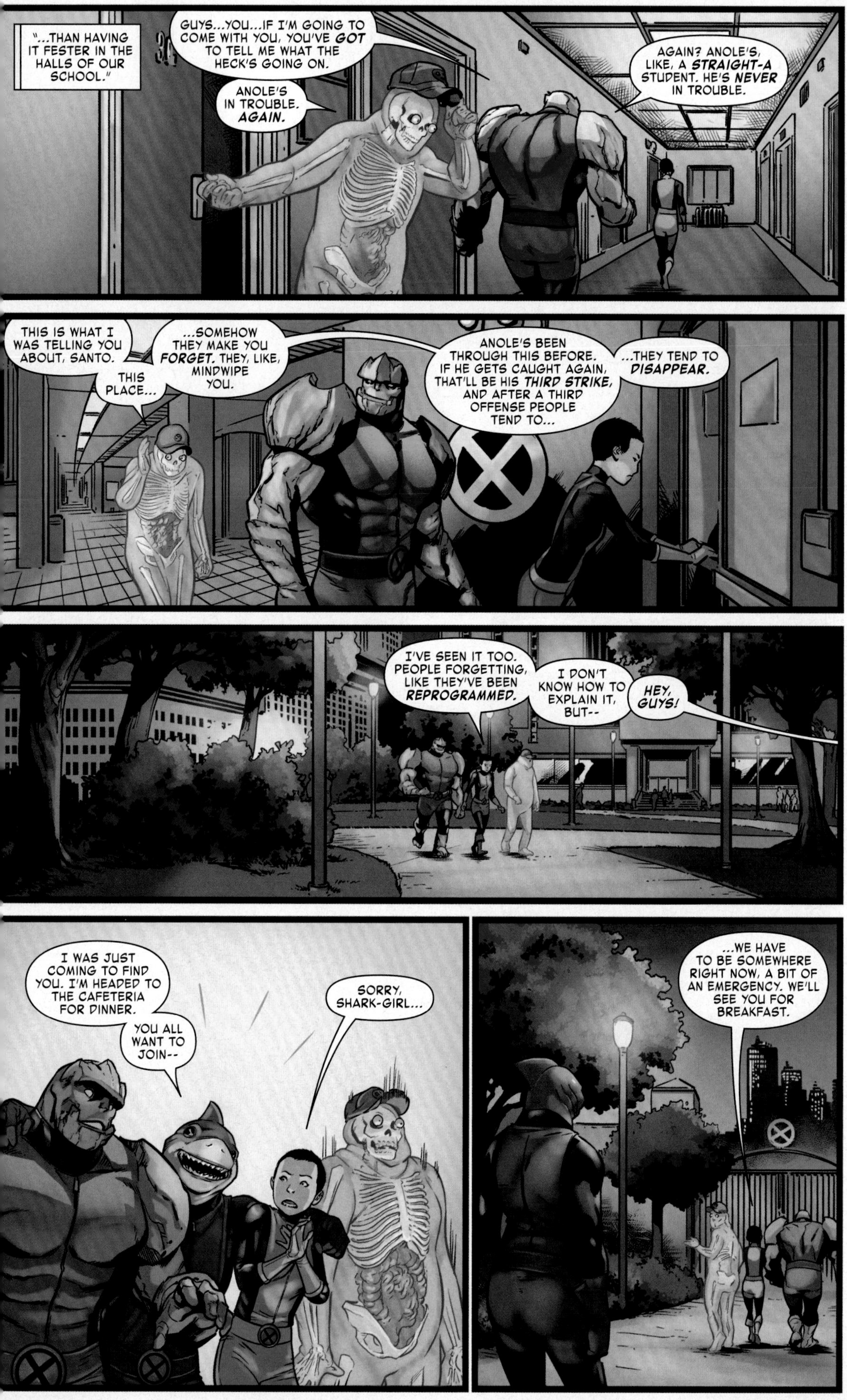
"...THAN HAVING IT FESTER IN THE HALLS OF OUR SCHOOL."
GUYS...YOU...IF I'M GOING TO COME WITH YOU, YOU'VE GOT TO TELL ME WHAT THE HECK'S GOING ON.
ANOLE'S IN TROUBLE. AGAIN.
AGAIN? ANOLE'S, LIKE, A STRAIGHT-A STUDENT. HE'S NEVER IN TROUBLE.
THIS IS WHAT I WAS TELLING YOU ABOUT, SANTO.
THIS PLACE...
...SOMEHOW THEY MAKE YOU FORGET. THEY, LIKE, MINDWIPE YOU.
ANOLE'S BEEN THROUGH THIS BEFORE. IF HE GETS CAUGHT AGAIN, THAT'LL BE HIS THIRD STRIKE, AND AFTER A THIRD OFFENSE PEOPLE TEND TO...
...THEY TEND TO DISAPPEAR.
I'VE SEEN IT TOO. PEOPLE FORGETTING, LIKE THEY'VE BEEN REPROGRAMMED.
I DON'T KNOW HOW TO EXPLAIN IT, BUT--
HEY, GUYS!
I WAS JUST COMING TO FIND YOU. I'M HEADED TO THE CAFETERIA FOR DINNER.
YOU ALL WANT TO JOIN--
SORRY, SHARK-GIRL...
...WE HAVE TO BE SOMEWHERE RIGHT NOW, A BIT OF AN EMERGENCY. WE'LL SEE YOU FOR BREAKFAST.

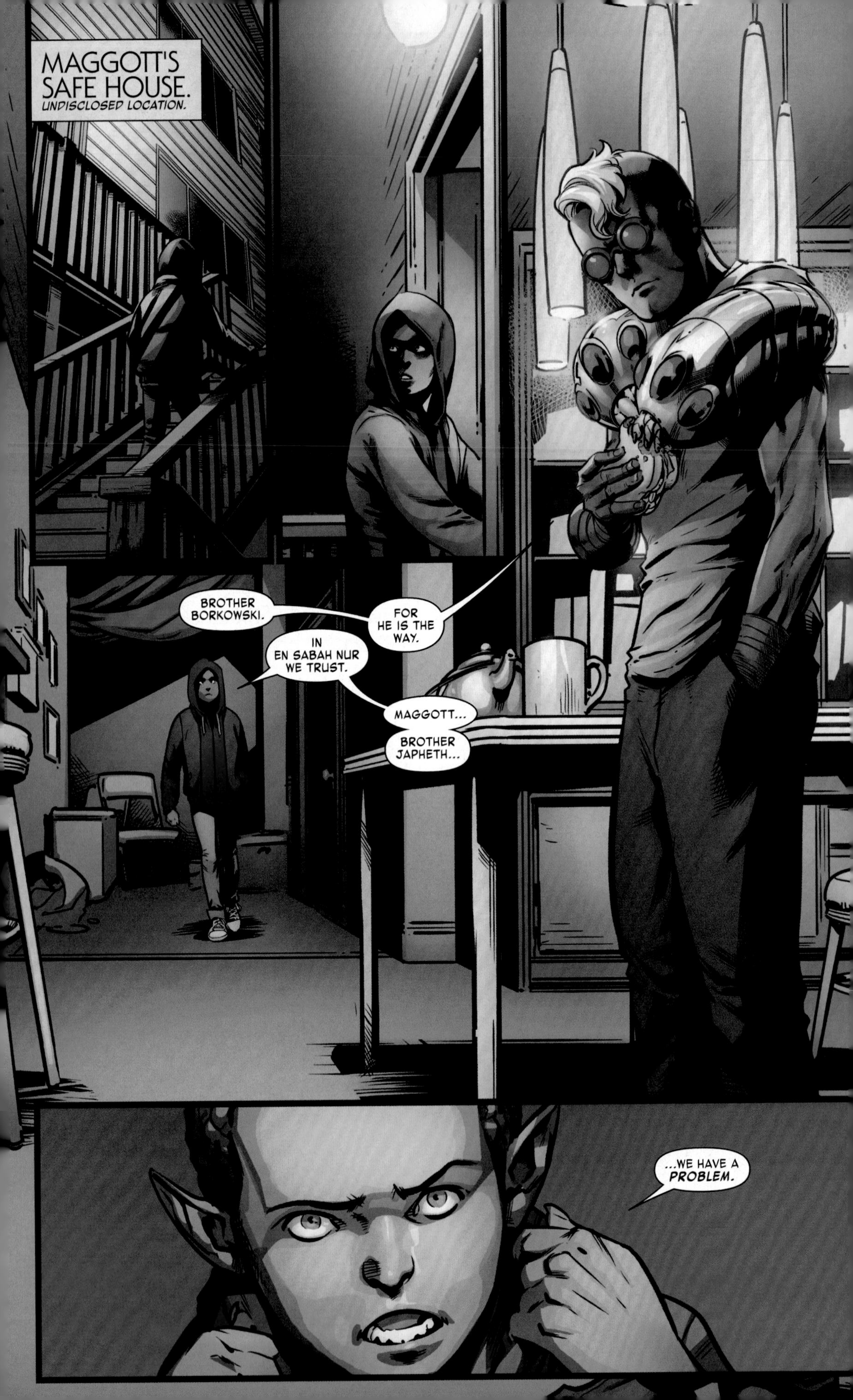
MAGGOTT'S SAFE HOUSE.
UNDISCLOSED LOCATION.
BROTHER BORKOWSKI.
FOR HE IS THE WAY.
IN EN SABAH NUR WE TRUST.
MAGGOTT...
BROTHER JAPHETH...
...WE HAVE A PROBLEM.

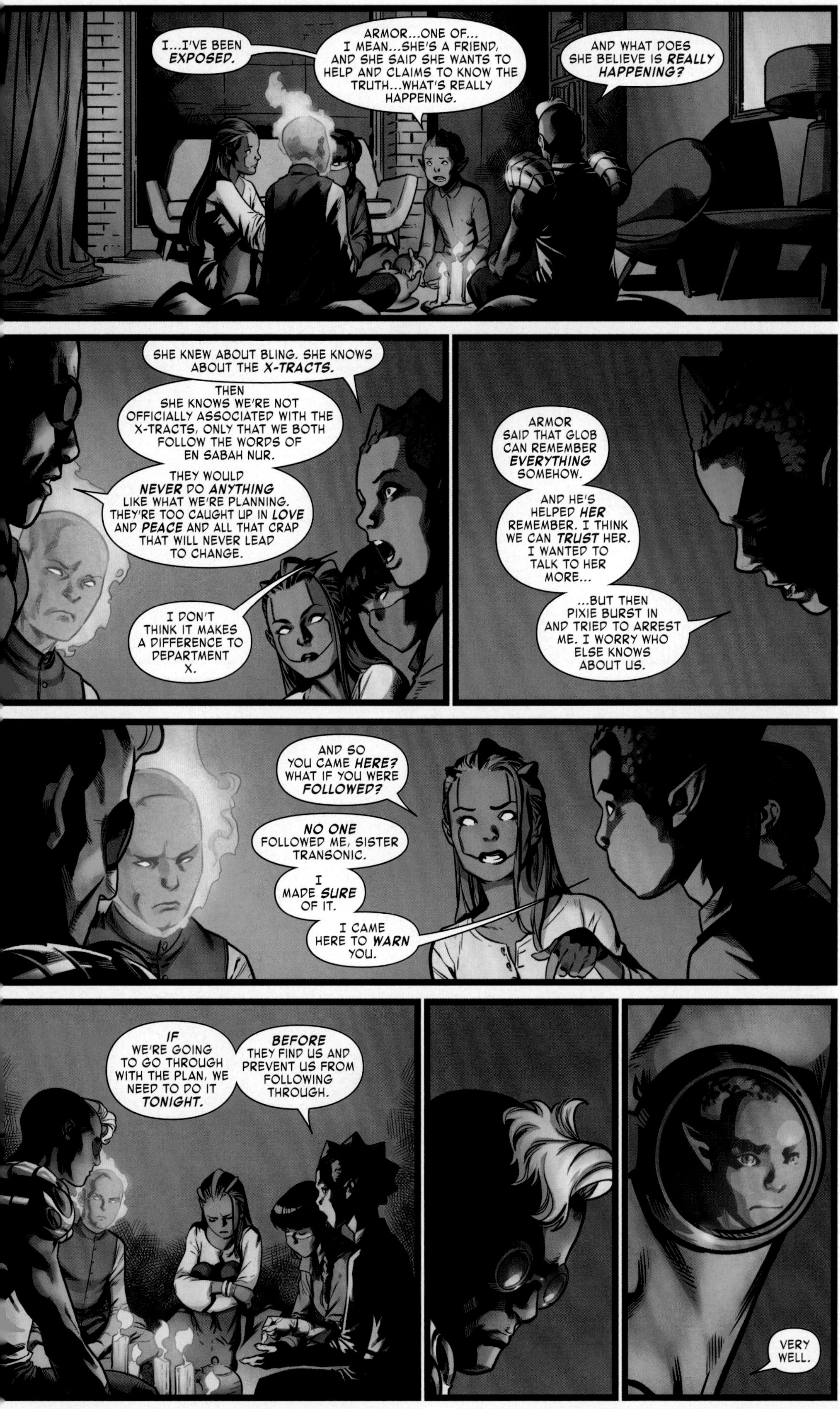
I...I'VE BEEN EXPOSED.
ARMOR...ONE OF... I MEAN...SHE'S A FRIEND, AND SHE SAID SHE WANTS TO HELP AND CLAIMS TO KNOW THE TRUTH...WHAT'S REALLY HAPPENING.
AND WHAT DOES SHE BELIEVE IS REALLY HAPPENING?
SHE KNEW ABOUT BLING. SHE KNOWS ABOUT THE X-TRACTS.
THEN SHE KNOWS WE'RE NOT OFFICIALLY ASSOCIATED WITH THE X-TRACTS, ONLY THAT WE BOTH FOLLOW THE WORDS OF EN SABAH NUR.
THEY WOULD NEVER DO ANYTHING LIKE WHAT WE'RE PLANNING. THEY'RE TOO CAUGHT UP IN LOVE AND PEACE AND ALL THAT CRAP THAT WILL NEVER LEAD TO CHANGE.
I DON'T THINK IT MAKES A DIFFERENCE TO DEPARTMENT X.
ARMOR SAID THAT GLOB CAN REMEMBER EVERYTHING SOMEHOW.
AND HE'S HELPED HER REMEMBER. I THINK WE CAN TRUST HER. I WANTED TO TALK TO HER MORE...
...BUT THEN PIXIE BURST IN AND TRIED TO ARREST ME. I WORRY WHO ELSE KNOWS ABOUT US.
AND SO YOU CAME HERE? WHAT IF YOU WERE FOLLOWED?
NO ONE FOLLOWED ME, SISTER TRANSONIC.
I MADE SURE OF IT.
I CAME HERE TO WARN YOU.
IF WE'RE GOING TO GO THROUGH WITH THE PLAN, WE NEED TO DO IT TONIGHT.
BEFORE THEY FIND US AND PREVENT US FROM FOLLOWING THROUGH.
VERY WELL.

AND YOU HAVE NO IDEA WHERE THEY WENT?

SUMMERS INSTITUTE FOR HIGHER LEARNING.

NO. ARMOR WALLOPED ME PRETTY GOOD.

WHEN I CAME TO, THE ROOM WAS *EMPTY.* I WENT STRAIGHT TO PROFESSOR YOSHIDA AND DEAN ANGEL.

AND I CALLED DEPARTMENT X DIRECTLY.

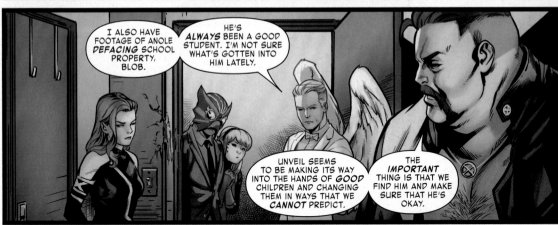

I ALSO HAVE FOOTAGE OF ANOLE *DEFACING* SCHOOL PROPERTY, BLOB.

HE'S *ALWAYS* BEEN A GOOD STUDENT. I'M NOT SURE WHAT'S GOTTEN INTO HIM LATELY.

UNVEIL SEEMS TO BE MAKING ITS WAY INTO THE HANDS OF *GOOD* CHILDREN AND CHANGING THEM IN WAYS THAT WE *CANNOT* PREDICT.

THE *IMPORTANT* THING IS THAT WE FIND HIM AND MAKE SURE THAT HE'S OKAY.

PIXIE, CAN YOU SHOW ME ARMOR'S ROOM? MAYBE THERE'S SOMETHING IN THERE THAT WILL GIVE US SOME INDICATION OF HOW TO HELP YOUR FRIEND.

SURE.

BLOB, YOU FINISH UP IN HERE. I'LL REPORT IF I FIND ANYTHING.

SURE THING, PSYLOCKE.

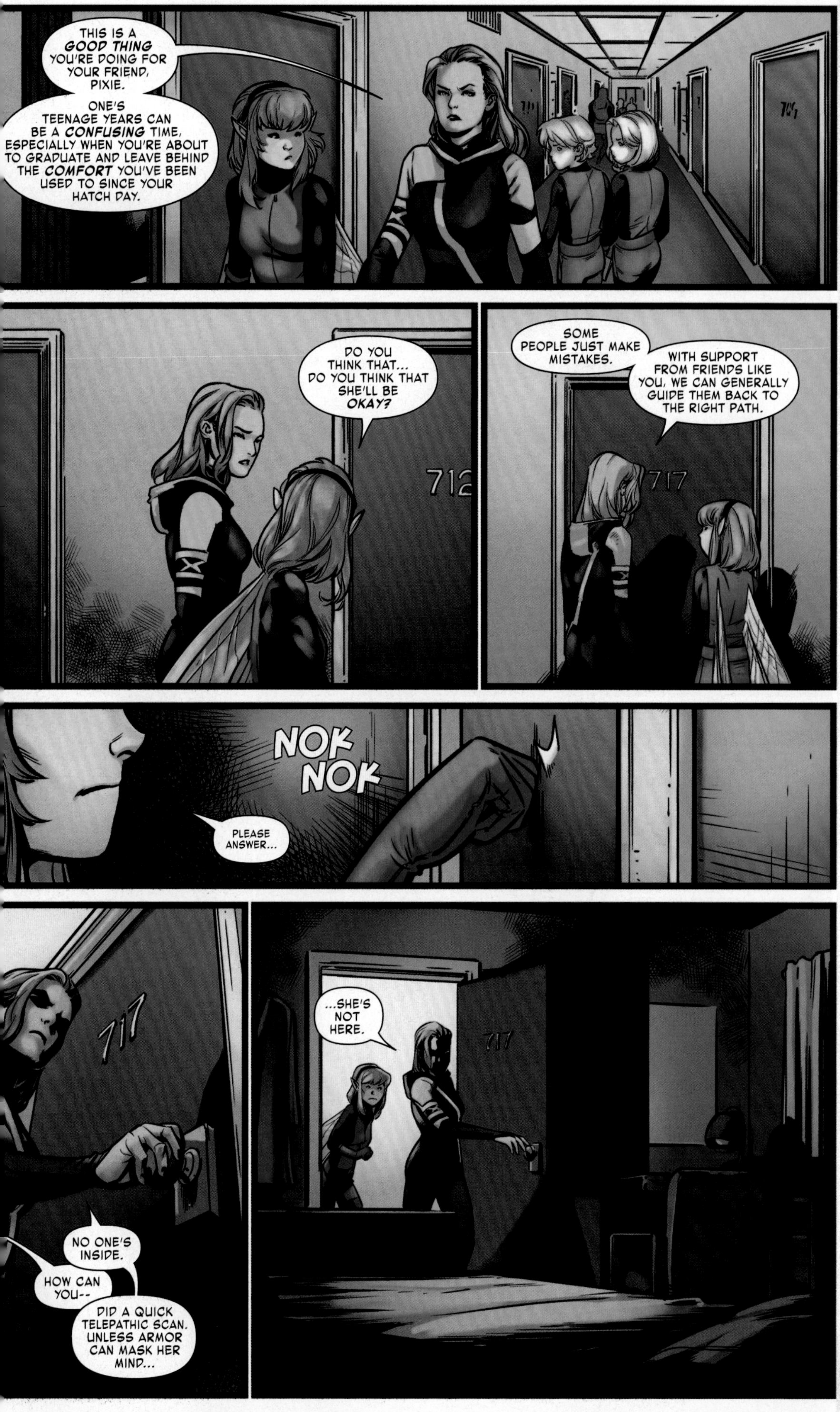
THIS IS A GOOD THING YOU'RE DOING FOR YOUR FRIEND, PIXIE.
ONE'S TEENAGE YEARS CAN BE A CONFUSING TIME, ESPECIALLY WHEN YOU'RE ABOUT TO GRADUATE AND LEAVE BEHIND THE COMFORT YOU'VE BEEN USED TO SINCE YOUR HATCH DAY.
DO YOU THINK THAT... DO YOU THINK THAT SHE'LL BE OKAY?
712
SOME PEOPLE JUST MAKE MISTAKES.
WITH SUPPORT FROM FRIENDS LIKE YOU, WE CAN GENERALLY GUIDE THEM BACK TO THE RIGHT PATH.
717
NOK NOK
PLEASE ANSWER...
717
...SHE'S NOT HERE.
717
NO ONE'S INSIDE.
HOW CAN YOU--
DID A QUICK TELEPATHIC SCAN. UNLESS ARMOR CAN MASK HER MIND...

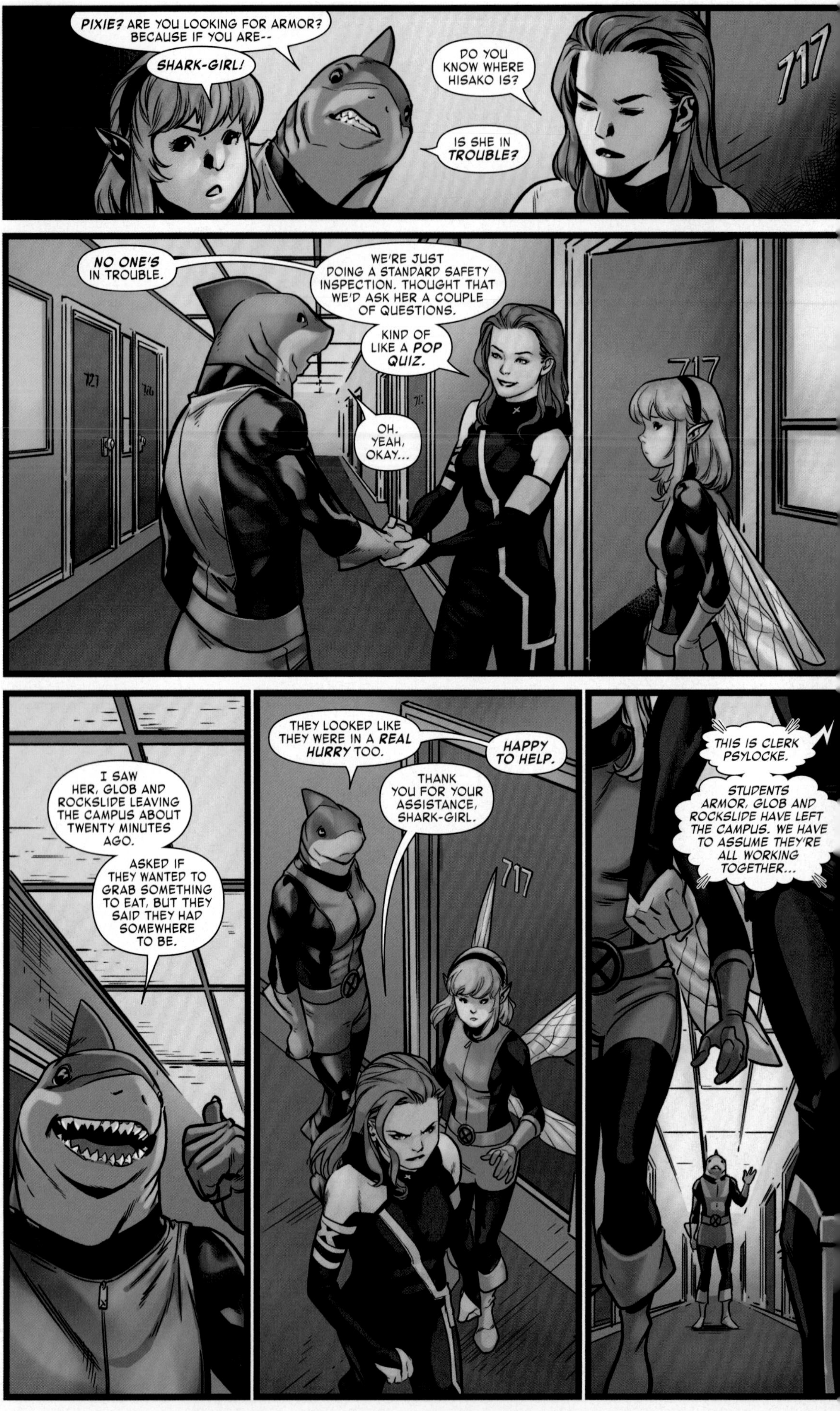
PIXIE? ARE YOU LOOKING FOR ARMOR? BECAUSE IF YOU ARE--
SHARK-GIRL!
DO YOU KNOW WHERE HISAKO IS?
IS SHE IN TROUBLE?
717
NO ONE'S IN TROUBLE.
WE'RE JUST DOING A STANDARD SAFETY INSPECTION. THOUGHT THAT WE'D ASK HER A COUPLE OF QUESTIONS.
KIND OF LIKE A POP QUIZ.
OH. YEAH, OKAY...
717
I SAW HER, GLOB AND ROCKSLIDE LEAVING THE CAMPUS ABOUT TWENTY MINUTES AGO.
ASKED IF THEY WANTED TO GRAB SOMETHING TO EAT, BUT THEY SAID THEY HAD SOMEWHERE TO BE.
THEY LOOKED LIKE THEY WERE IN A REAL HURRY TOO.
HAPPY TO HELP.
THANK YOU FOR YOUR ASSISTANCE, SHARK-GIRL.
717
THIS IS CLERK PSYLOCKE.
STUDENTS ARMOR, GLOB AND ROCKSLIDE HAVE LEFT THE CAMPUS. WE HAVE TO ASSUME THEY'RE ALL WORKING TOGETHER...

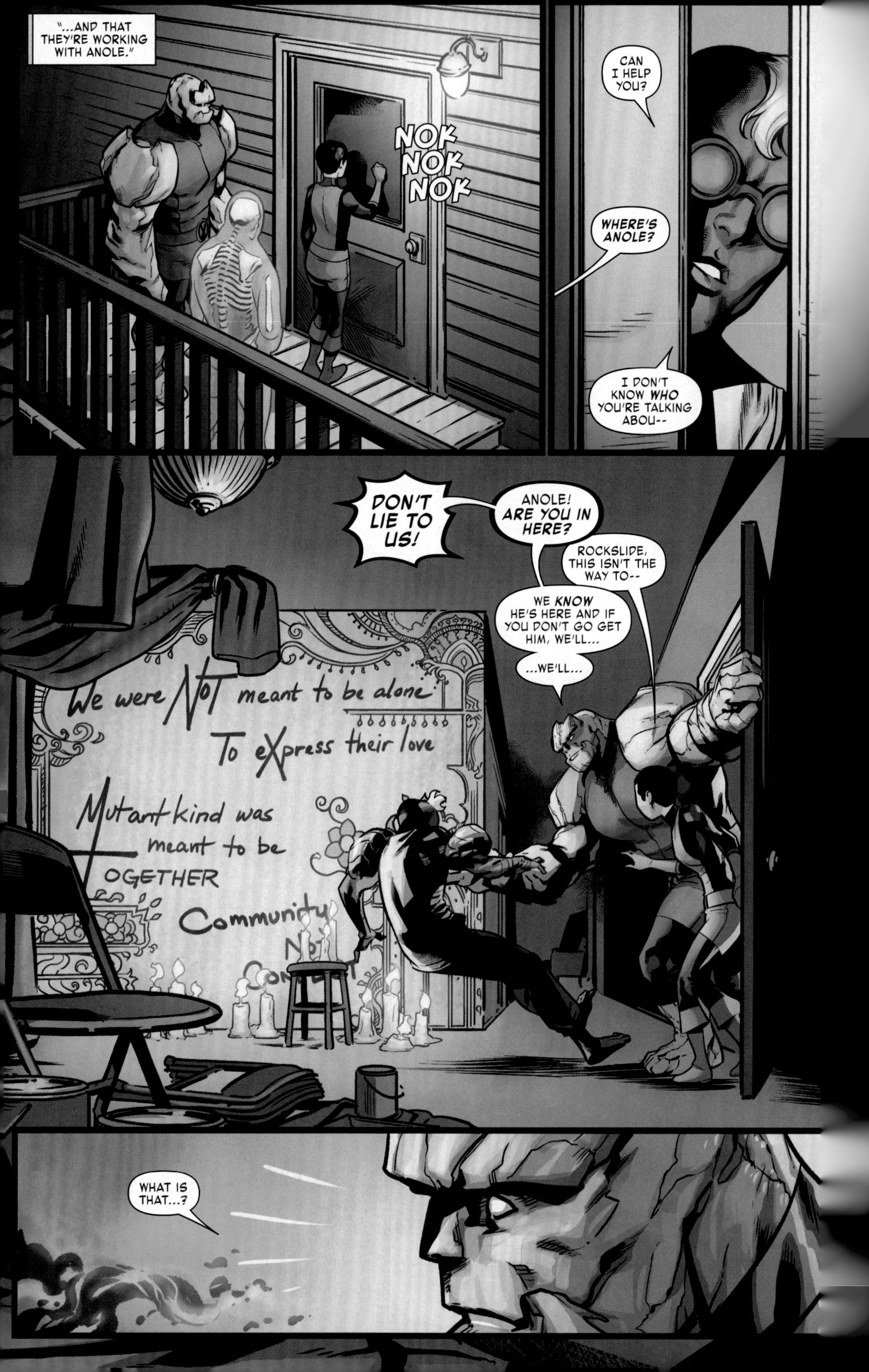
"...AND THAT THEY'RE WORKING WITH ANOLE."
NOK NOK NOK
CAN I HELP YOU?
WHERE'S ANOLE?
I DON'T KNOW WHO YOU'RE TALKING ABOU--
DON'T LIE TO US!
ANOLE! ARE YOU IN HERE?
ROCKSLIDE, THIS ISN'T THE WAY TO--
WE KNOW HE'S HERE AND IF YOU DON'T GO GET HIM, WE'LL...
...WE'LL...
We were NOT meant to be alone
To eXpress their love
Mutantkind was meant to be TOGETHER
Community
WHAT IS THAT...?

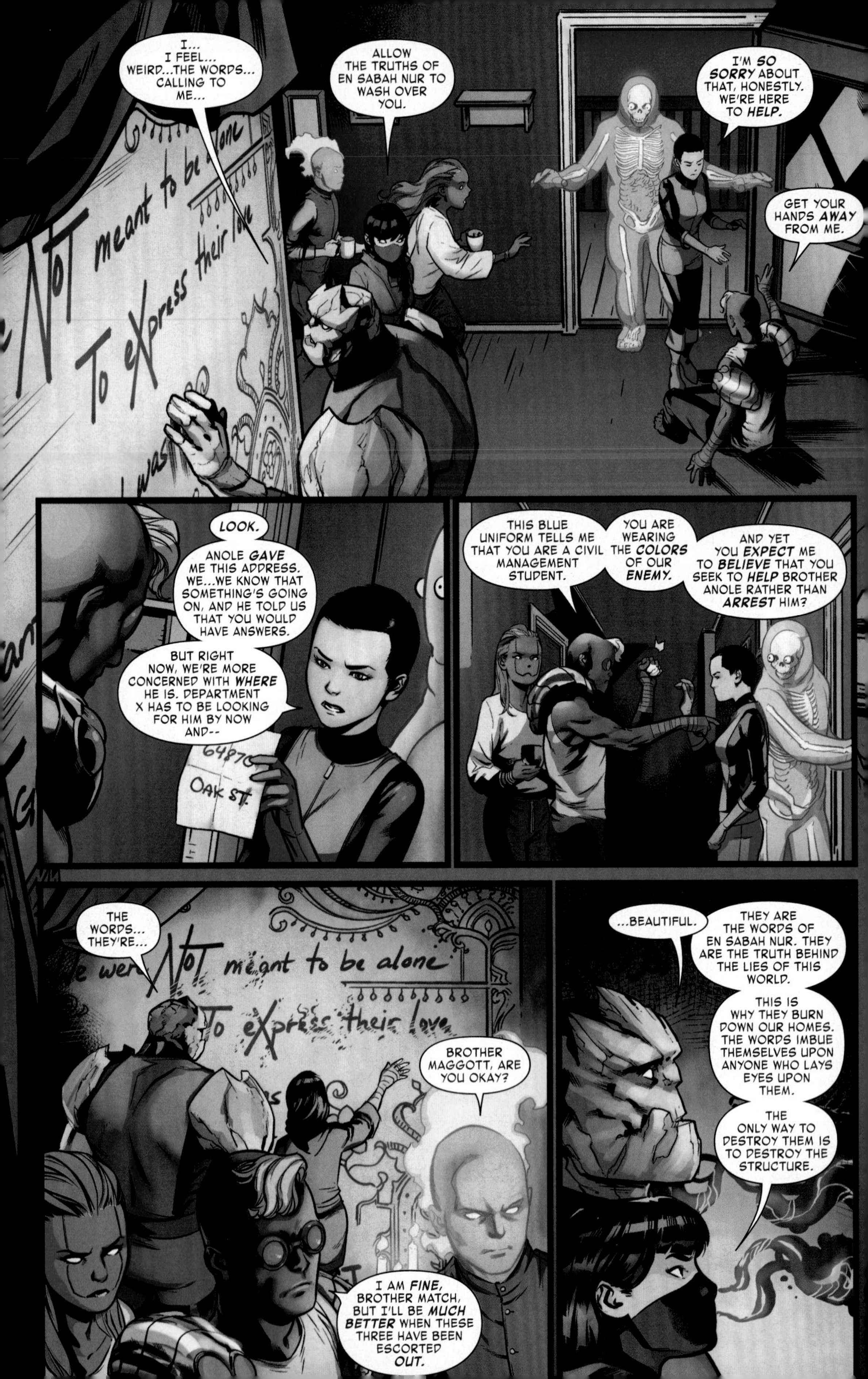
I... I FEEL... WEIRD...THE WORDS... CALLING TO ME...
ALLOW THE TRUTHS OF EN SABAH NUR TO WASH OVER YOU.
I'M SO SORRY ABOUT THAT, HONESTLY. WE'RE HERE TO HELP.
GET YOUR HANDS AWAY FROM ME.
NOT meant to be alone
To eXpress their love
LOOK.
ANOLE GAVE ME THIS ADDRESS. WE...WE KNOW THAT SOMETHING'S GOING ON, AND HE TOLD US THAT YOU WOULD HAVE ANSWERS.
BUT RIGHT NOW, WE'RE MORE CONCERNED WITH WHERE HE IS. DEPARTMENT X HAS TO BE LOOKING FOR HIM BY NOW AND--
OAK ST.
THIS BLUE UNIFORM TELLS ME THAT YOU ARE A CIVIL MANAGEMENT STUDENT.
YOU ARE WEARING THE COLORS OF OUR ENEMY.
AND YET YOU EXPECT ME TO BELIEVE THAT YOU SEEK TO HELP BROTHER ANOLE RATHER THAN ARREST HIM?
THE WORDS... THEY'RE...
...BEAUTIFUL.
We were NOT meant to be alone
To eXpress their love
THEY ARE THE WORDS OF EN SABAH NUR. THEY ARE THE TRUTH BEHIND THE LIES OF THIS WORLD.
THIS IS WHY THEY BURN DOWN OUR HOMES. THE WORDS IMBUE THEMSELVES UPON ANYONE WHO LAYS EYES UPON THEM.
THE ONLY WAY TO DESTROY THEM IS TO DESTROY THE STRUCTURE.
BROTHER MAGGOTT, ARE YOU OKAY?
I AM FINE, BROTHER MATCH, BUT I'LL BE MUCH BETTER WHEN THESE THREE HAVE BEEN ESCORTED OUT.

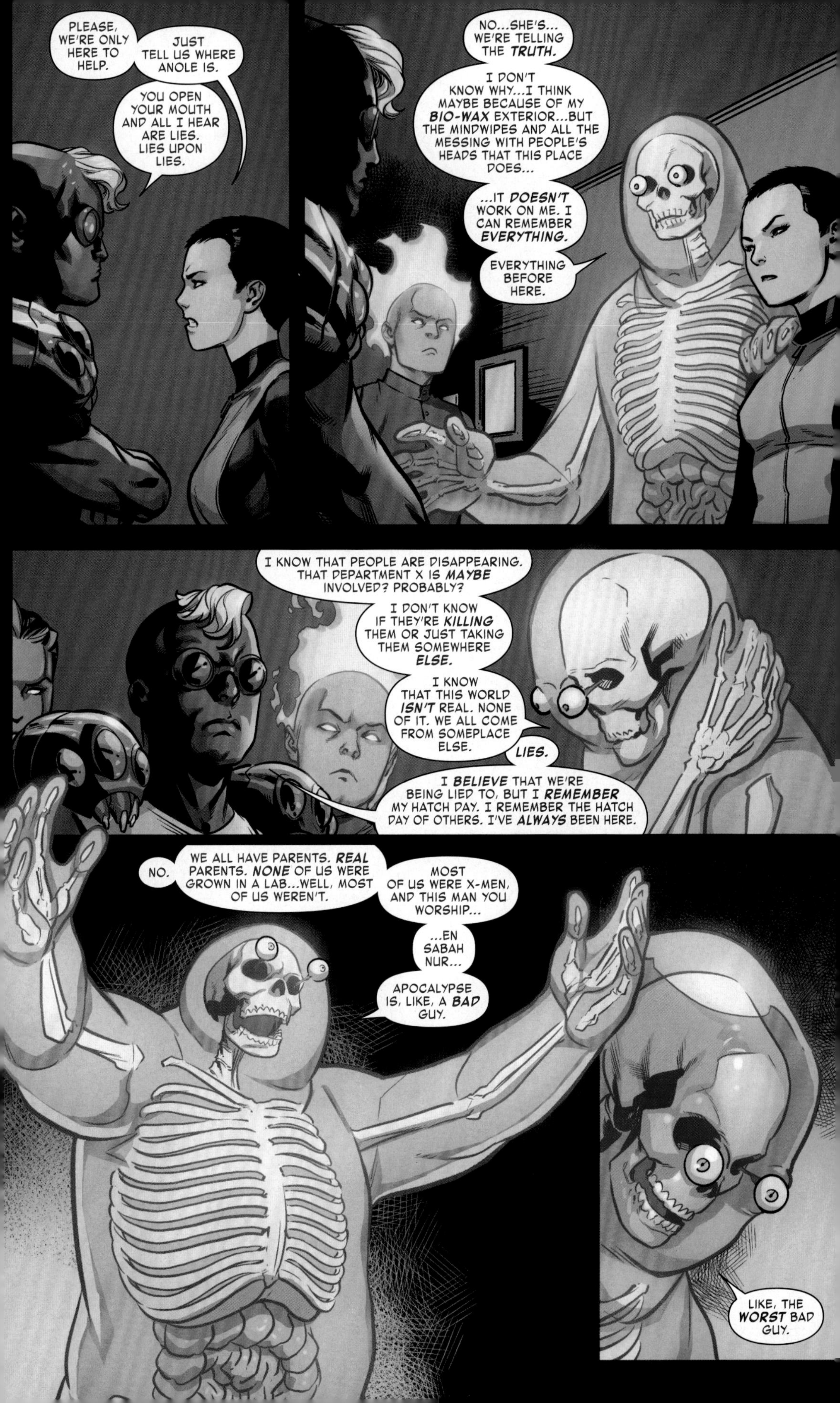
PLEASE, WE'RE ONLY HERE TO HELP.
JUST TELL US WHERE ANOLE IS.
YOU OPEN YOUR MOUTH AND ALL I HEAR ARE LIES. LIES UPON LIES.
NO...SHE'S... WE'RE TELLING THE TRUTH.
I DON'T KNOW WHY...I THINK MAYBE BECAUSE OF MY BIO-WAX EXTERIOR...BUT THE MINDWIPES AND ALL THE MESSING WITH PEOPLE'S HEADS THAT THIS PLACE DOES...
...IT DOESN'T WORK ON ME. I CAN REMEMBER EVERYTHING.
EVERYTHING BEFORE HERE.
I KNOW THAT PEOPLE ARE DISAPPEARING. THAT DEPARTMENT X IS MAYBE INVOLVED? PROBABLY?
I DON'T KNOW IF THEY'RE KILLING THEM OR JUST TAKING THEM SOMEWHERE ELSE.
I KNOW THAT THIS WORLD ISN'T REAL. NONE OF IT. WE ALL COME FROM SOMEPLACE ELSE.
LIES.
I BELIEVE THAT WE'RE BEING LIED TO, BUT I REMEMBER MY HATCH DAY. I REMEMBER THE HATCH DAY OF OTHERS. I'VE ALWAYS BEEN HERE.
NO.
WE ALL HAVE PARENTS. REAL PARENTS. NONE OF US WERE GROWN IN A LAB...WELL, MOST OF US WEREN'T.
MOST OF US WERE X-MEN, AND THIS MAN YOU WORSHIP...
...EN SABAH NUR...
APOCALYPSE IS, LIKE, A BAD GUY.
LIKE, THE WORST BAD GUY.

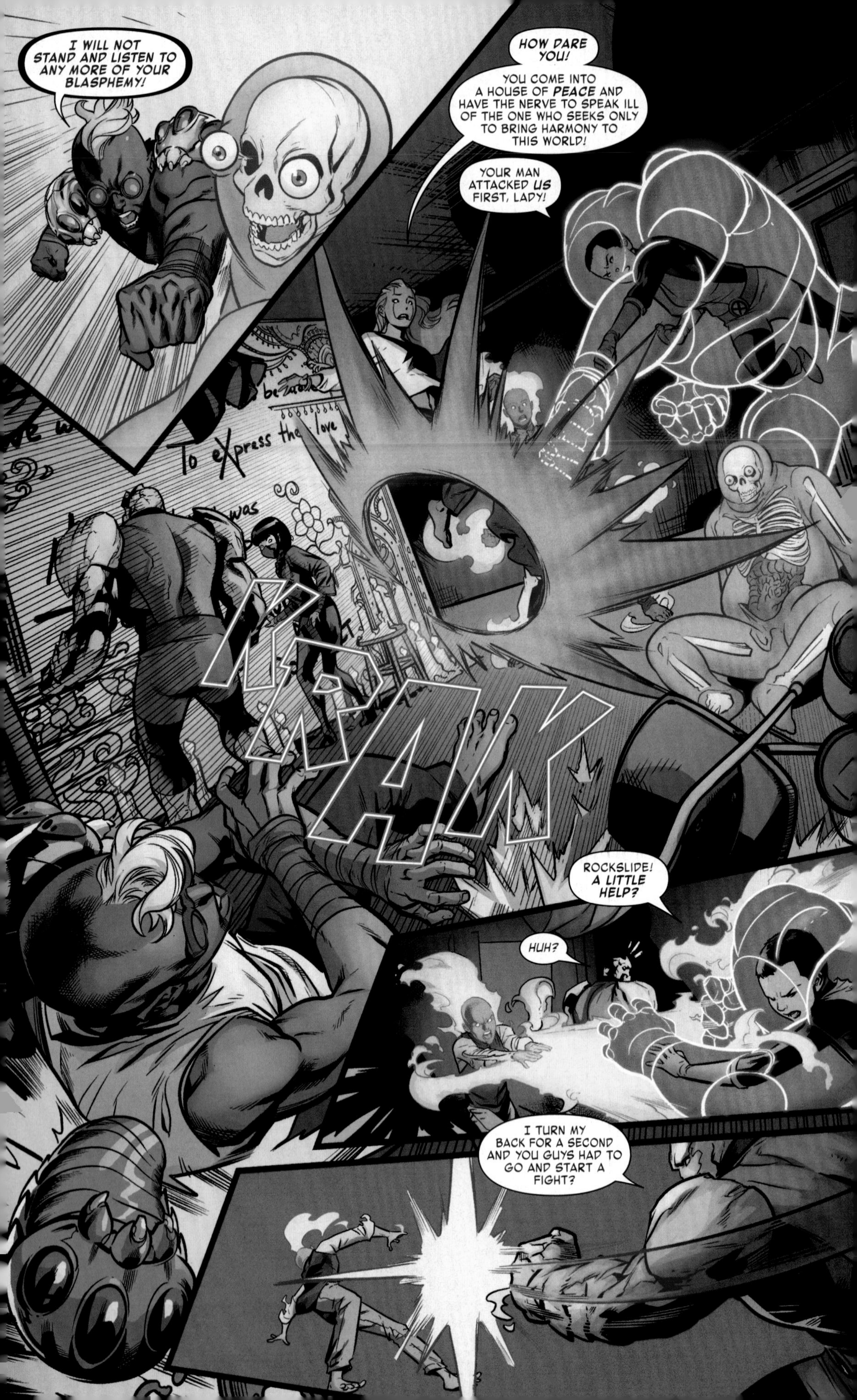
I WILL NOT STAND AND LISTEN TO ANY MORE OF YOUR BLASPHEMY!
HOW DARE YOU!
YOU COME INTO A HOUSE OF PEACE AND HAVE THE NERVE TO SPEAK ILL OF THE ONE WHO SEEKS ONLY TO BRING HARMONY TO THIS WORLD!
YOUR MAN ATTACKED US FIRST, LADY!
To eXpress the love
K-RAK
ROCKSLIDE! A LITTLE HELP?
HUH?
I TURN MY BACK FOR A SECOND AND YOU GUYS HAD TO GO AND START A FIGHT?

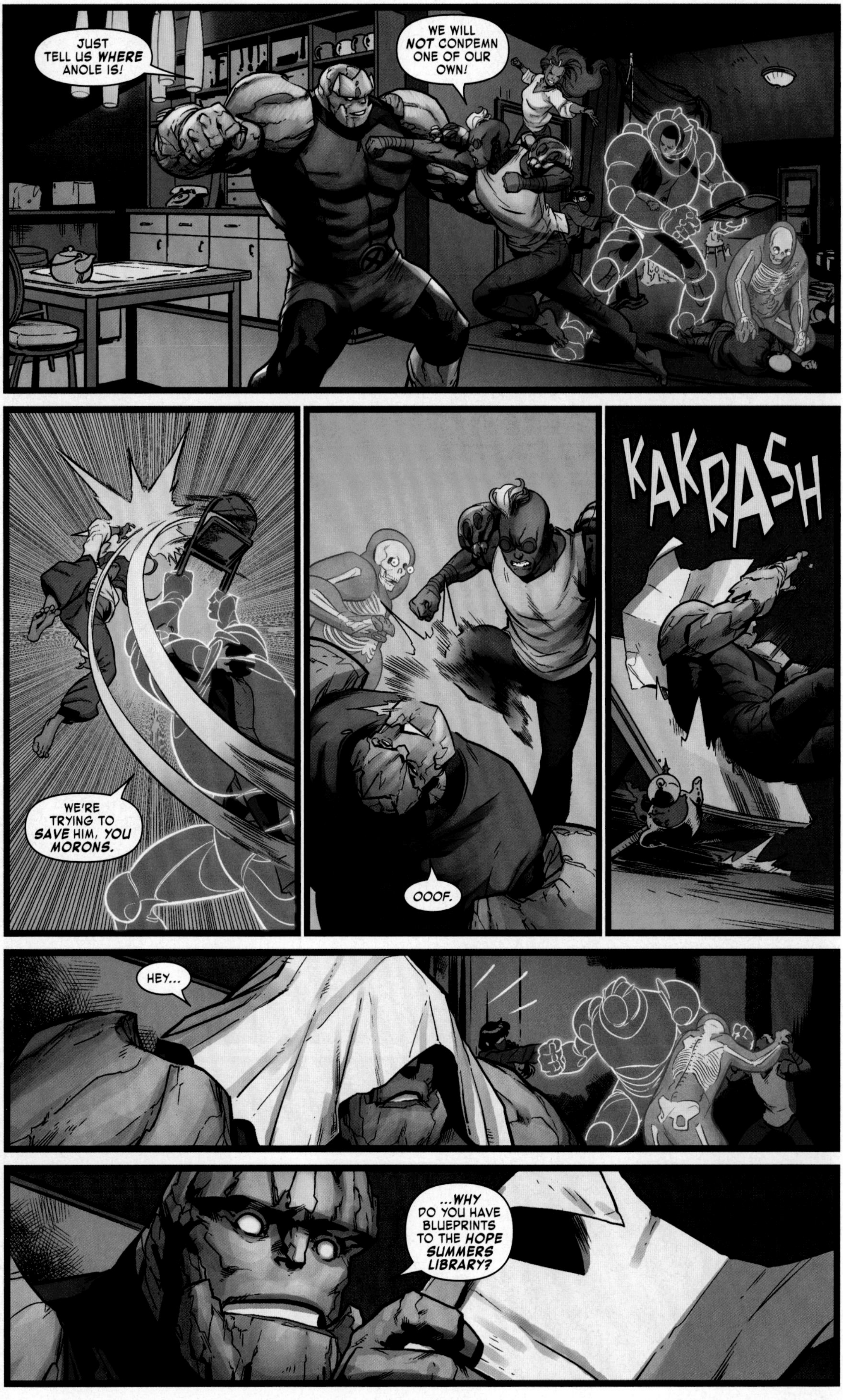
JUST TELL US WHERE ANOLE IS!
WE WILL NOT CONDEMN ONE OF OUR OWN!
WE'RE TRYING TO SAVE HIM, YOU MORONS.
OOOF.
KAKRASH
HEY...
...WHY DO YOU HAVE BLUEPRINTS TO THE HOPE SUMMERS LIBRARY?

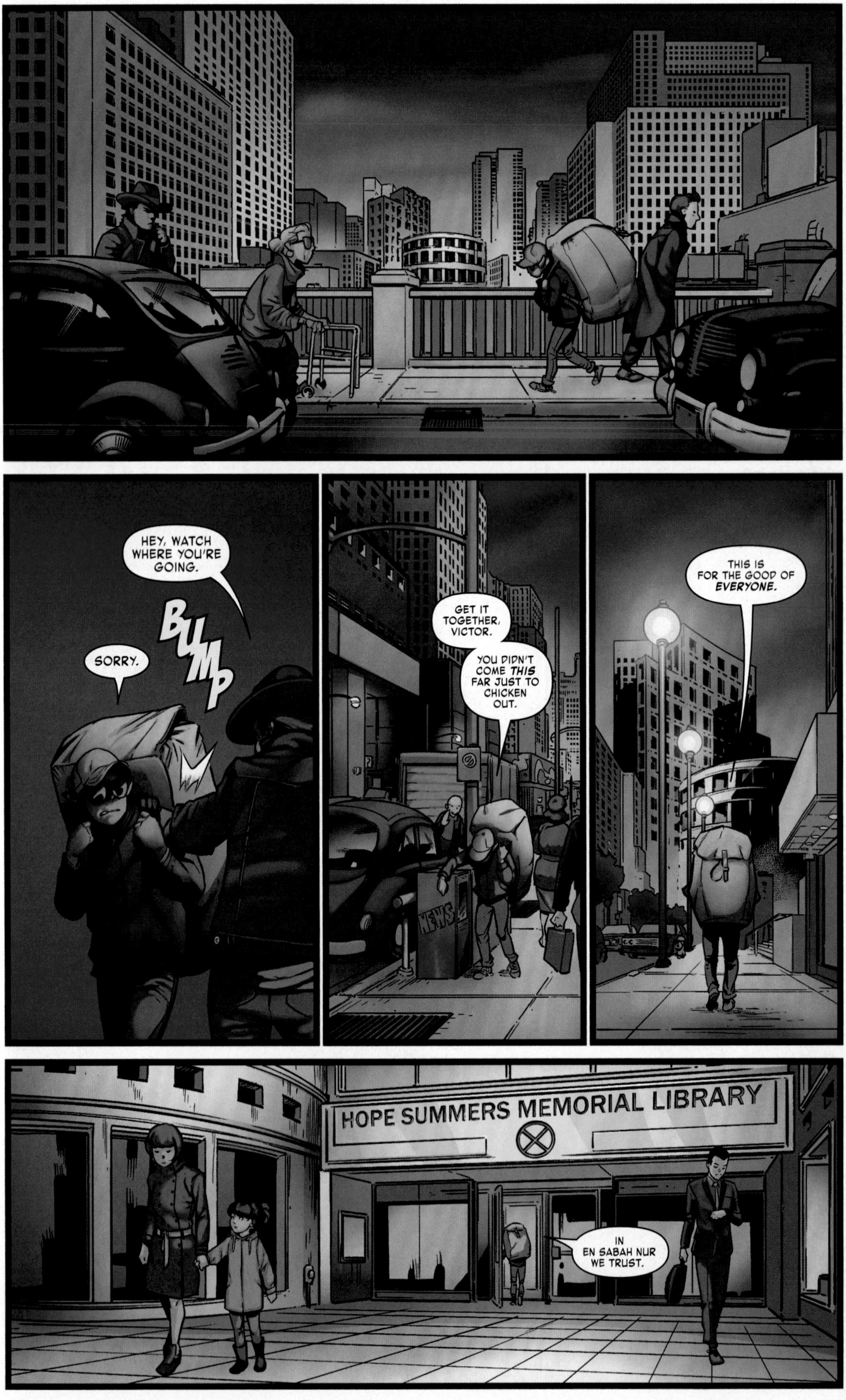
HEY, WATCH WHERE YOU'RE GOING.
BUMP
SORRY.
GET IT TOGETHER, VICTOR.
YOU DIDN'T COME THIS FAR JUST TO CHICKEN OUT.
NEWS
THIS IS FOR THE GOOD OF EVERYONE.
HOPE SUMMERS MEMORIAL LIBRARY
IN EN SABAH NUR WE TRUST.

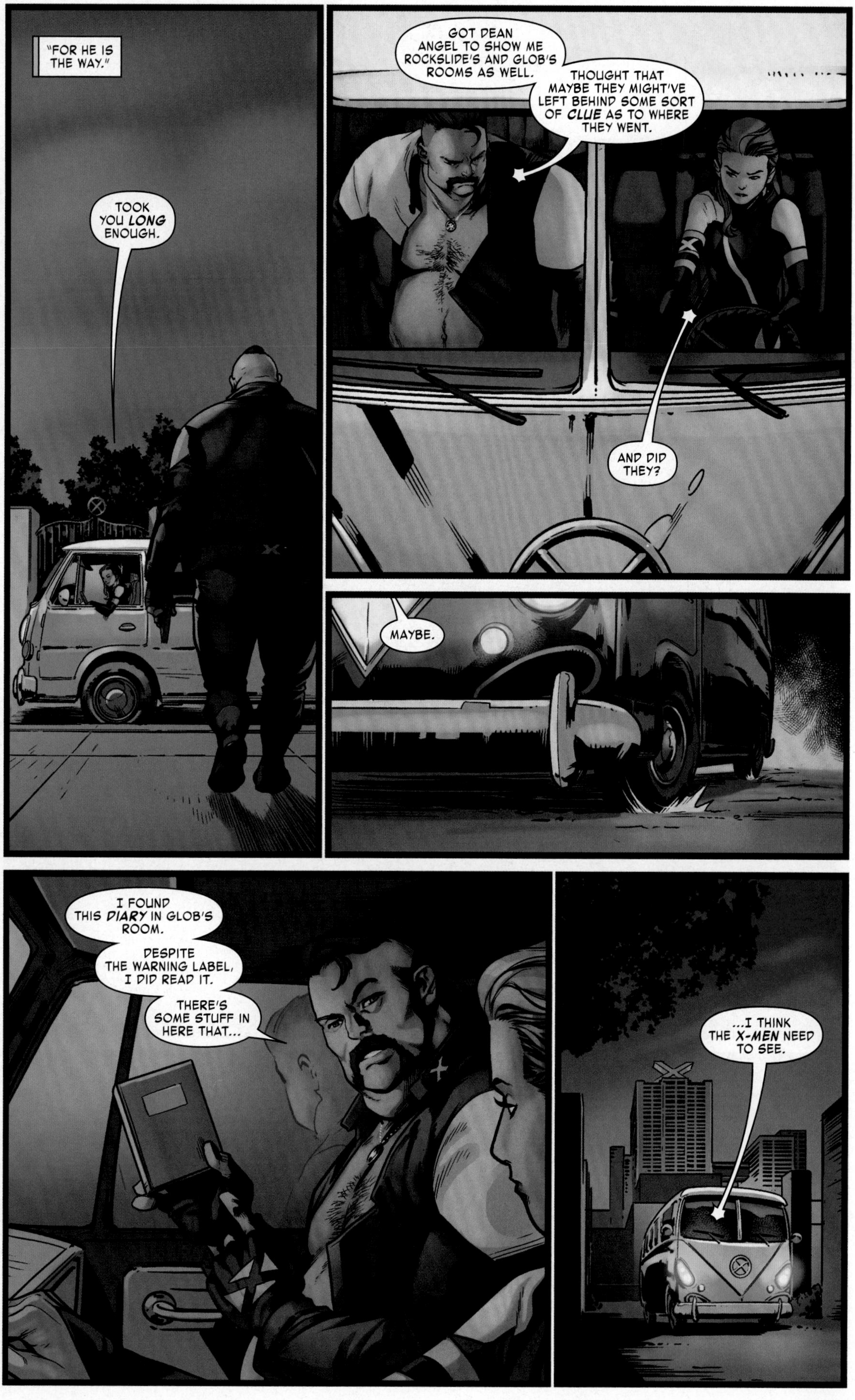
"FOR HE IS THE WAY."
TOOK YOU LONG ENOUGH.
GOT DEAN ANGEL TO SHOW ME ROCKSLIDE'S AND GLOB'S ROOMS AS WELL.
THOUGHT THAT MAYBE THEY MIGHT'VE LEFT BEHIND SOME SORT OF CLUE AS TO WHERE THEY WENT.
AND DID THEY?
MAYBE.
I FOUND THIS DIARY IN GLOB'S ROOM.
DESPITE THE WARNING LABEL, I DID READ IT.
THERE'S SOME STUFF IN HERE THAT...
...I THINK THE X-MEN NEED TO SEE.

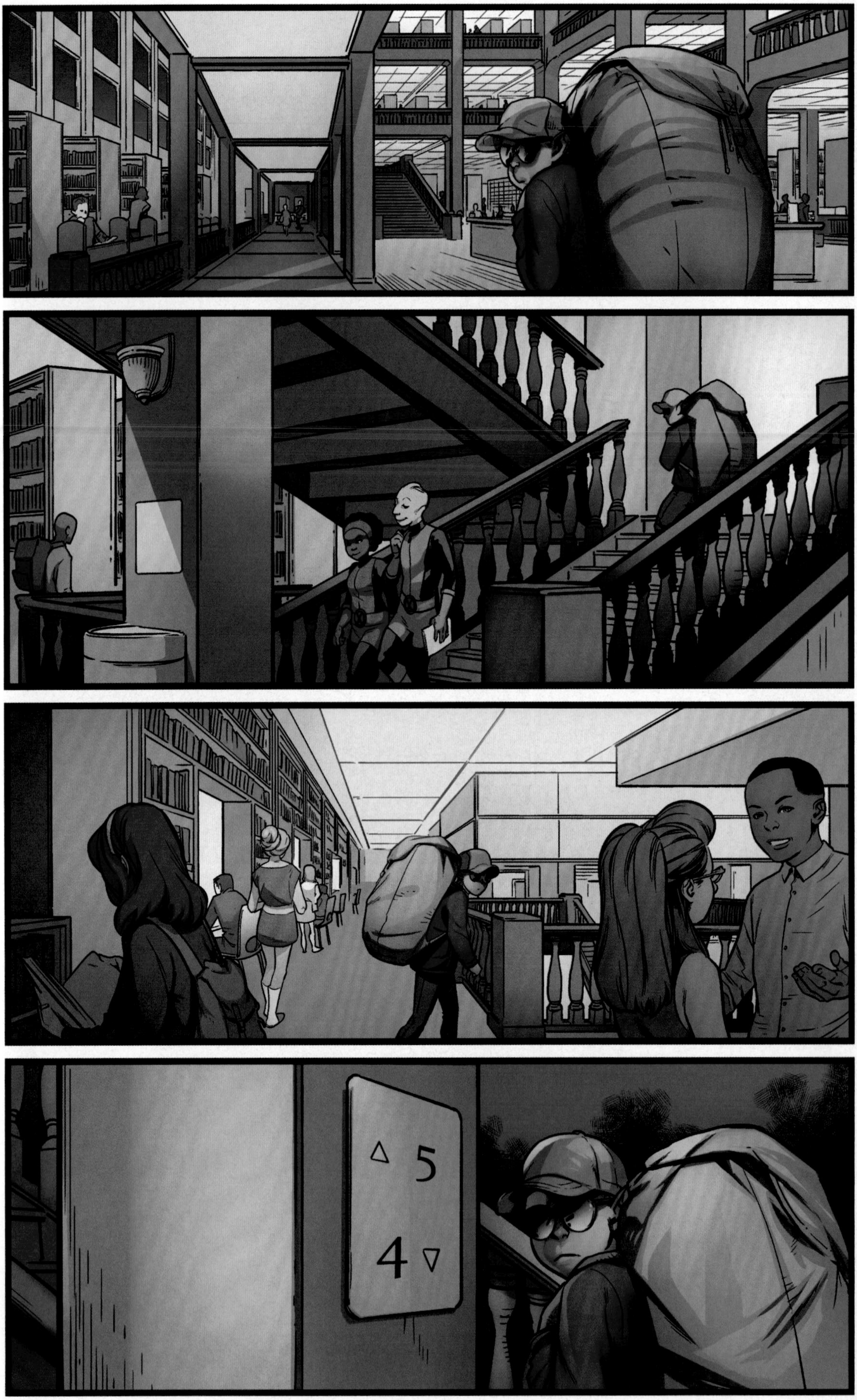
5
4

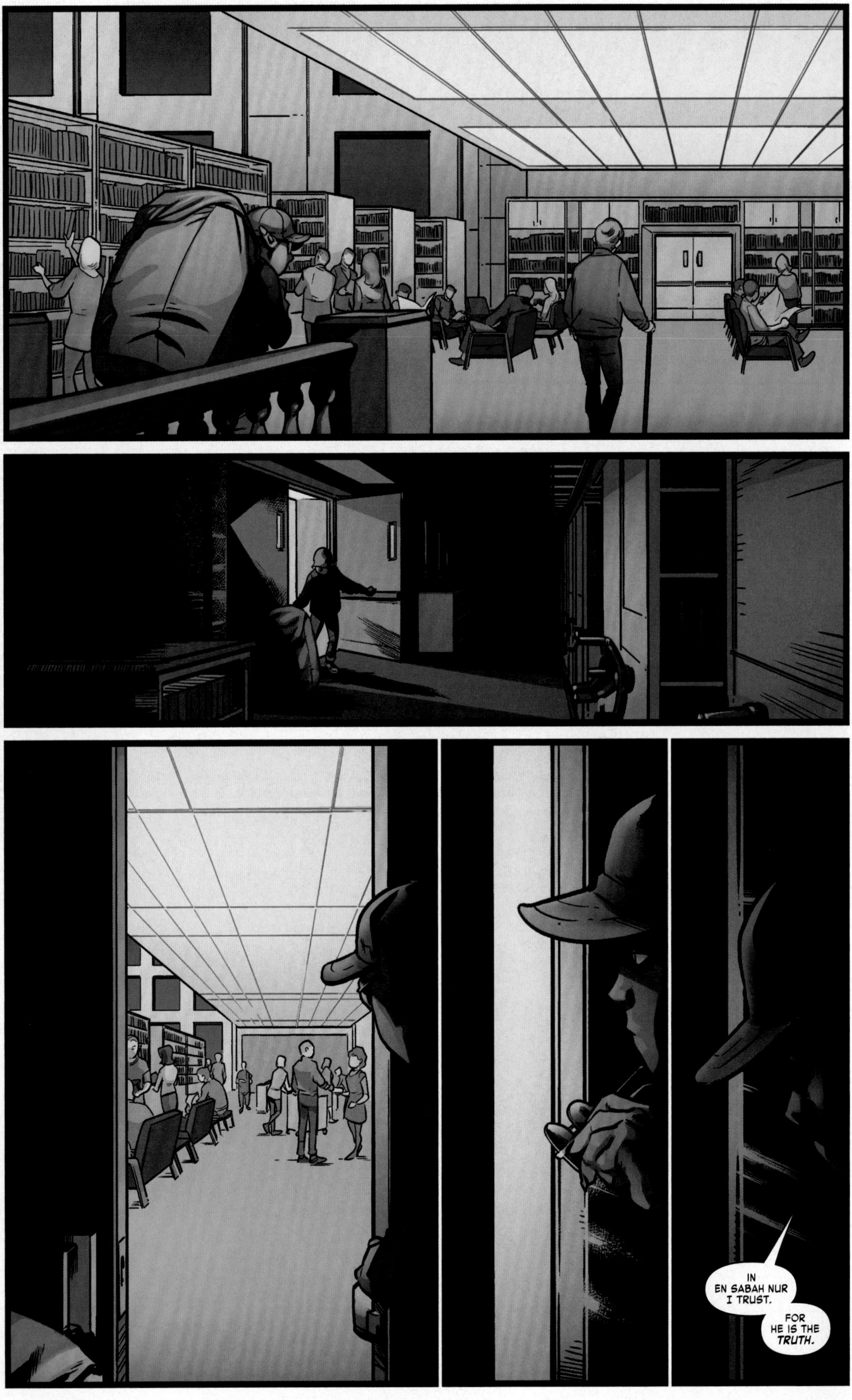

IN EN SABAH NUR I TRUST.
FOR HE IS THE *TRUTH.*

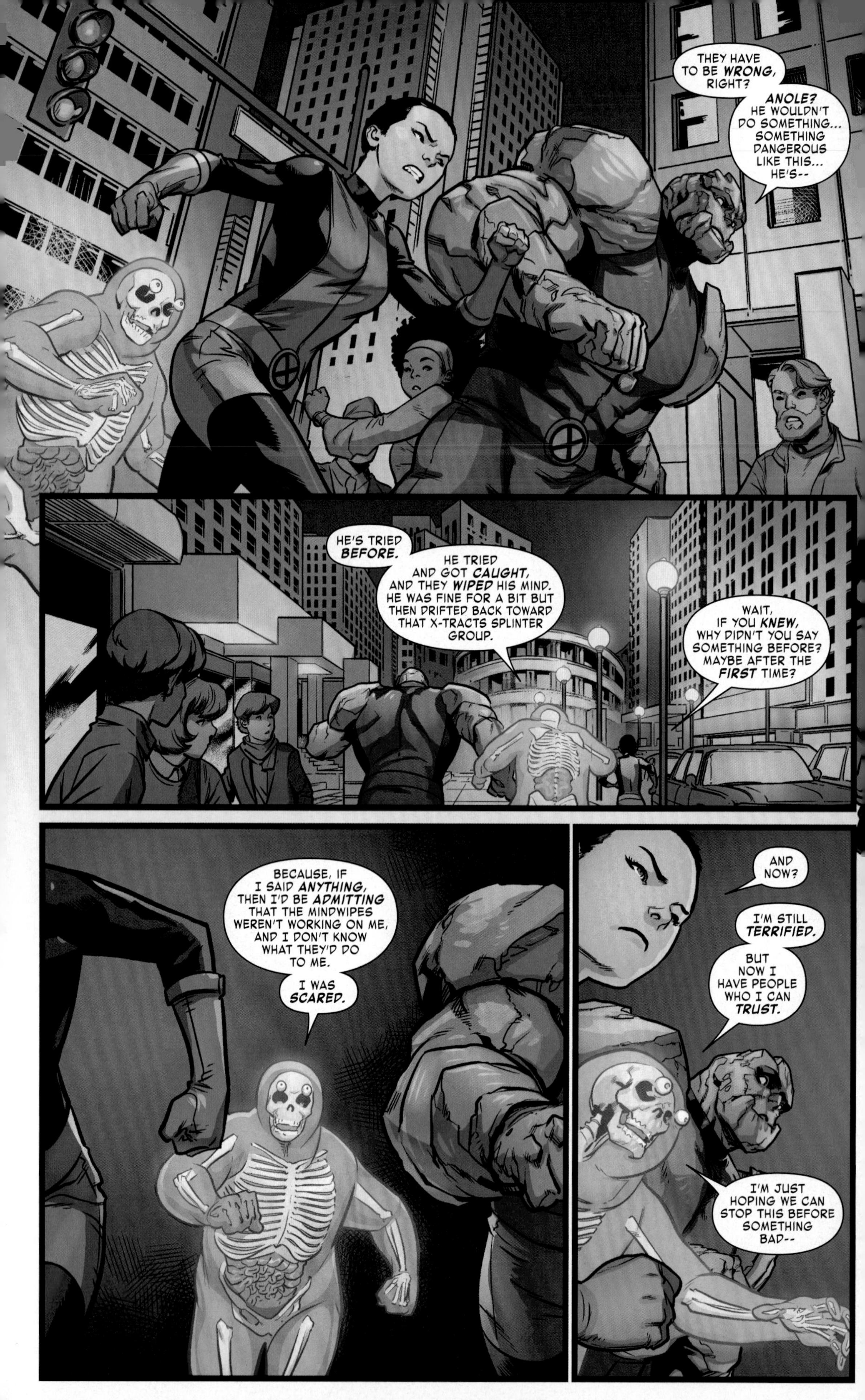

THEY HAVE TO BE WRONG, RIGHT?
ANOLE? HE WOULDN'T DO SOMETHING... SOMETHING DANGEROUS LIKE THIS... HE'S--
HE'S TRIED BEFORE.
HE TRIED AND GOT CAUGHT, AND THEY WIPED HIS MIND. HE WAS FINE FOR A BIT BUT THEN DRIFTED BACK TOWARD THAT X-TRACTS SPLINTER GROUP.
WAIT, IF YOU KNEW, WHY DIDN'T YOU SAY SOMETHING BEFORE? MAYBE AFTER THE FIRST TIME?
BECAUSE, IF I SAID ANYTHING, THEN I'D BE ADMITTING THAT THE MINDWIPES WEREN'T WORKING ON ME, AND I DON'T KNOW WHAT THEY'D DO TO ME.
I WAS SCARED.
AND NOW?
I'M STILL TERRIFIED.
BUT NOW I HAVE PEOPLE WHO I CAN TRUST.
I'M JUST HOPING WE CAN STOP THIS BEFORE SOMETHING BAD--

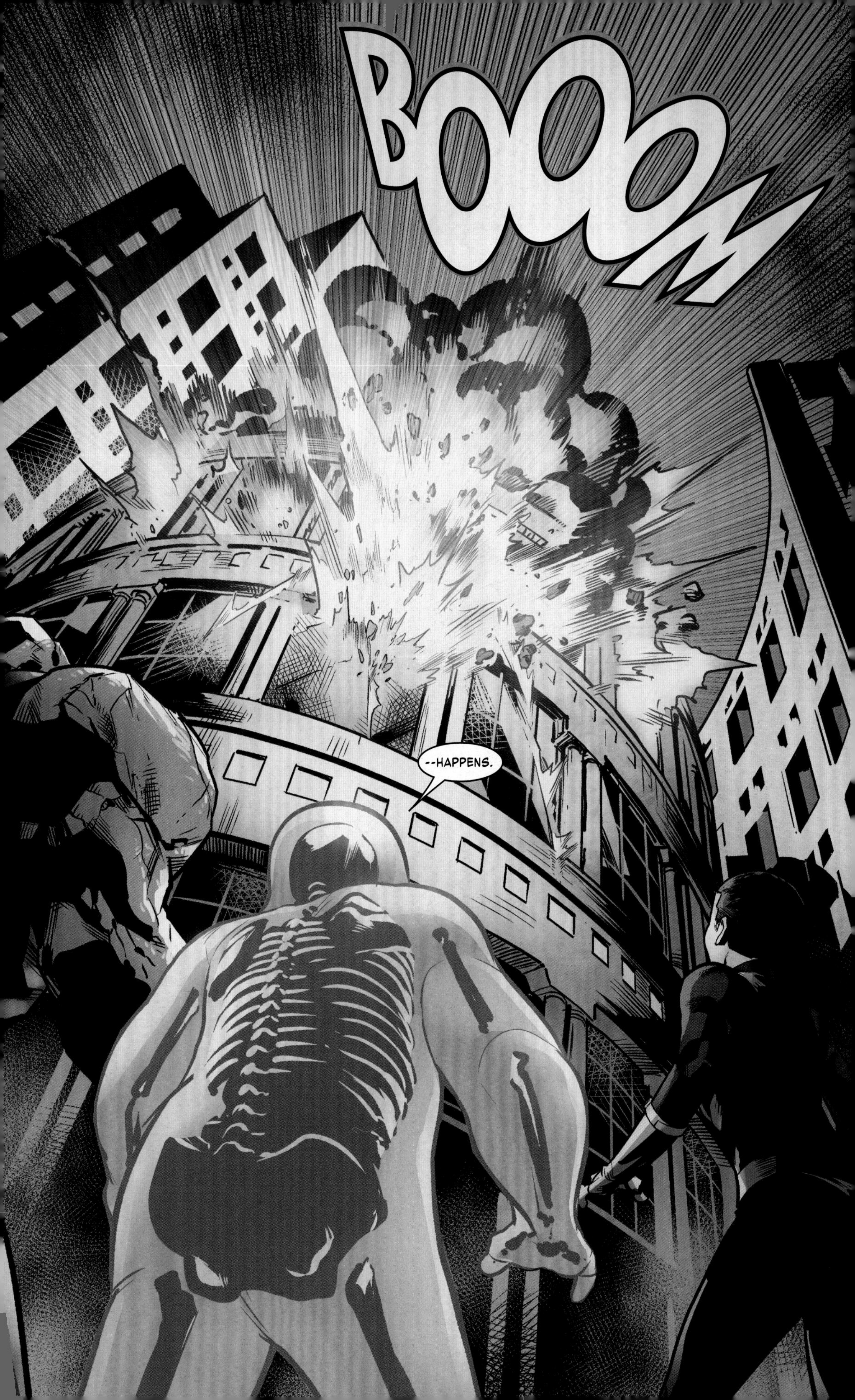
BOOOM
--HAPPENS.

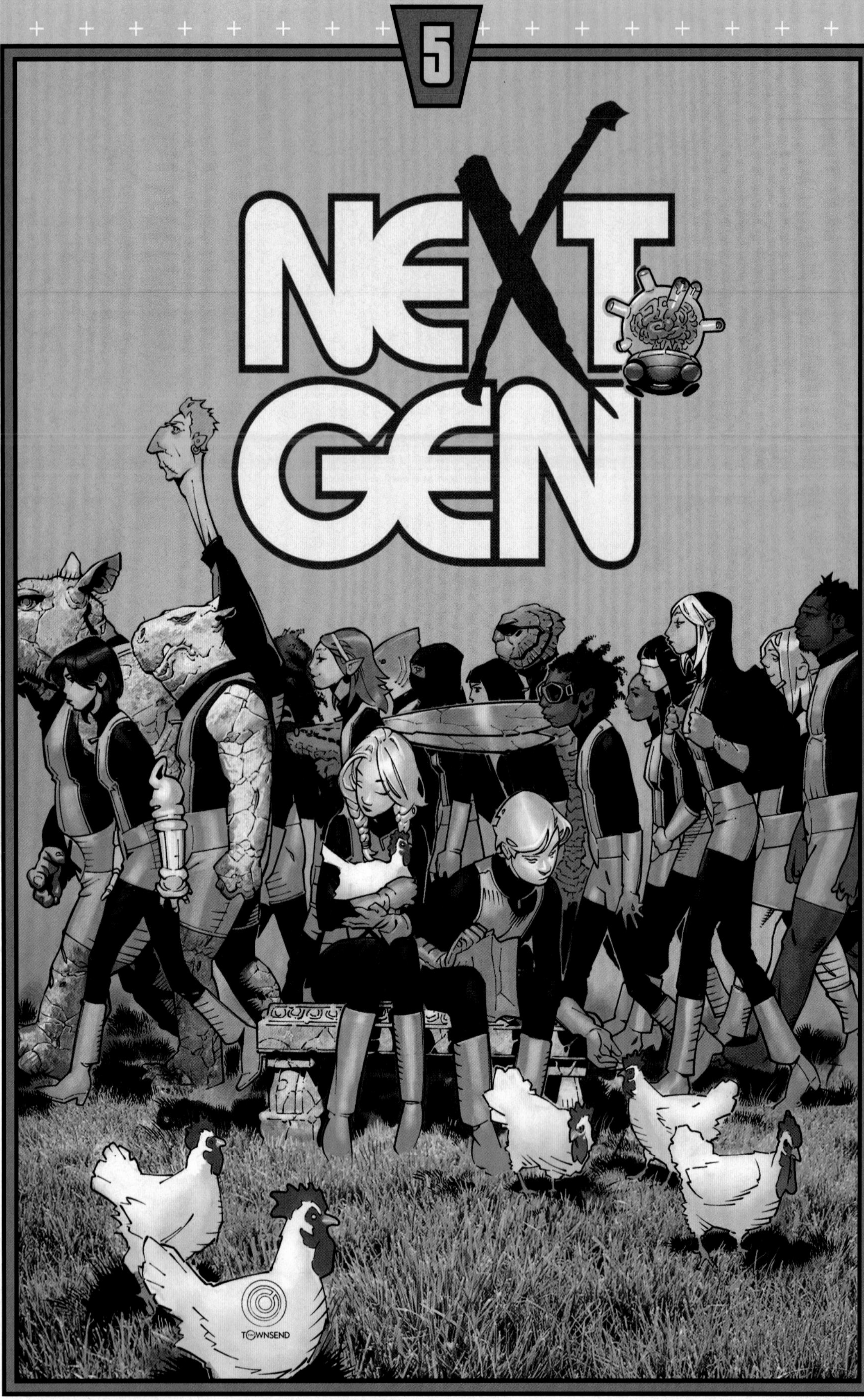
5
NEXT GEN

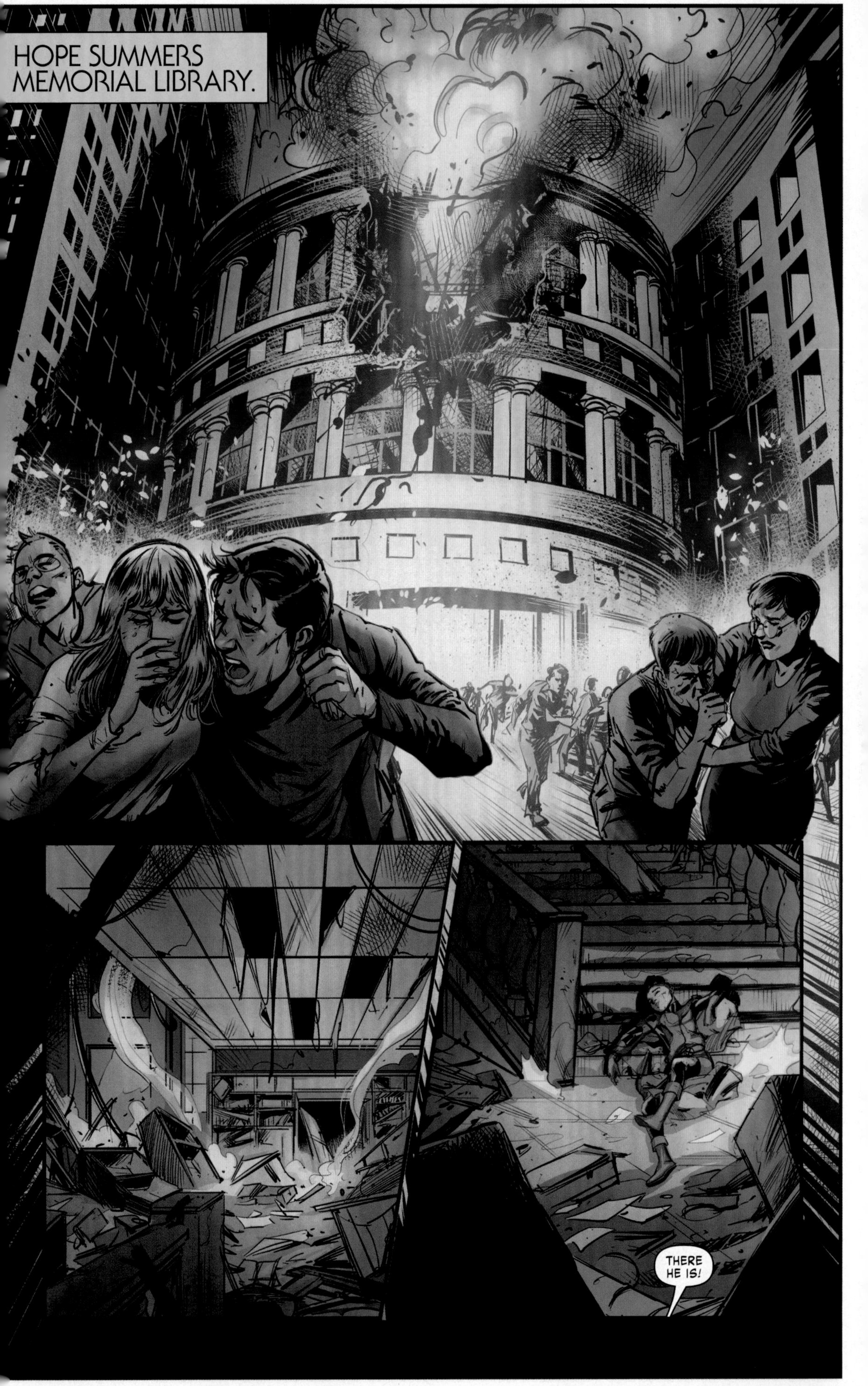
HOPE SUMMERS MEMORIAL LIBRARY.
THERE HE IS!

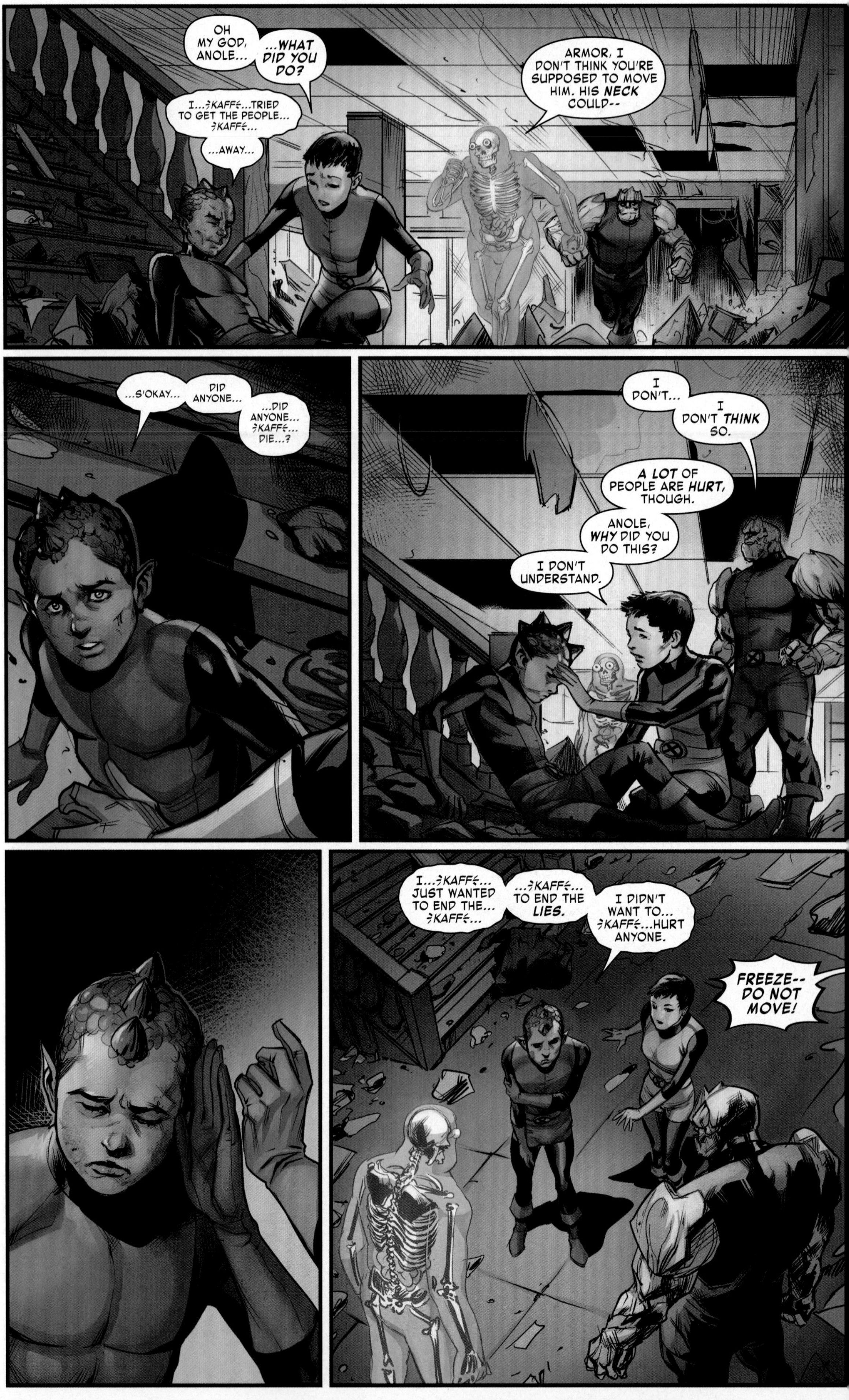
OH MY GOD, ANOLE...
...WHAT DID YOU DO?
I...KAFF...TRIED TO GET THE PEOPLE... KAFF...
...AWAY...
ARMOR, I DON'T THINK YOU'RE SUPPOSED TO MOVE HIM. HIS NECK COULD--
...S'OKAY...
DID ANYONE...
...DID ANYONE... KAFF... DIE...?
I DON'T...
I DON'T THINK SO.
A LOT OF PEOPLE ARE HURT, THOUGH.
ANOLE, WHY DID YOU DO THIS?
I DON'T UNDERSTAND.
I...KAFF... JUST WANTED TO END THE... KAFF...
...KAFF... TO END THE LIES.
I DIDN'T WANT TO... KAFF...HURT ANYONE.
FREEZE-- DO NOT MOVE!

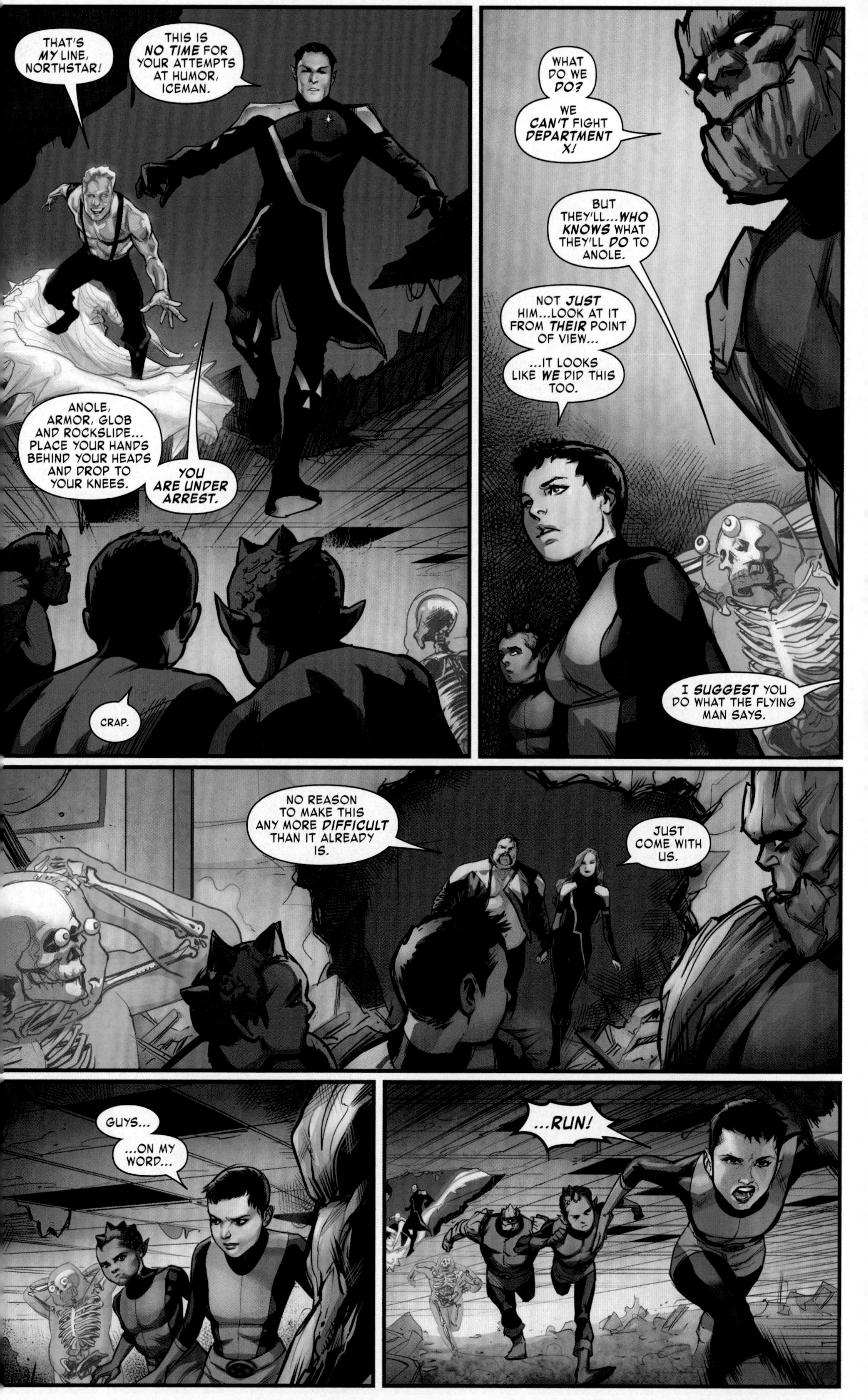
THAT'S MY LINE, NORTHSTAR!
THIS IS NO TIME FOR YOUR ATTEMPTS AT HUMOR, ICEMAN.
ANOLE, ARMOR, GLOB AND ROCKSLIDE... PLACE YOUR HANDS BEHIND YOUR HEADS AND DROP TO YOUR KNEES.
YOU ARE UNDER ARREST.
CRAP.
WHAT DO WE DO?
WE CAN'T FIGHT DEPARTMENT X!
BUT THEY'LL...WHO KNOWS WHAT THEY'LL DO TO ANOLE.
NOT JUST HIM...LOOK AT IT FROM THEIR POINT OF VIEW...
...IT LOOKS LIKE WE DID THIS TOO.
I SUGGEST YOU DO WHAT THE FLYING MAN SAYS.
NO REASON TO MAKE THIS ANY MORE DIFFICULT THAN IT ALREADY IS.
JUST COME WITH US.
GUYS...
...ON MY WORD...
...RUN!

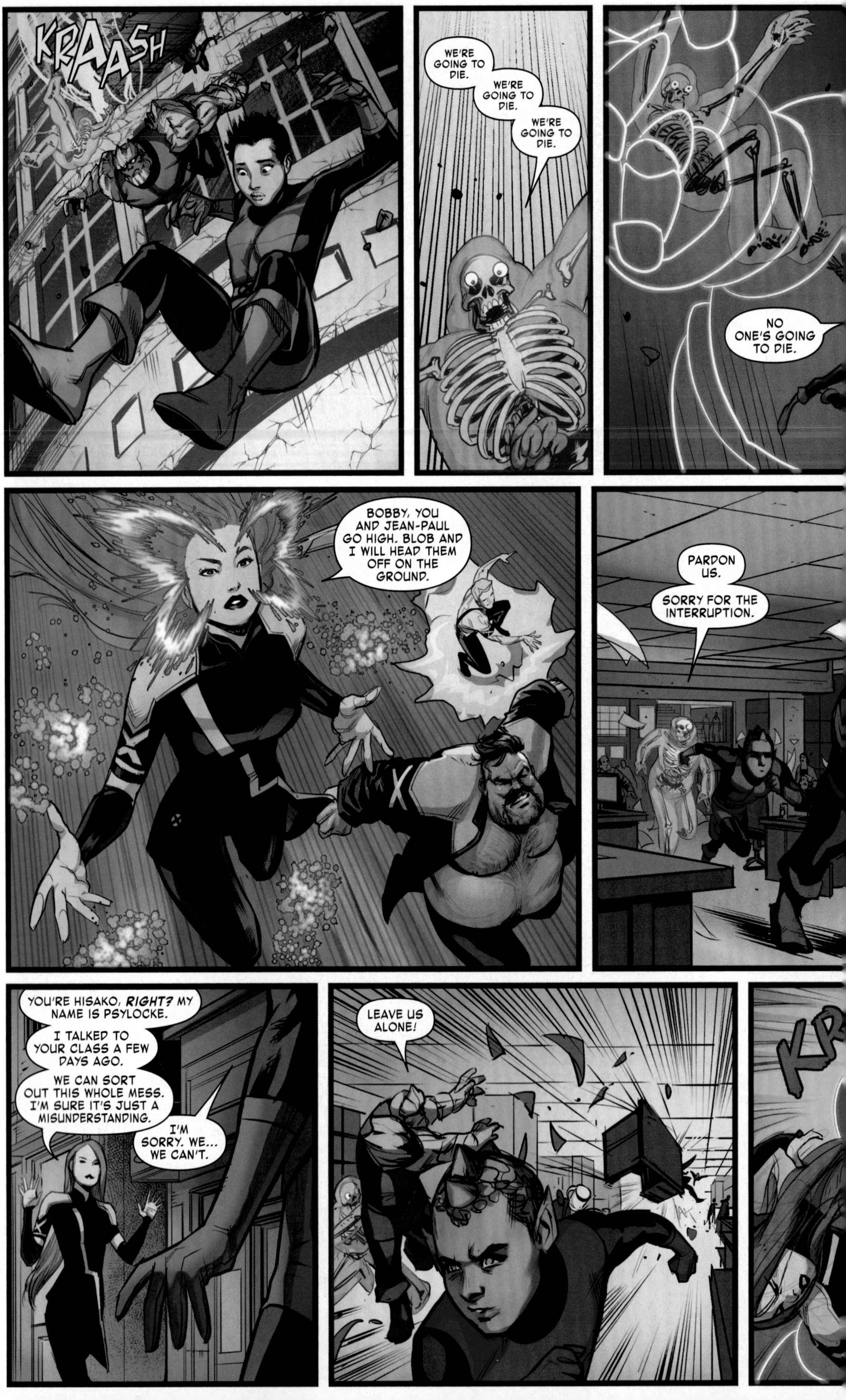
KRAASH
WE'RE GOING TO DIE.
WE'RE GOING TO DIE.
WE'RE GOING TO DIE.
NO ONE'S GOING TO DIE.
BOBBY, YOU AND JEAN-PAUL GO HIGH. BLOB AND I WILL HEAD THEM OFF ON THE GROUND.
PARDON US.
SORRY FOR THE INTERRUPTION.
YOU'RE HISAKO, RIGHT? MY NAME IS PSYLOCKE.
I TALKED TO YOUR CLASS A FEW DAYS AGO.
WE CAN SORT OUT THIS WHOLE MESS. I'M SURE IT'S JUST A MISUNDERSTANDING.
I'M SORRY. WE... WE CAN'T.
LEAVE US ALONE!

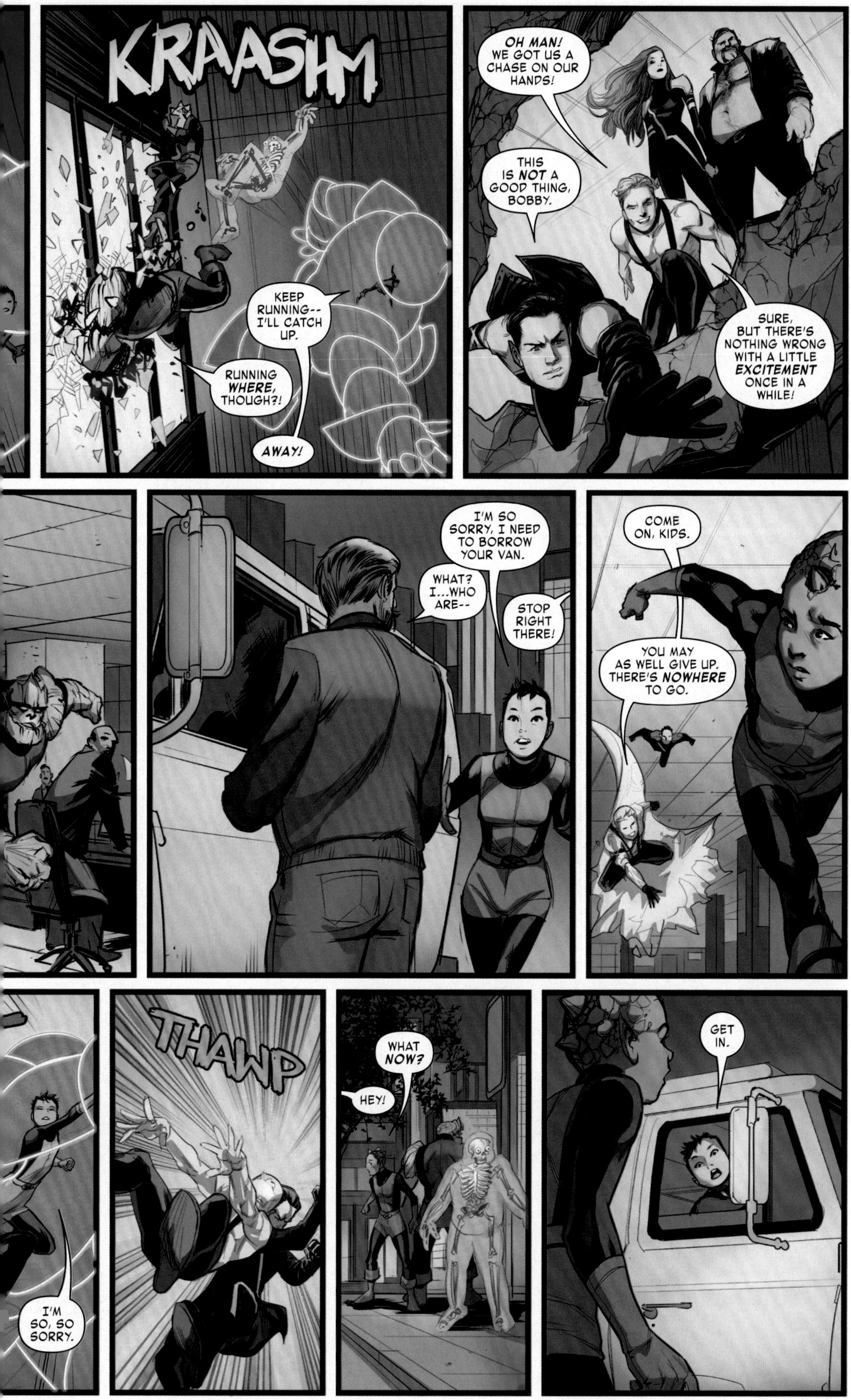
KRAASHM
KEEP RUNNING-- I'LL CATCH UP.
RUNNING WHERE, THOUGH?!
AWAY!
OH MAN! WE GOT US A CHASE ON OUR HANDS!
THIS IS NOT A GOOD THING, BOBBY.
SURE, BUT THERE'S NOTHING WRONG WITH A LITTLE EXCITEMENT ONCE IN A WHILE!
I'M SO SORRY, I NEED TO BORROW YOUR VAN.
WHAT? I...WHO ARE--
STOP RIGHT THERE!
COME ON, KIDS.
YOU MAY AS WELL GIVE UP. THERE'S NOWHERE TO GO.
I'M SO, SO SORRY.
THAWP
WHAT NOW?
HEY!
GET IN.

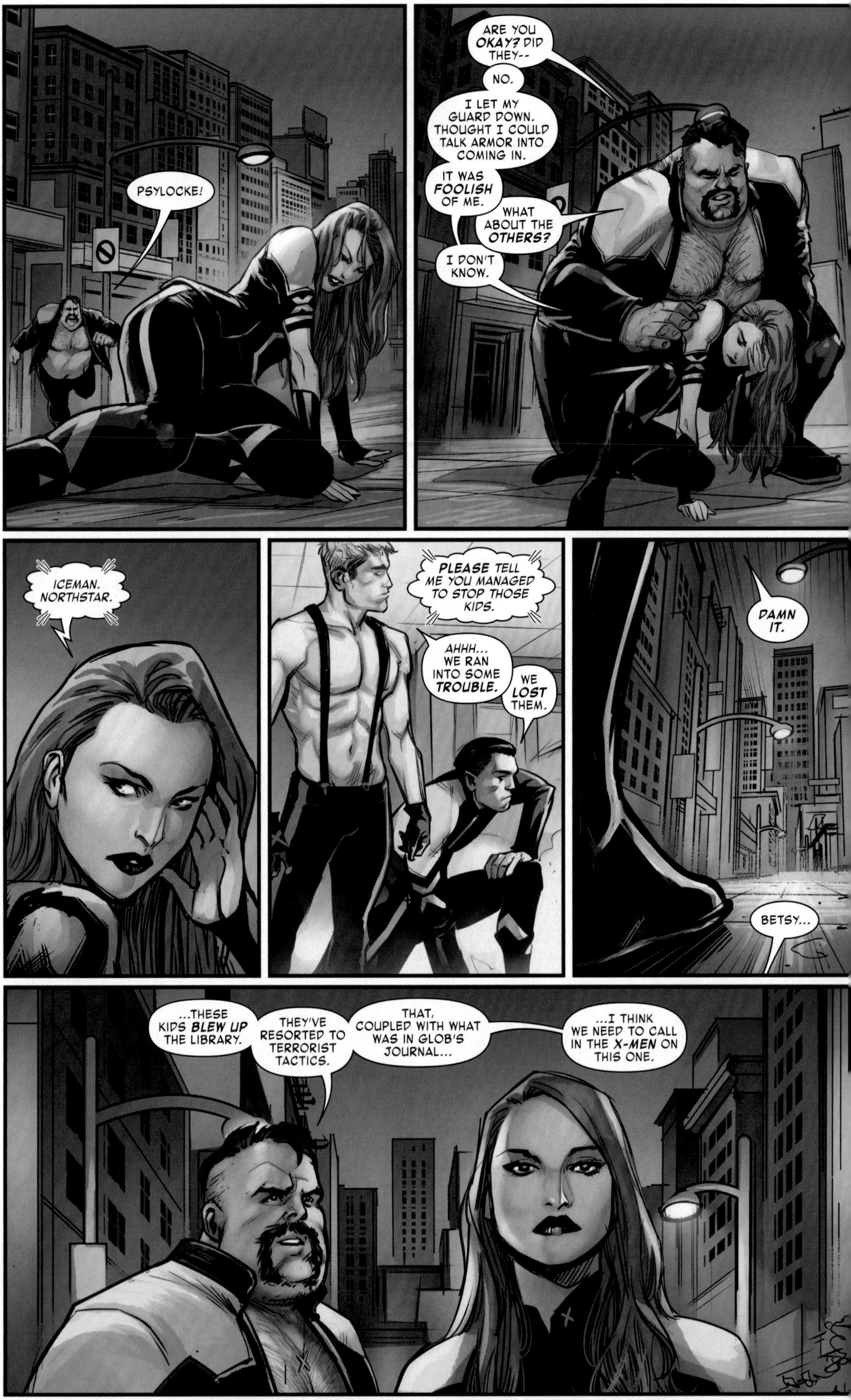
PSYLOCKE!
ARE YOU OKAY? DID THEY--
NO.
I LET MY GUARD DOWN. THOUGHT I COULD TALK ARMOR INTO COMING IN.
IT WAS FOOLISH OF ME.
WHAT ABOUT THE OTHERS?
I DON'T KNOW.
ICEMAN. NORTHSTAR.
PLEASE TELL ME YOU MANAGED TO STOP THOSE KIDS.
AHHH... WE RAN INTO SOME TROUBLE.
WE LOST THEM.
DAMN IT.
BETSY...
...THESE KIDS BLEW UP THE LIBRARY.
THEY'VE RESORTED TO TERRORIST TACTICS.
THAT, COUPLED WITH WHAT WAS IN GLOB'S JOURNAL...
...I THINK WE NEED TO CALL IN THE X-MEN ON THIS ONE.

DEPARTMENT X IS STILL ON THE LOOKOUT FOR FOUR SUMMERS INSTITUTE STUDENTS WHO WENT MISSING LAST WEEK.

WE GO NOW TO ANGEL, DEAN OF THE SUMMERS INSTITUTE.

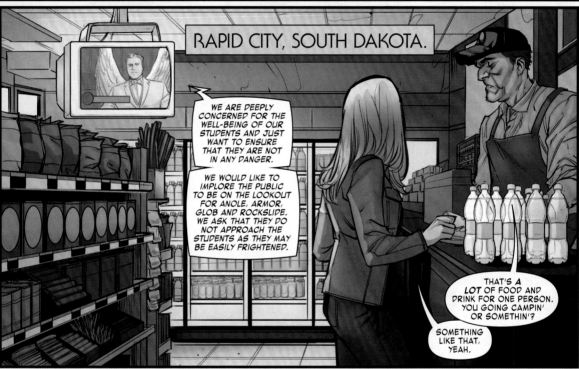

RAPID CITY, SOUTH DAKOTA.

WE ARE DEEPLY CONCERNED FOR THE WELL-BEING OF OUR STUDENTS AND JUST WANT TO ENSURE THAT THEY ARE NOT IN ANY DANGER.

WE WOULD LIKE TO IMPLORE THE PUBLIC TO BE ON THE LOOKOUT FOR ANOLE, ARMOR, GLOB AND ROCKSLIDE. WE ASK THAT THEY DO NOT APPROACH THE STUDENTS AS THEY MAY BE EASILY FRIGHTENED.

THAT'S A LOT OF FOOD AND DRINK FOR ONE PERSON. YOU GOING CAMPIN' OR SOMETHIN'?

SOMETHING LIKE THAT, YEAH.

IF YOU DO SEE THEM, CONTACT DEPARTMENT X IMMEDIATELY. AND, STUDENTS, IF YOU'RE OUT THERE--

ALL RIGHT. THE GAS PLUS THE DRINKS AND SANDWICHES, YOU'RE LOOKING AT NINETEEN DOLLARS AND 63 CENTS.

HERE.

--PLEASE GET IN TOUCH WITH US. LET US KNOW WHERE YOU ARE.

KEEP THE CHANGE.

WE JUST WANT TO HELP.

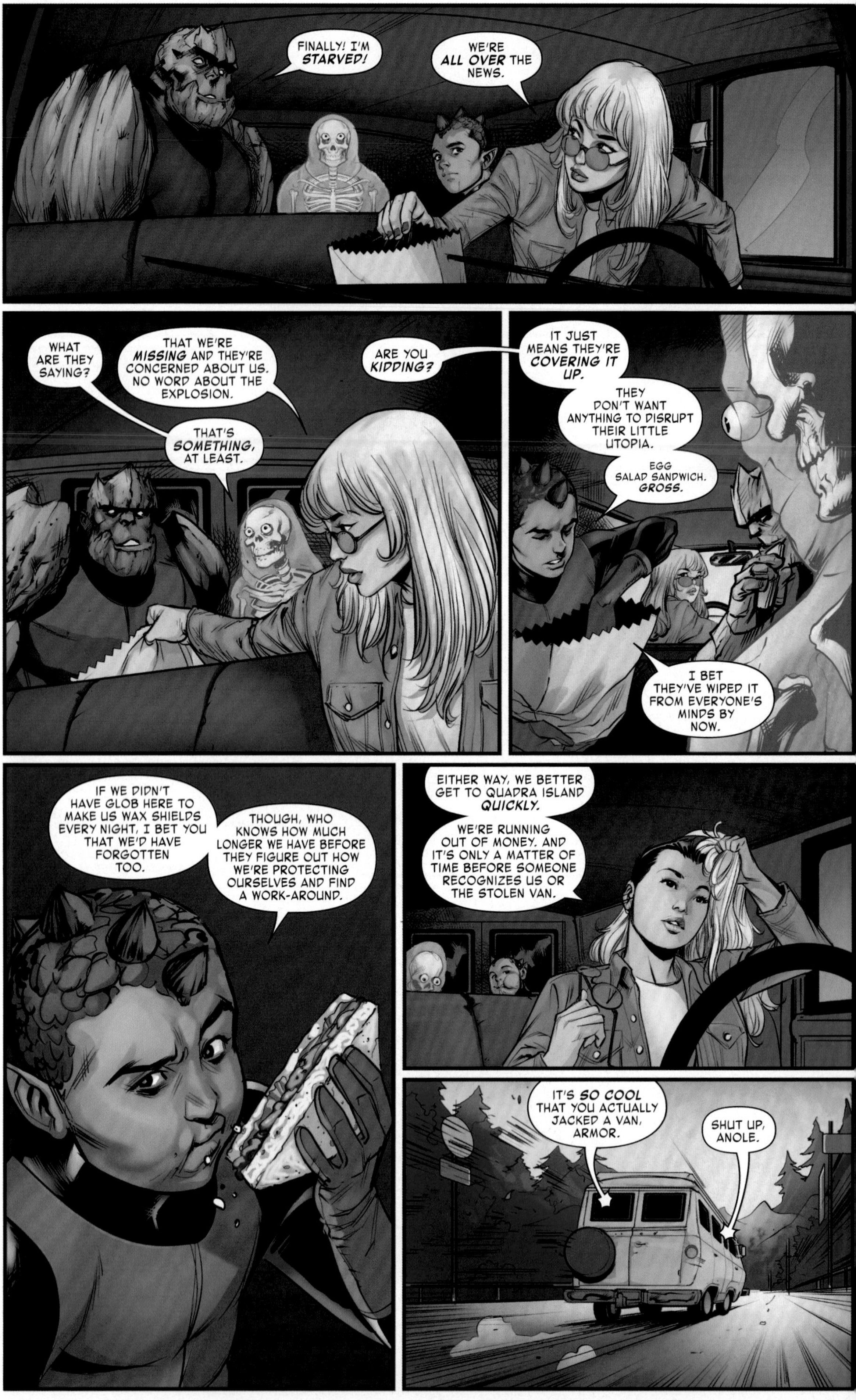
FINALLY! I'M STARVED!
WE'RE ALL OVER THE NEWS.
WHAT ARE THEY SAYING?
THAT WE'RE MISSING AND THEY'RE CONCERNED ABOUT US. NO WORD ABOUT THE EXPLOSION.
THAT'S SOMETHING, AT LEAST.
ARE YOU KIDDING?
IT JUST MEANS THEY'RE COVERING IT UP.
THEY DON'T WANT ANYTHING TO DISRUPT THEIR LITTLE UTOPIA.
EGG SALAD SANDWICH. GROSS.
I BET THEY'VE WIPED IT FROM EVERYONE'S MINDS BY NOW.
IF WE DIDN'T HAVE GLOB HERE TO MAKE US WAX SHIELDS EVERY NIGHT, I BET YOU THAT WE'D HAVE FORGOTTEN TOO.
THOUGH, WHO KNOWS HOW MUCH LONGER WE HAVE BEFORE THEY FIGURE OUT HOW WE'RE PROTECTING OURSELVES AND FIND A WORK-AROUND.
EITHER WAY, WE BETTER GET TO QUADRA ISLAND QUICKLY.
WE'RE RUNNING OUT OF MONEY. AND IT'S ONLY A MATTER OF TIME BEFORE SOMEONE RECOGNIZES US OR THE STOLEN VAN.
IT'S SO COOL THAT YOU ACTUALLY JACKED A VAN, ARMOR.
SHUT UP, ANOLE.

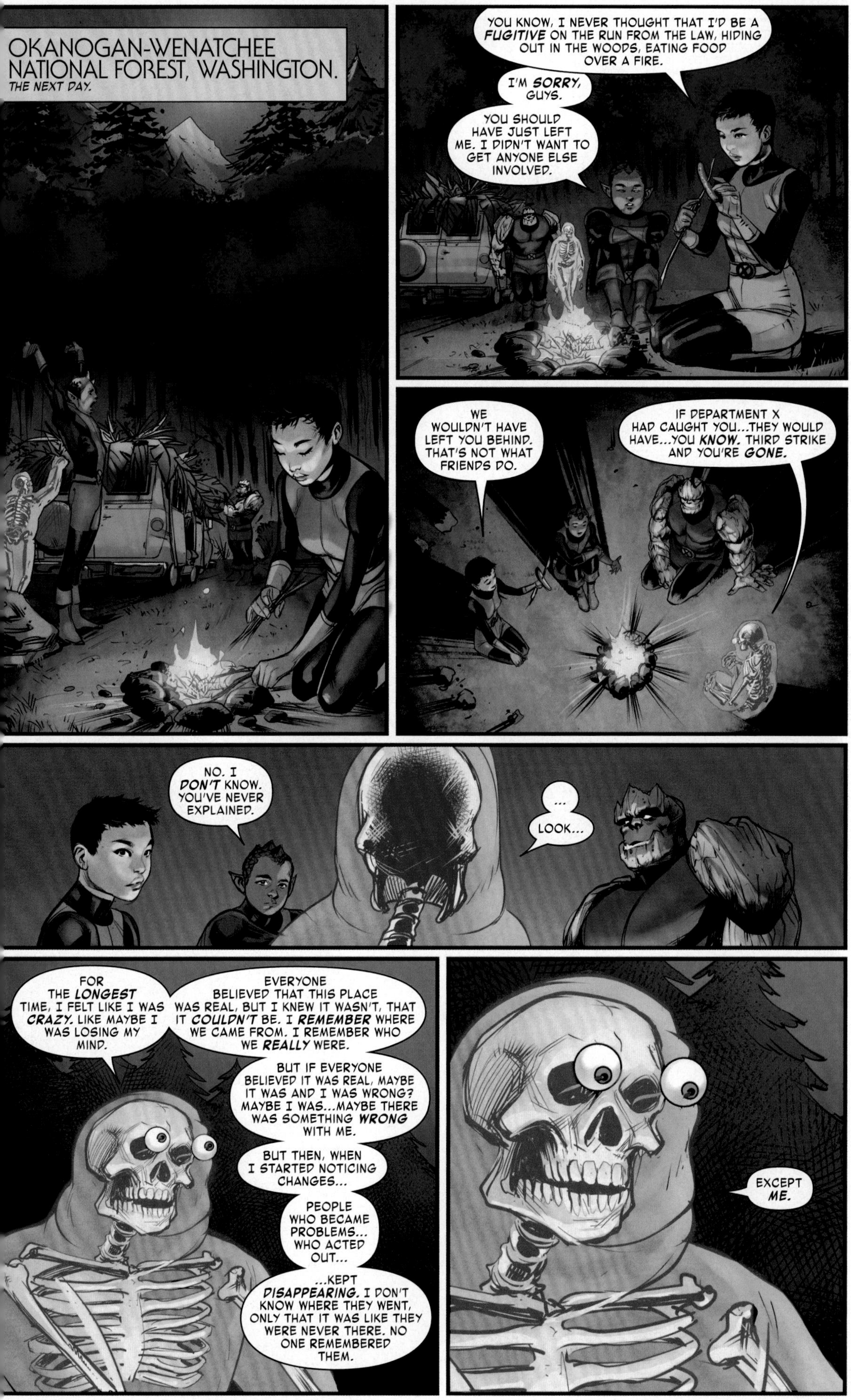
OKANOGAN-WENATCHEE NATIONAL FOREST, WASHINGTON.
THE NEXT DAY.
YOU KNOW, I NEVER THOUGHT THAT I'D BE A FUGITIVE ON THE RUN FROM THE LAW, HIDING OUT IN THE WOODS, EATING FOOD OVER A FIRE.
I'M SORRY, GUYS.
YOU SHOULD HAVE JUST LEFT ME. I DIDN'T WANT TO GET ANYONE ELSE INVOLVED.
WE WOULDN'T HAVE LEFT YOU BEHIND. THAT'S NOT WHAT FRIENDS DO.
IF DEPARTMENT X HAD CAUGHT YOU...THEY WOULD HAVE...YOU KNOW. THIRD STRIKE AND YOU'RE GONE.
NO. I DON'T KNOW. YOU'VE NEVER EXPLAINED.
...
LOOK...
FOR THE LONGEST TIME, I FELT LIKE I WAS CRAZY. LIKE MAYBE I WAS LOSING MY MIND.
EVERYONE BELIEVED THAT THIS PLACE WAS REAL, BUT I KNEW IT WASN'T, THAT IT COULDN'T BE. I REMEMBER WHERE WE CAME FROM. I REMEMBER WHO WE REALLY WERE.
BUT IF EVERYONE BELIEVED IT WAS REAL, MAYBE IT WAS AND I WAS WRONG? MAYBE I WAS...MAYBE THERE WAS SOMETHING WRONG WITH ME.
BUT THEN, WHEN I STARTED NOTICING CHANGES...
PEOPLE WHO BECAME PROBLEMS... WHO ACTED OUT...
...KEPT DISAPPEARING. I DON'T KNOW WHERE THEY WENT, ONLY THAT IT WAS LIKE THEY WERE NEVER THERE. NO ONE REMEMBERED THEM.
EXCEPT ME.

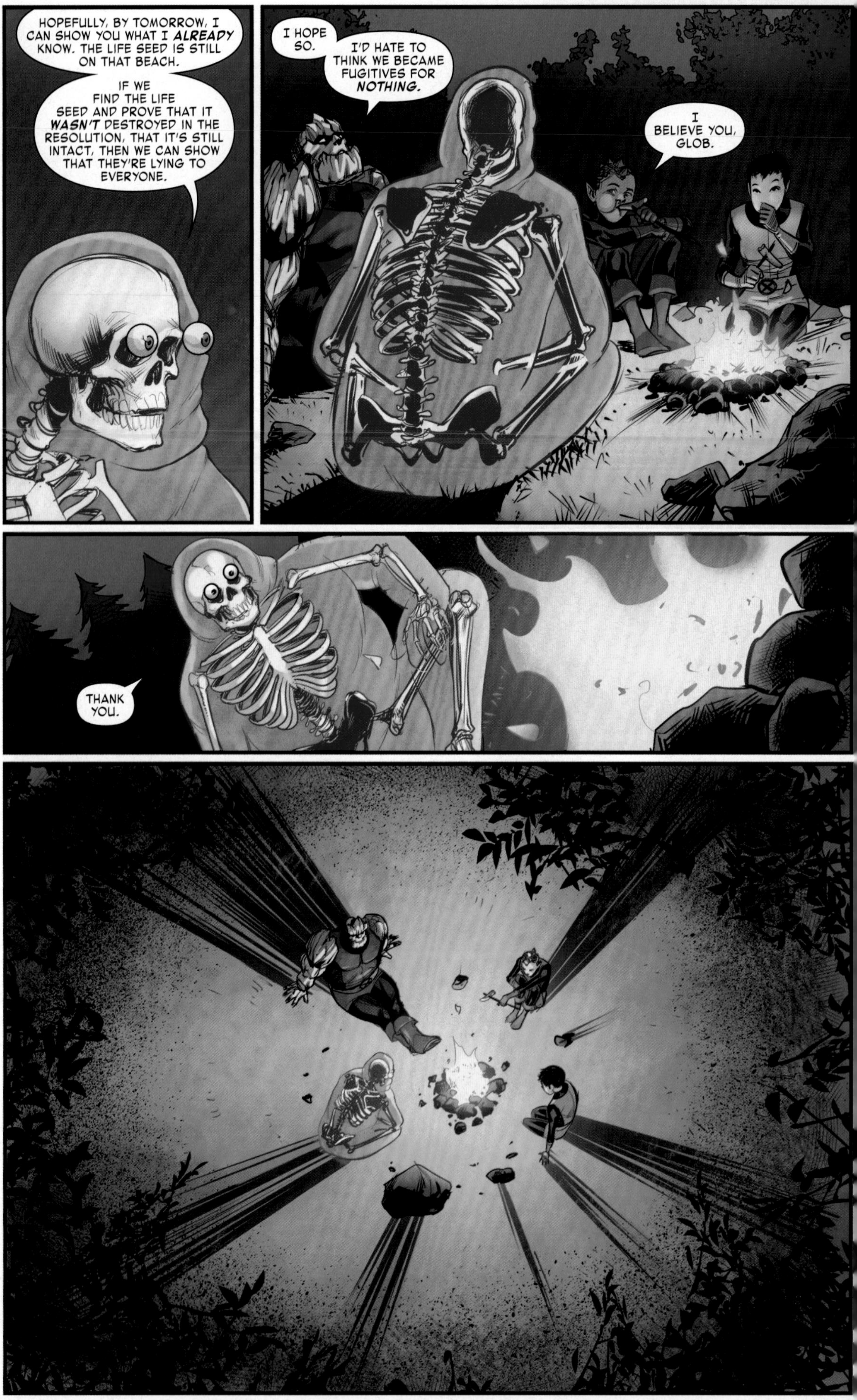
HOPEFULLY, BY TOMORROW, I CAN SHOW YOU WHAT I *ALREADY* KNOW. THE LIFE SEED IS STILL ON THAT BEACH.
IF WE FIND THE LIFE SEED AND PROVE THAT IT *WASN'T* DESTROYED IN THE RESOLUTION, THAT IT'S STILL INTACT, THEN WE CAN SHOW THAT THEY'RE LYING TO EVERYONE.
I HOPE SO.
I'D HATE TO THINK WE BECAME FUGITIVES FOR *NOTHING.*
I BELIEVE YOU, GLOB.
THANK YOU.

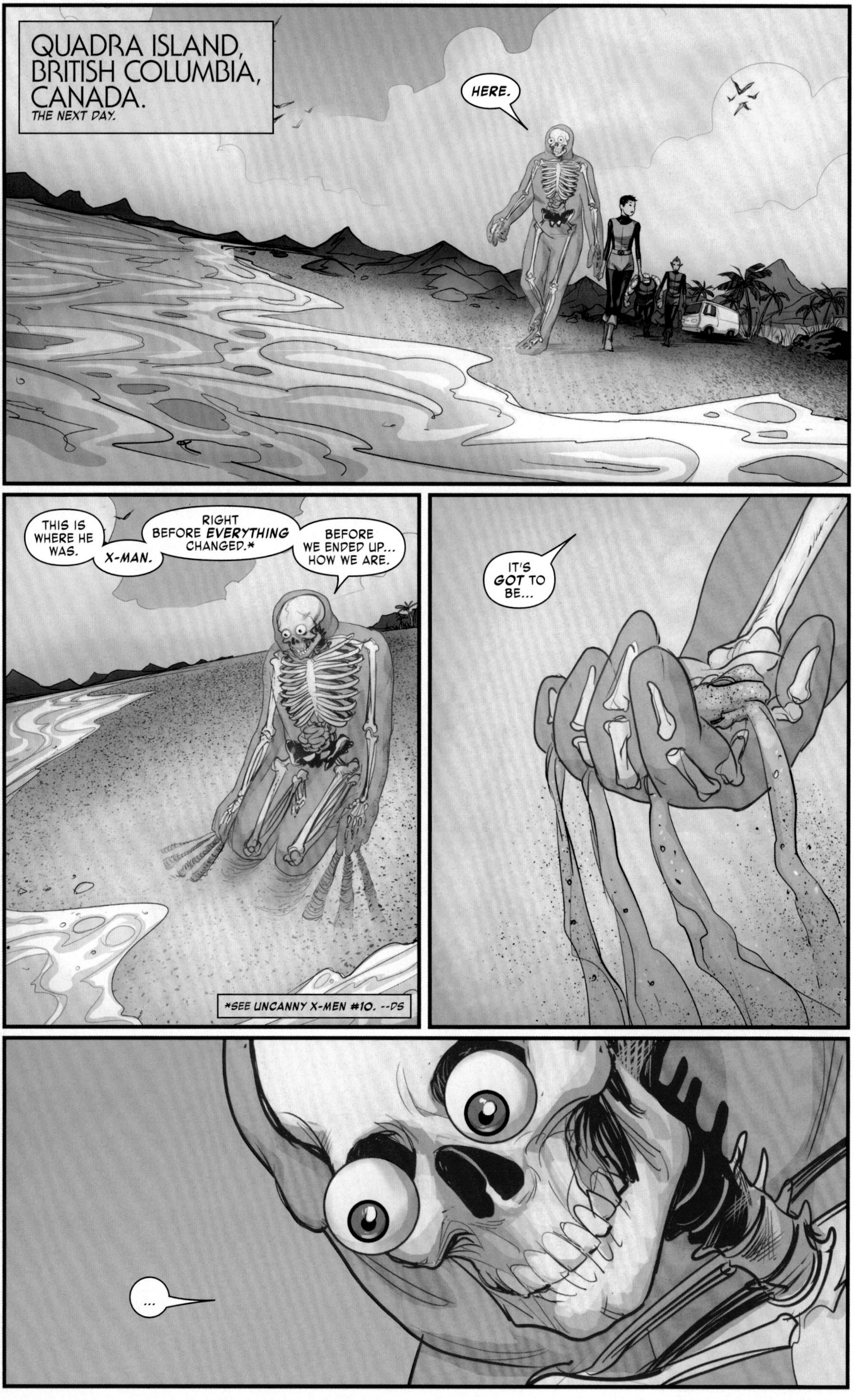

QUADRA ISLAND, BRITISH COLUMBIA, CANADA.
THE NEXT DAY.
HERE.
THIS IS WHERE HE WAS.
X-MAN.
RIGHT BEFORE EVERYTHING CHANGED.*
BEFORE WE ENDED UP... HOW WE ARE.
*SEE UNCANNY X-MEN #10. --DS
IT'S GOT TO BE...
...

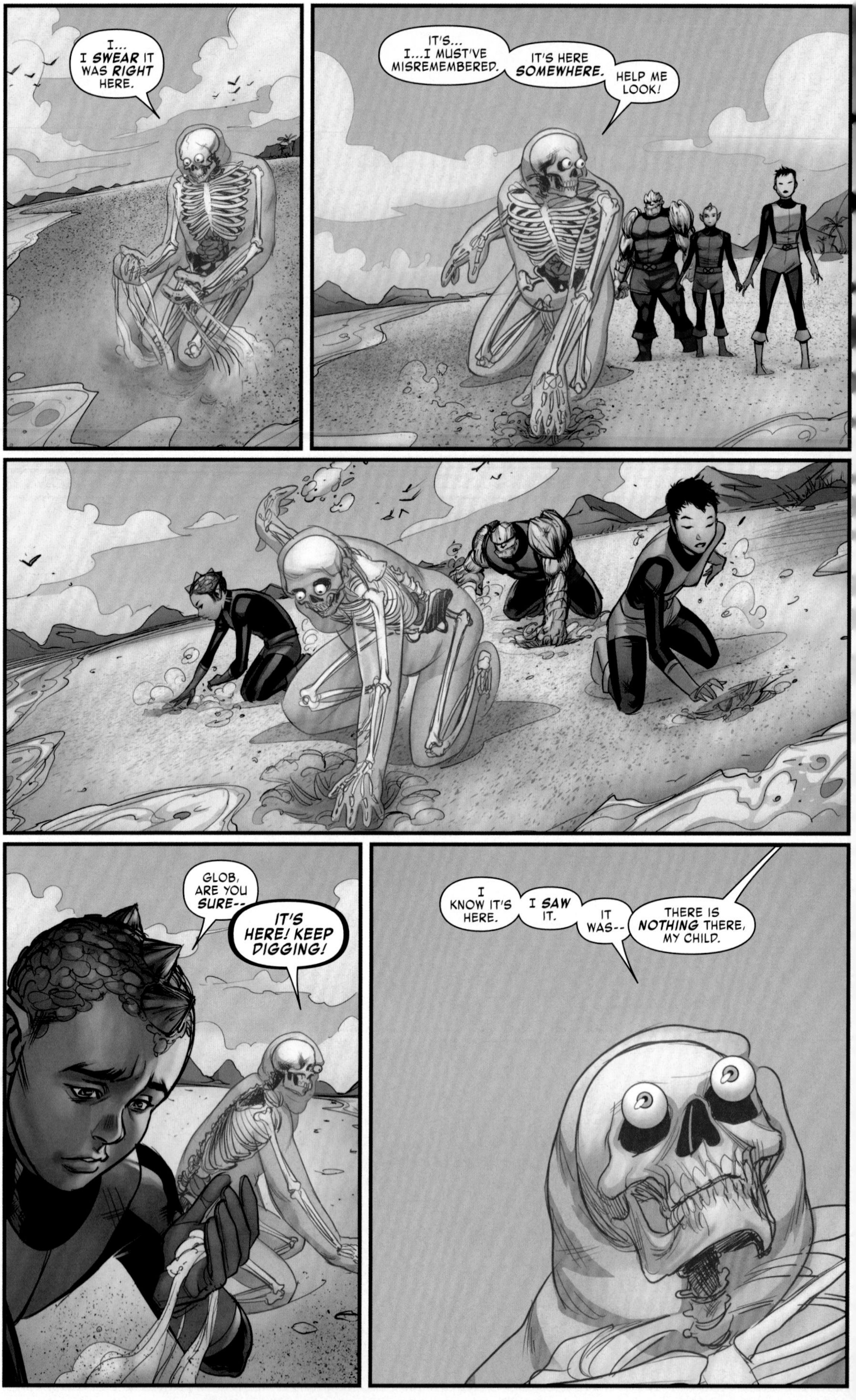
I... I SWEAR IT WAS RIGHT HERE.
IT'S... I...I MUST'VE MISREMEMBERED.
IT'S HERE SOMEWHERE.
HELP ME LOOK!
GLOB, ARE YOU SURE--
IT'S HERE! KEEP DIGGING!
I KNOW IT'S HERE.
I SAW IT.
IT WAS--
THERE IS NOTHING THERE, MY CHILD.

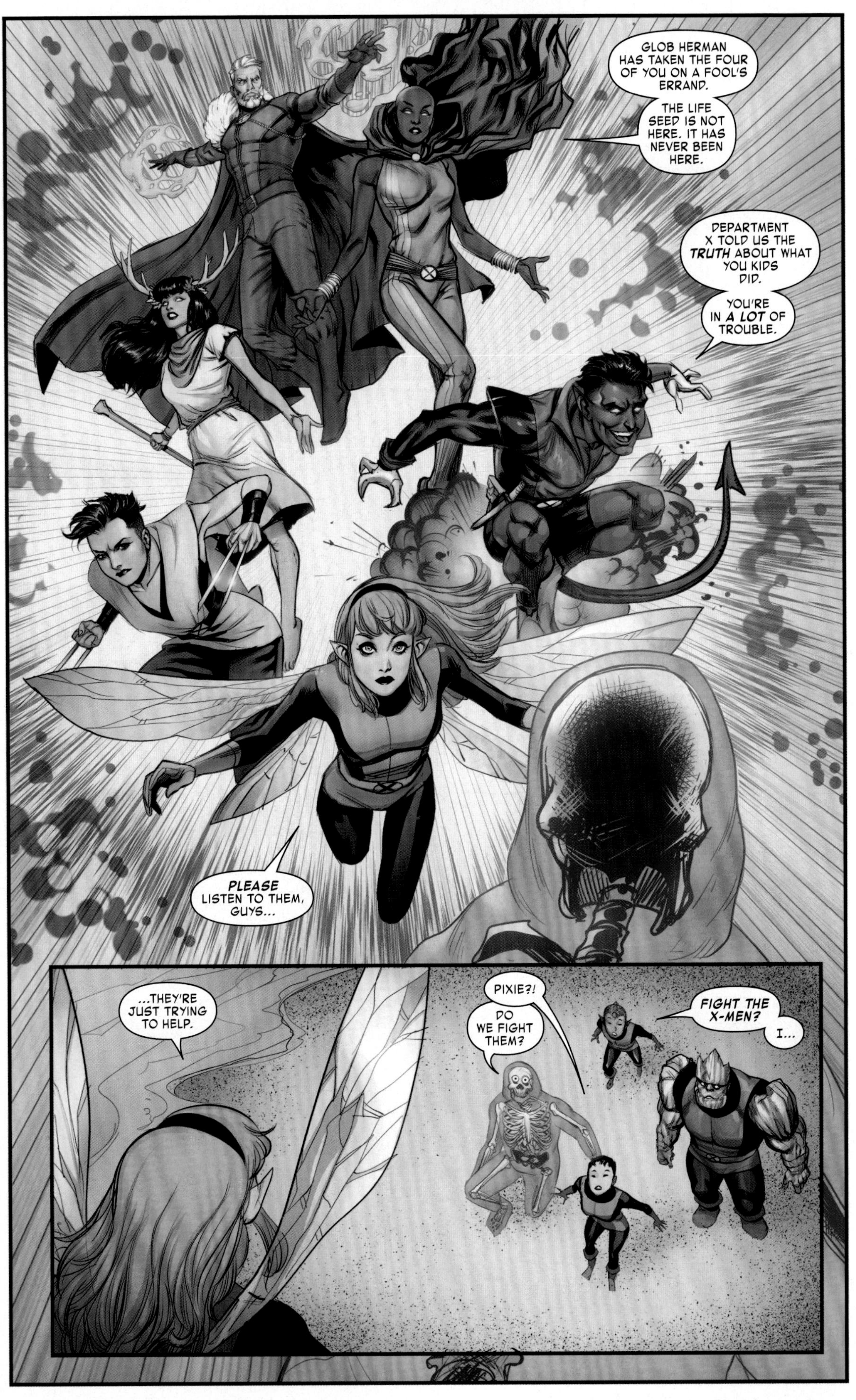
GLOB HERMAN HAS TAKEN THE FOUR OF YOU ON A FOOL'S ERRAND.
THE LIFE SEED IS NOT HERE. IT HAS NEVER BEEN HERE.
DEPARTMENT X TOLD US THE TRUTH ABOUT WHAT YOU KIDS DID.
YOU'RE IN A LOT OF TROUBLE.
PLEASE LISTEN TO THEM, GUYS...
...THEY'RE JUST TRYING TO HELP.
PIXIE?!
DO WE FIGHT THEM?
FIGHT THE X-MEN?
I...

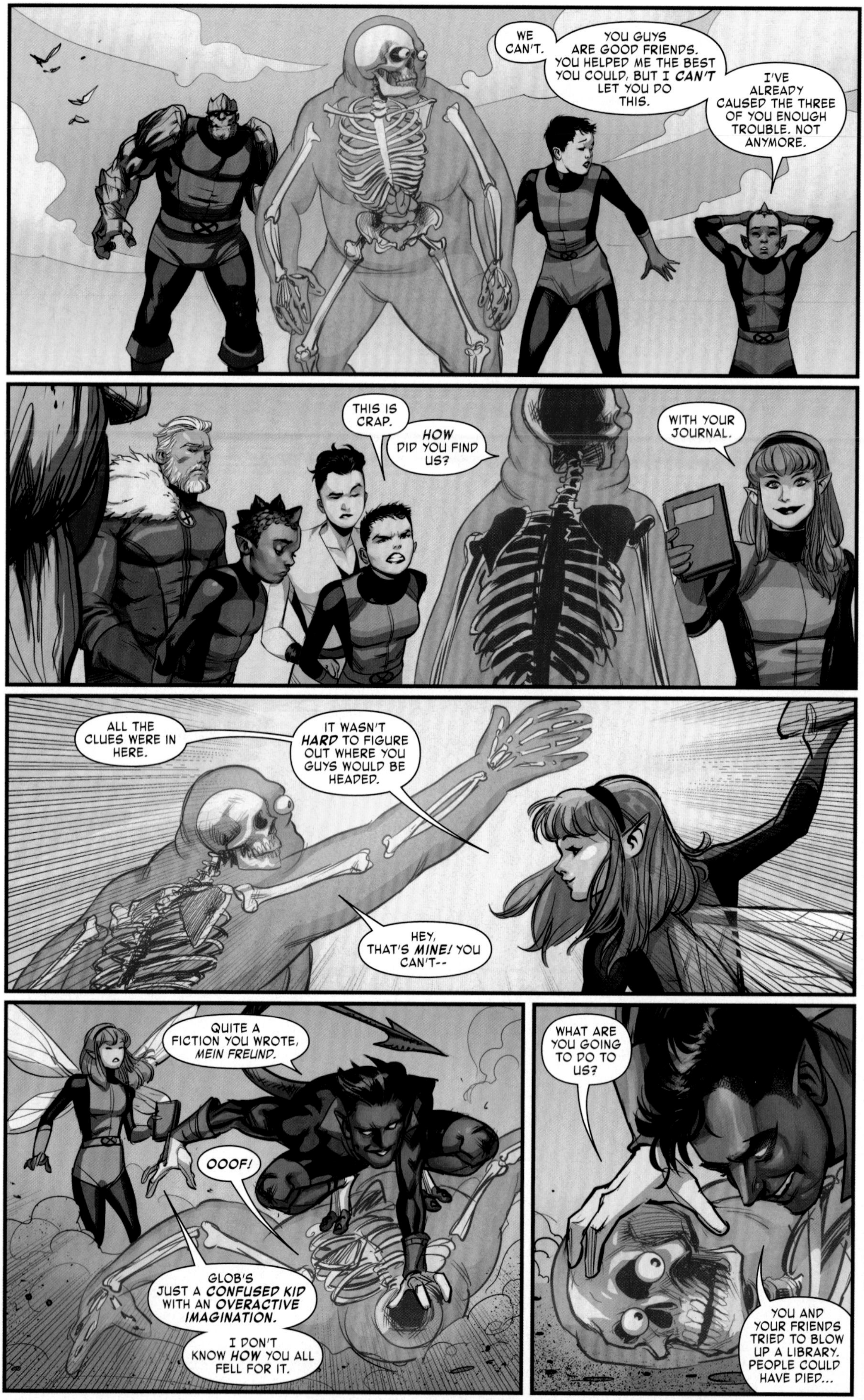
WE CAN'T.
YOU GUYS ARE GOOD FRIENDS. YOU HELPED ME THE BEST YOU COULD, BUT I CAN'T LET YOU DO THIS.
I'VE ALREADY CAUSED THE THREE OF YOU ENOUGH TROUBLE. NOT ANYMORE.
THIS IS CRAP.
HOW DID YOU FIND US?
WITH YOUR JOURNAL.
ALL THE CLUES WERE IN HERE.
IT WASN'T HARD TO FIGURE OUT WHERE YOU GUYS WOULD BE HEADED.
HEY, THAT'S MINE! YOU CAN'T--
QUITE A FICTION YOU WROTE, MEIN FREUND.
OOOF!
GLOB'S JUST A CONFUSED KID WITH AN OVERACTIVE IMAGINATION.
I DON'T KNOW HOW YOU ALL FELL FOR IT.
WHAT ARE YOU GOING TO DO TO US?
YOU AND YOUR FRIENDS TRIED TO BLOW UP A LIBRARY. PEOPLE COULD HAVE DIED...

THE DANGER ROOM PRISON COMPLEX.
LOCATION: UNKNOWN. SEVERAL DAYS LATER.

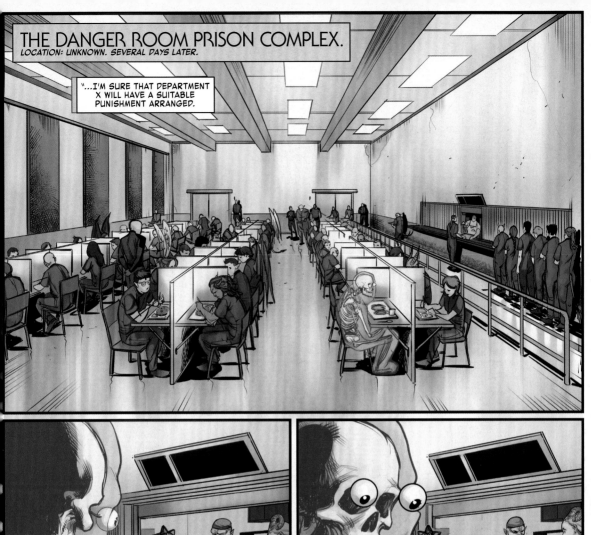

"...I'M SURE THAT DEPARTMENT X WILL HAVE A SUITABLE PUNISHMENT ARRANGED.

HEY THERE.

MIND IF I SIT HERE?

UH...

YEAH... I MEAN... SURE...

...PLEASE.

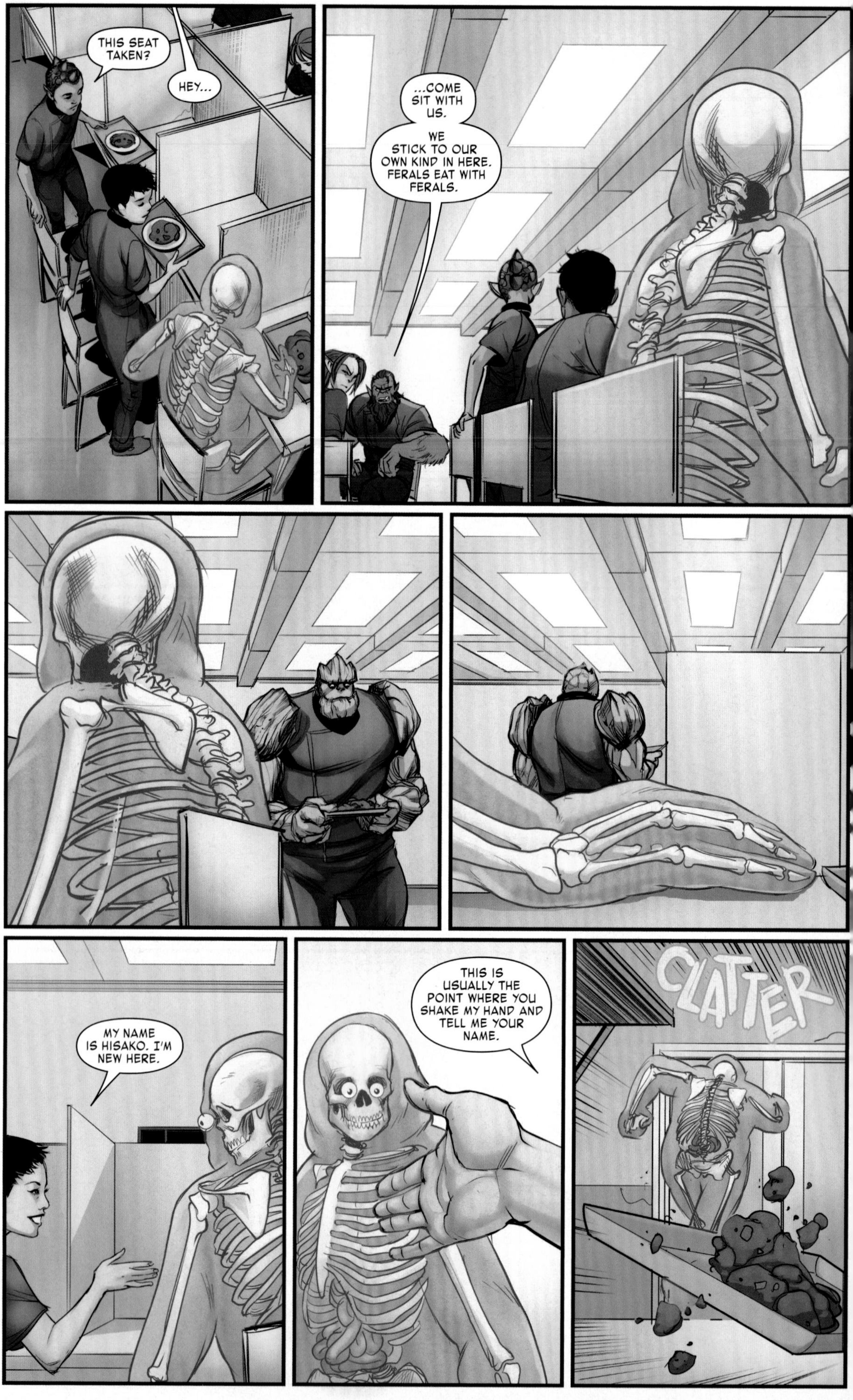
THIS SEAT TAKEN?
HEY...
...COME SIT WITH US.
WE STICK TO OUR OWN KIND IN HERE. FERALS EAT WITH FERALS.
MY NAME IS HISAKO. I'M NEW HERE.
THIS IS USUALLY THE POINT WHERE YOU SHAKE MY HAND AND TELL ME YOUR NAME.
CLATTER

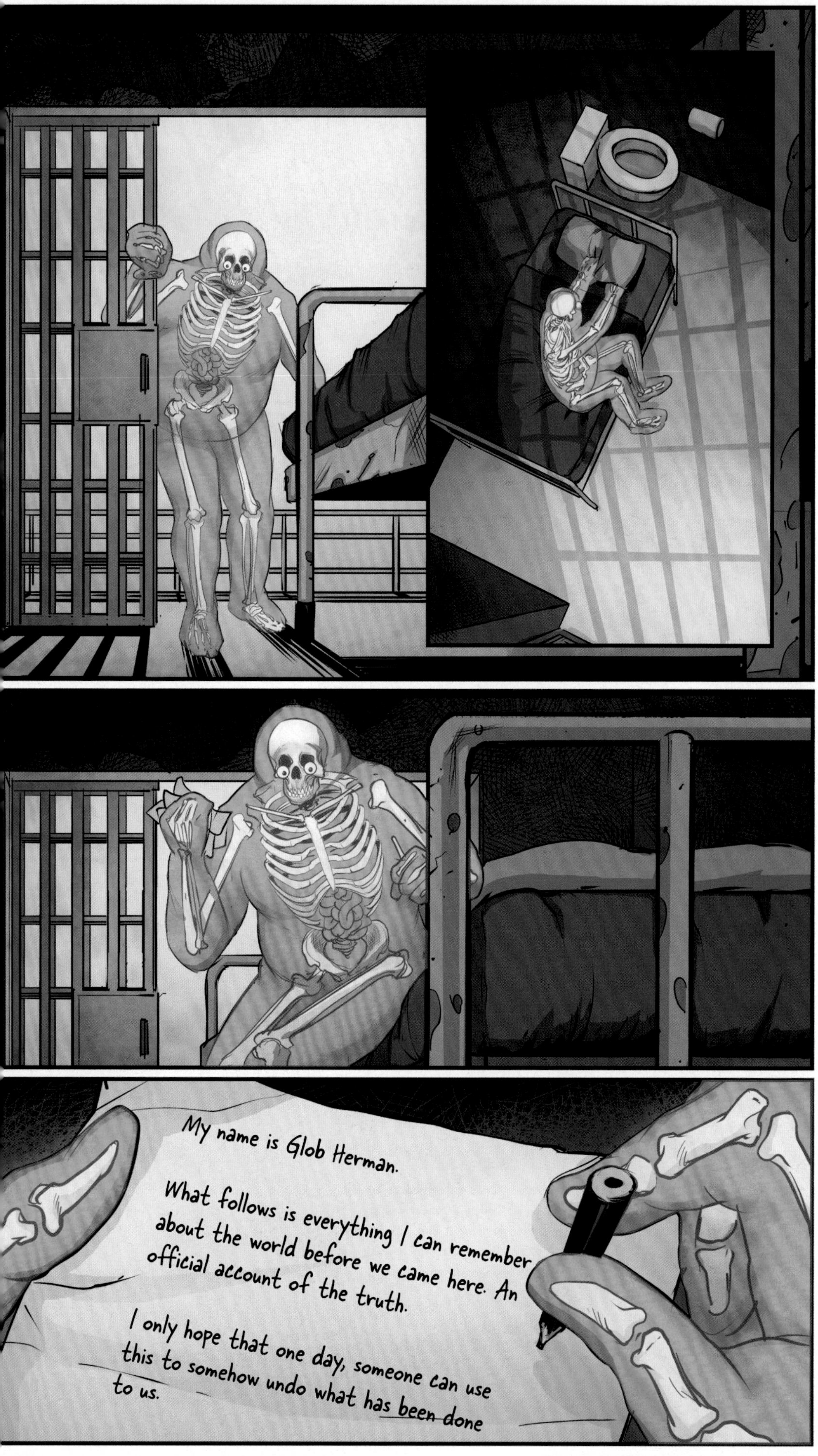
My name is Glob Herman.
What follows is everything I can remember about the world before we came here. An official account of the truth.
I only hope that one day, someone can use this to somehow undo what has been done to us.

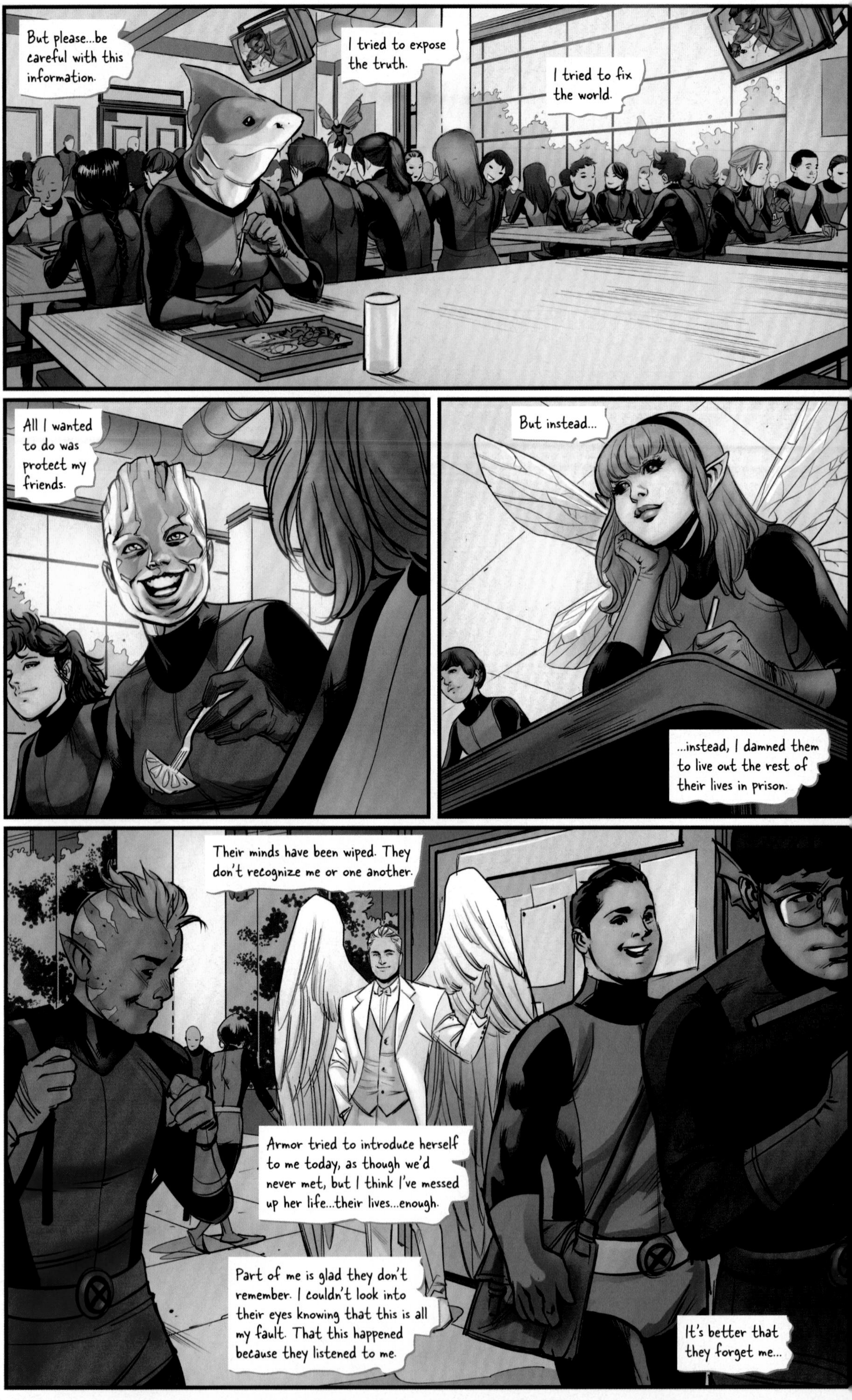

But please...be careful with this information.
I tried to expose the truth.
I tried to fix the world.
All I wanted to do was protect my friends.
But instead...
...instead, I damned them to live out the rest of their lives in prison.
Their minds have been wiped. They don't recognize me or one another.
Armor tried to introduce herself to me today, as though we'd never met, but I think I've messed up her life...their lives...enough.
Part of me is glad they don't remember. I couldn't look into their eyes knowing that this is all my fault. That this happened because they listened to me.
It's better that they forget me...

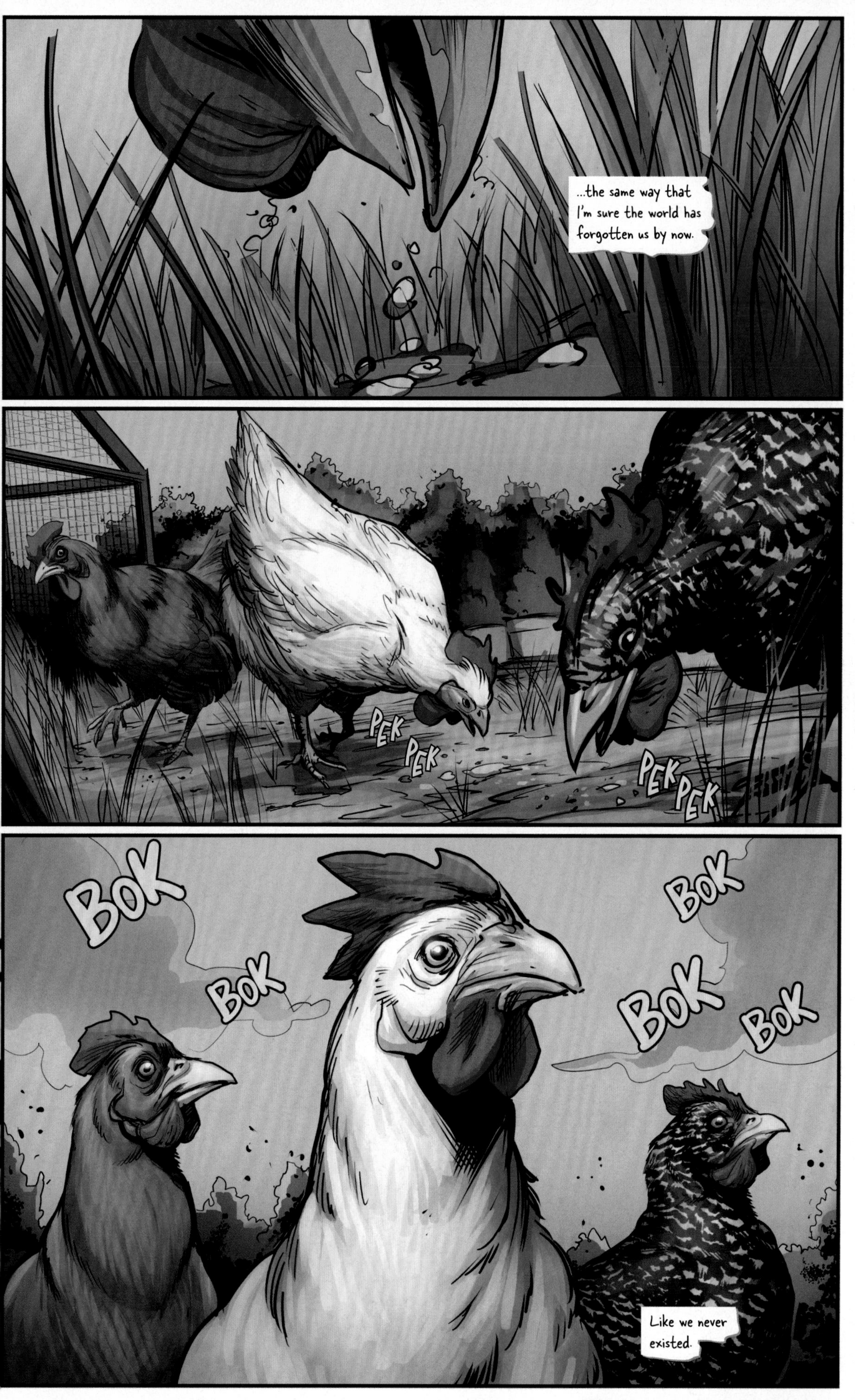
...the same way that I'm sure the world has forgotten us by now.
PEK
PEK
PEK PEK
BOK
BOK
BOK
BOK
BOK
Like we never existed.

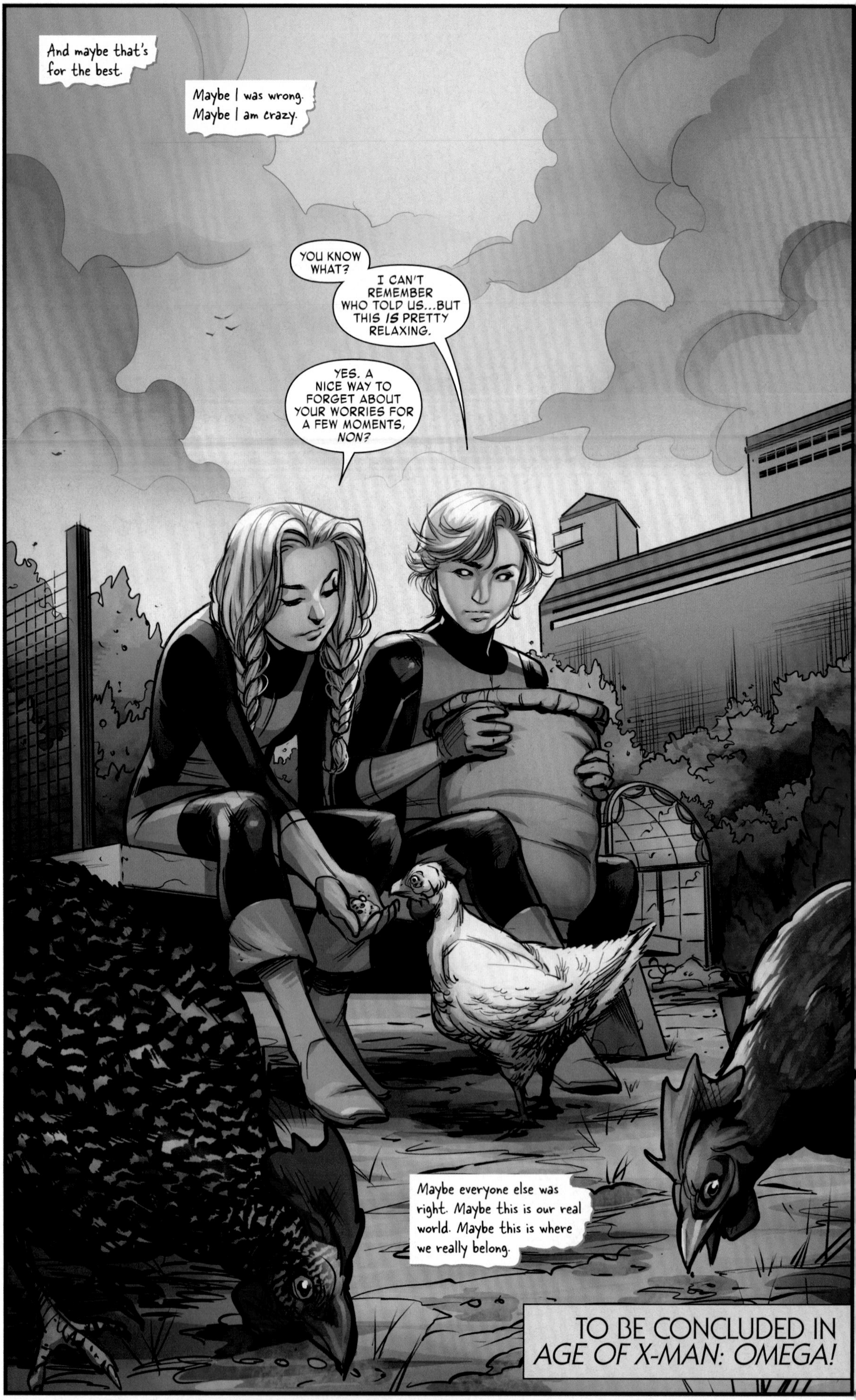
And maybe that's for the best.
Maybe I was wrong. Maybe I am crazy.
YOU KNOW WHAT?
I CAN'T REMEMBER WHO TOLD US...BUT THIS *IS* PRETTY RELAXING.
YES. A NICE WAY TO FORGET ABOUT YOUR WORRIES FOR A FEW MOMENTS, *NON?*
Maybe everyone else was right. Maybe this is our real world. Maybe this is where we really belong.
TO BE CONCLUDED IN *AGE OF X-MAN: OMEGA!*

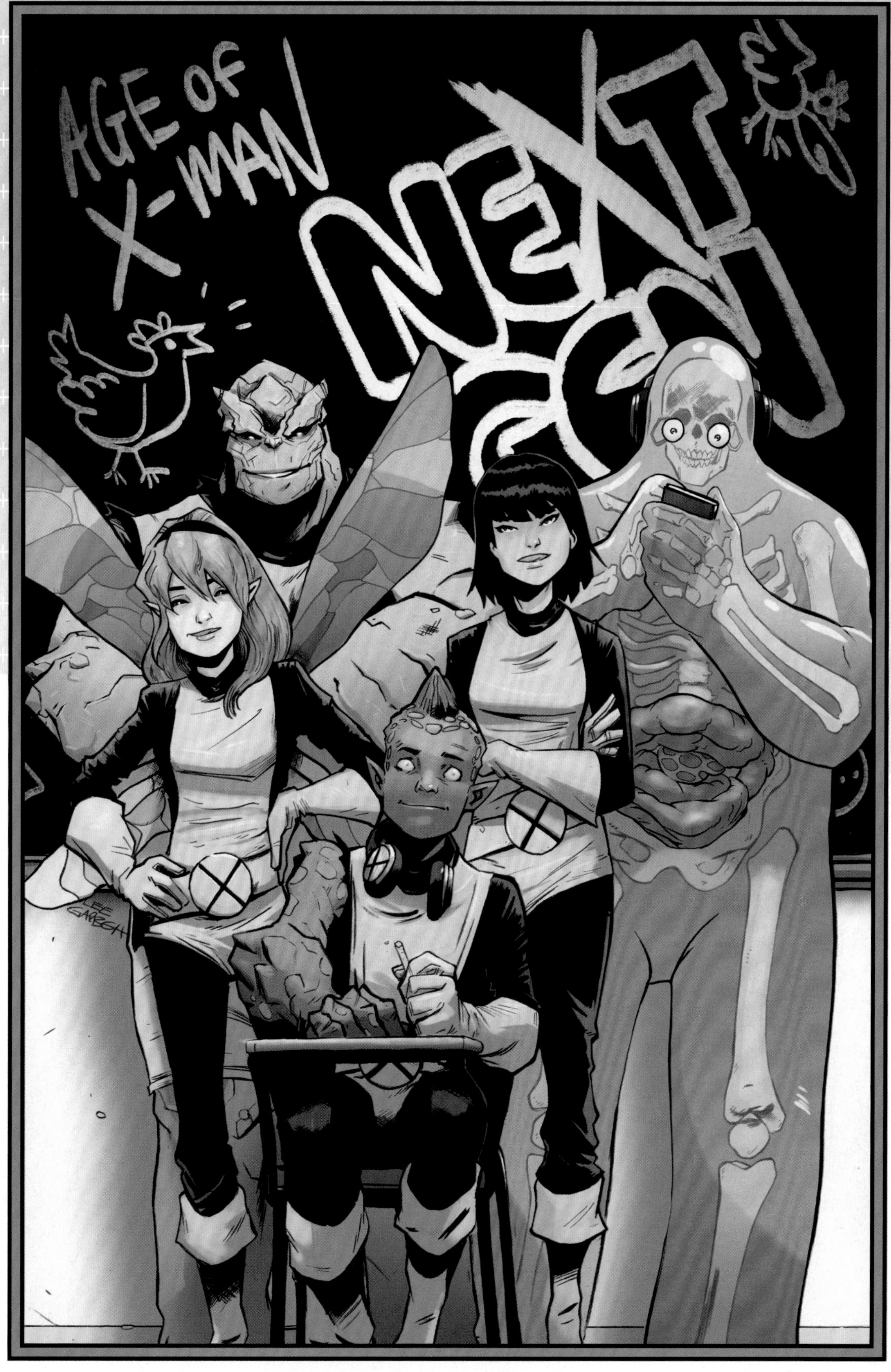
AGE OF
X-MAN
NEXT
GEN
LEE
GARBETT

#1 VARIANT BY **LEE GARBETT**

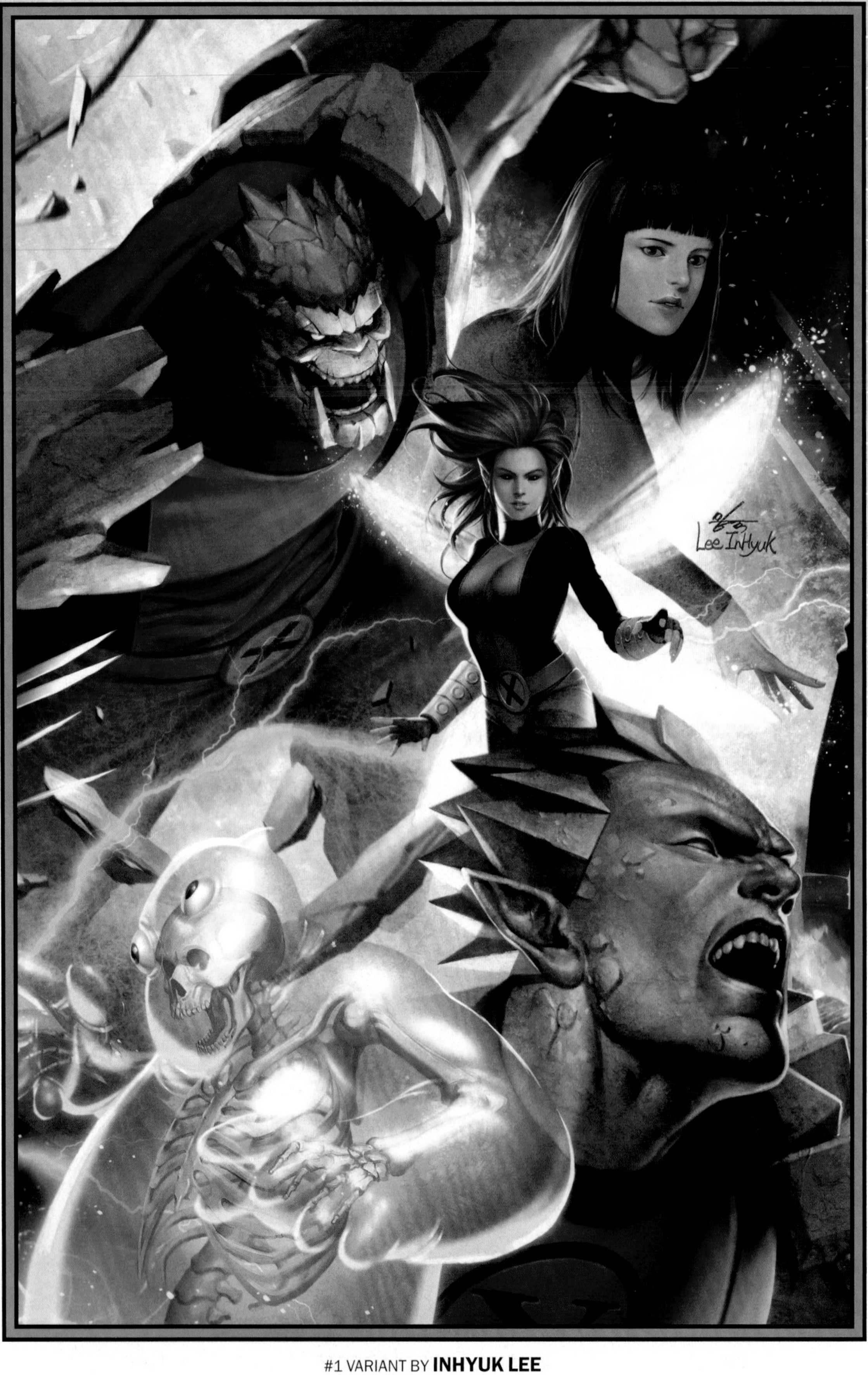
Lee InHyuk

#1 VARIANT BY **INHYUK LEE**

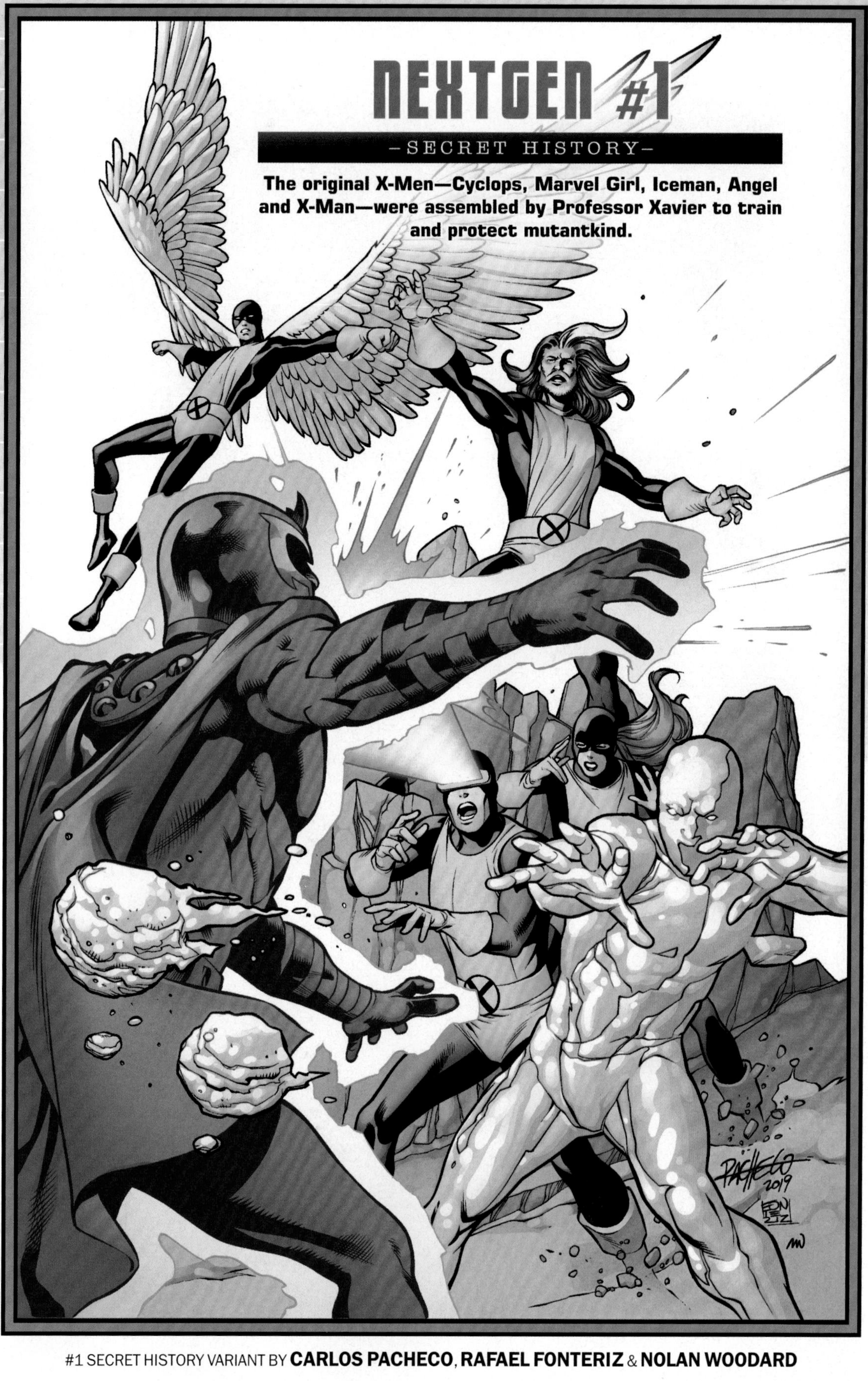
NEXTGEN #1
–SECRET HISTORY–
The original X-Men—Cyclops, Marvel Girl, Iceman, Angel and X-Man—were assembled by Professor Xavier to train and protect mutantkind.

#1 SECRET HISTORY VARIANT BY **CARLOS PACHECO**, **RAFAEL FONTERIZ** & **NOLAN WOODARD**

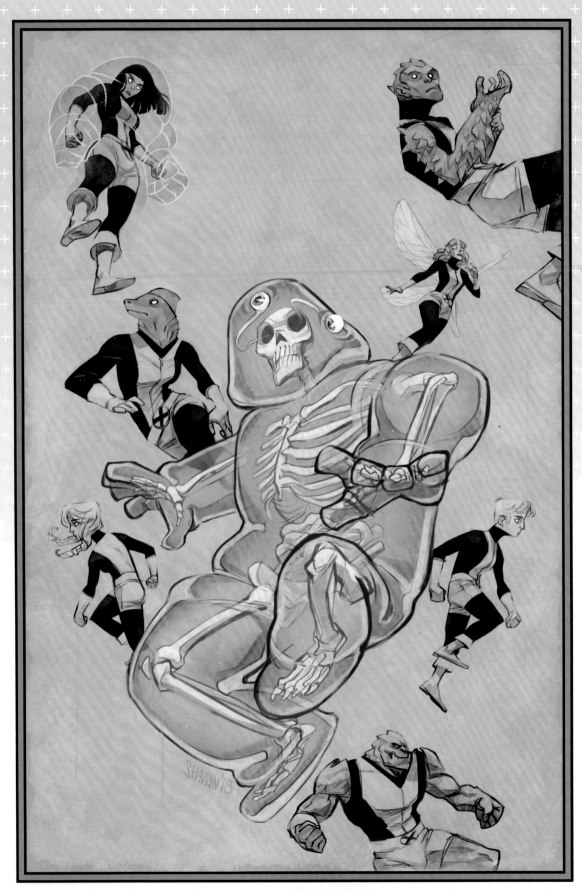

#2 VARIANT BY **IVAN SHAVRIN**